Asylum Seekers, Sovereignty, and the Senses of the International

The confrontation between asylum seeking and sovereignty has mainly focused on ways in which the movement and possibilities of refugees and migrants are limited. In this volume, instead of departing from the practices of governance and surveillance, Puumala begins with the moving body, its engagements and relations, and examines different ways of seeing and sensing the struggle between asylum seekers and sovereign practices.

Puumala asserts that our political imagination is being challenged in its ways of ordering, practicing and thinking about the international and those relations we call international. The issues relating to asylum seekers are one example of the deficiencies in the spatiotemporal logic upon which these relations were originally built; words such as 'nation', 'people', 'sovereignty' and 'community' are challenged. Conventional methods of governing, regulating and administering increased forms of mobility are in trouble, which gives rise to the invention of new technologies at borders and introduces regulations and spaces of exception.

Based on extensive fieldwork that sheds light on a range of Europe-wide practices in the field of asylum and migration policies, this book will be of interest to scholars of IR theory, biopolitics and migration, as well as critical security more broadly.

Eeva Puumala is a post-doctoral researcher at the Tampere Peace Research Institute at the University of Tampere, Finland.

Interventions
Edited by: Jenny Edkins, *Aberystwyth University* and
Nick Vaughan-Williams, *University of Warwick*

The Series provides a forum for innovative and interdisciplinary work that engages with alternative critical, post-structural, feminist, postcolonial, psychoanalytic and cultural approaches to international relations and global politics. In our first 5 years we have published 60 volumes.

We aim to advance understanding of the key areas in which scholars working within broad critical post-structural traditions have chosen to make their interventions, and to present innovative analyses of important topics. Titles in the series engage with critical thinkers in philosophy, sociology, politics and other disciplines and provide situated historical, empirical and textual studies in international politics.

For a full list of available titles please visit https://www.routledge.com/series/INT

The most recent titles in this series are:

Security Without Weapons
Rethinking Violence, Nonviolent Actions, and Civilian Protection
M. S. Wallace

Disorienting Democracy
Politics of Emancipation
Clare Woodford

Democracy Promotion as Foreign Policy
Temporal Othering in International Relations
Cathy Elliott

Asylum Seekers, Sovereignty, and the Senses of the International
A Politico-corporeal Struggle
Eeva Puumala

Global Powers of Horror
Security, Politics, and the Body in Pieces
François Debrix

Asylum Seekers, Sovereignty, and the Senses of the International
A politico-corporeal struggle

Eeva Puumala

LONDON AND NEW YORK

First published 2017
by Routledge
2 Park Square, Milton Park, Abingdon, Oxon OX14 4RN

and by Routledge
711 Third Avenue, New York, NY 10017

Routledge is an imprint of the Taylor & Francis Group, an informa business

© 2017 Eeva Puumala

The right of Eeva Puumala to be identified as author of this work has been asserted by her in accordance with sections 77 and 78 of the Copyright, Designs and Patents Act 1988.

All rights reserved. No part of this book may be reprinted or reproduced or utilised in any form or by any electronic, mechanical, or other means, now known or hereafter invented, including photocopying and recording, or in any information storage or retrieval system, without permission in writing from the publishers.

Trademark notice: Product or corporate names may be trademarks or registered trademarks, and are used only for identification and explanation without intent to infringe.

British Library Cataloguing in Publication Data
A catalogue record for this book is available from the British Library

Library of Congress Cataloging in Publication Data
Names: Puumala, Eeva, author.
Title: Asylum seekers, sovereignty, and the senses of the international :
   a politico-corporeal struggle / Eeva Puumala.
Description: Abingdon, Oxon ; New York, NY : Routledge, 2017. | Series:
   Interventions | Includes bibliographical references and index.
Identifiers: LCCN 2016037869 | ISBN 9781138944886 (hardback) |
   ISBN 9781315671215 (ebook)
Subjects: LCSH: Refugees—Government policy—European Union
   countries. | Asylum, Right of—European Union countries. |
   Human body—Political aspects. | Biopolitics.
Classification: LCC HV640.4.E8 P88 2017 | DDC 362.87/561094—dc23
LC record available at https://lccn.loc.gov/2016037869

ISBN: 978-1-138-94488-6 (hbk)
ISBN: 978-1-315-67121-5 (ebk)

Typeset in Times New Roman
by Apex CoVantage, LLC

Contents

Acknowledgements   viii
Preface   x
  The international xii
  Relational ethics xiii
  Collaging research xiv
  Responsible scholarship xv

EVENT 1
Ethnographic experiences   1

1   **Exposure**   5

Points of departure 5
The field 6
Research motivation 9
The demand 10
Sensuous scholarship and ethnographic seduction 13
Lines of life 18
The writing 'I' 22
A hermeneutics of the ontologically potent body 25

EVENT 2
Political lives, professional ethics, and sovereign practices   29

2   **Sovereignty, mobility, the body**   33

In search of solid ground 33
Sovereign control and the body 35
Approaching asylum through exposure 38
A politics of voice, the politics of the body 41
The ontological body 44

vi   *Contents*

Compearance – beyond essentialist politics 46
Exploring the event of exposure 48
Towards the senses of the international 51

EVENT 3
Asylum, a monologist narrative of the state?   55

3   A struggle over the body   59

Contestation and connection 59
Gaping discord 60
Equal discontent towards the process 65
Representation and articulation 70
The body as a point of reflection 73
The dynamics of asylum interviews 76
Evented positionalities 80
The body matters 89
In-different positionalities 93

EVENT 4
Passages and dislocations   97

4   Moving (in) space   101

Seeing movement like a state 101
Movement as corporeal articulation 105
Sovereignty in transition 108
The body as a limit 111
Seeing states through movement 114
Sensing space 121
The bodily event of the political 128

EVENT 5
The feltness of sovereignty   133

5   Sensuous politics, political sentiments   137

On sense and sensing 137
Local colour 141
Making sense of the senses and sentiment 145
Sensuous protests 148

A shared sense of vulnerability 153
Corporeal refusals and aversion 157
Sensuous articulations of the political 160

Collage of a politico-corporeal struggle 165

References 171
Appendix 190
Index 191

Acknowledgements

For me, writing this book in this way with this particular emphasis has seemed a necessity. The necessity emerged on the one hand from the belief and enthusiasm that my research participants showed towards my work. Asylum seekers who over the years shared their experiences with me hoped to see their stories finally in print. The vague promise of that happening brought them a sense of making a difference, seeing some kind of a purpose in what they were going through. On the other hand, the necessity has represented a disciplinary effort with regard to International Relations. The ultimate focus of this book results from a circular process that started with my doctoral dissertation. This book builds on, widens and systematises the methodological input that began to take shape in the thesis. In so doing, it draws less on the discipline of IR and focuses more on comprehending the politico-corporeal struggle that characterises asylum seeking. Hence, it is not so much what I had to say that kept the sometimes agonising research process alive, but how I wanted to write about that struggle and the sensed value of such exploration. The book is perhaps best characterised as a theoretico-methodological exploration into the inadequacy of both learnt concepts and ways of conceptualising in describing what is at stake in the struggle between asylum seeking and the enactments of sovereignty. The pressing question of the book is: *could a different methodology also account for a different ontology?*

I am indebted to all those who have shared their stories and perspectives with me: asylum seekers, failed asylum seekers and detainees, as well as legal advisers, interpreters, mental health workers, migration officials and professionals at the various reception centres for asylum seekers. Furthermore, I wish to express my deep appreciation particularly to Tarja Väyrynen, Stephen Chan, Anitta Kynsilehto and Elina Penttinen. Your comments, support and belief in my work has encouraged me to carry on with it. In addition, your courage and uncompromising passion towards research have greatly inspired me and also urged me to challenge my own ways of thinking and knowing.

The research community at the Tampere Peace Research Institute (TAPRI) at the University of Tampere has been an academic home for me for the greater part of this project. I have learned a lot during the discussions and debates with both former and current Taprians. My sincere thanks go to Samu Pehkonen, Tiina Vaittinen, Frank Möller, Matti Jutila, Élise Feron, Alina Curticapean, Ruth Illman,

Unto Vesa and Pirjo Jukarainen. Besides my colleagues at TAPRI, I am indebted to colleagues whom I have met on various occasions and with whom I have had the pleasure to discuss: Roland Bleiker, Jyrki Käkönen, Anna-Kaisa Kuusisto-Arponen, Elina Niinivaara, Riitta Ylikomi, Vicki Squire, Saara Särmä, Jaana Vuori, Taina Kinnunen, Marja Alastalo, Susanna Lindberg, Marjaana Jauhola and Kirsi Pauliina Kallio.

I wish to express my gratitude also to the resarch seminar on Corporeality, Movement and Politics for providing a collegial and constructive environment for reading and discussing research, and to the participants in the data sessions organised by Johanna Ruusuvuori and Aija Logren at the University of Tampere. The organisation and people behind the Floating Platforms project by New Performance Turku Festival and Aboagora Symposium also deserve a heartfelt thank you. I was very privileged to be invited to participate in such a collaboration between the arts and sciences and to have an opportunity to work with a brilliant young artist and curator, Márcio Carvalho. My talks with Márcio and the overall experience continues to inspire and puzzle me.

My research assistant Hanna-Leena Ristimäki deserves a special thank you. I appreciate tremendously her help during data collection in 2014–2015 and her efforts in transcribing the data from asylum interviews. In addition, I have learned a lot from her and greatly enjoyed our interdisciplinary discussions concerning the interactional play of institutional frameworks and personal experiences. Furthermore, I am grateful to my editorial assistant, Lydia DeCruz, at Routledge, and series editors Jenny Edkins and Nick Vaughan-Williams for their patience with me and my work and the support that they have given me throughout the process. In the final phases of the process, Michael Owston did a wonderful job with proofreading the text.

This research has been funded by the Tampere Peace Research Institute, the Kone Foundation, the University of Tampere Foundation and the Academy of Finland projects "The Body Politic of Migration" (132403) and "The Body as a Vocabulary of the Political" (266009). I consider myself very lucky that these organisations have seen a value in what I do.

However, if it was not for the support from my family, this work would have never been completed. I am deeply grateful to my parents, Helmi Puumala and Reijo Reuna, for always supporting me, to my husband Juha Koskela for his loving patience and to Severi, Eljas and Aarni for adding so many senses to my life.

Preface

> I have great and wonderful memories from my childhood. Life has changed totally, since the civil war began. Before, there were different cultures co-existing in my country. People were hospitable, invited you to their homes and considered you as a family member even if they didn't know you. I am proud to be Syrian.
>
> I am shocked about what's now happening around the world: all this cruelty and killing. I think some animals are more merciful to one another than human beings.
>
> (Housni, an asylum seeker from Syria, September 2015)

In raising the question of mercy, Housni's perception of the human condition started to resonate in my mind with the image of dead, 3-year-old Aylan from Syria, whose picture circulated widely in the media in the autumn of 2015. At about that time I, together with Márcio Carvalho, was involved in an art-science production, where we sought to form (im)possible points of contact between (hi)stories by engaging with people's personal narratives and memories. That is how we came across Housni, who was waiting at the police station for his wife to be registered as an asylum seeker. There, he shared with us his most cherished memories and views concerning the present. Housni had fled Syria to save his life and had managed to reach Finland. Aylan, on the other hand, had drowned when the refugee boat that had carried his family across the Mediterranean Sea sunk. European borders rise high for asylum seekers and the routes and methods of reaching Europe are perilous.

In Europe, states implement a horde of restrictive measures designed to control the movement of people. In the face of the refugee 'crisis' that began in 2015 in Europe, it has become obvious that no state alone can resolve the 'problem'. The notion of a crisis, claims Emma Haddad (2008: 168), results from an experiential reinterpretation of the past against asylum seekers. Refugees from outside Europe, states Haddad, have been made to represent a new experience, radically different from the factors and scale that led to the formation of the current asylum regime. As Benedict Anderson (1991) famously noted, all nations are imagined, which means that identities that are founded on the national – or statist – logic of belonging are imaginary as well. It also means, as Vicki Squire (2009) points out, that in order to constitute an identity for themselves political communities have to be based on a logic of selective opposition, which seeks to solve the problem of "ontological belonging" (Agnew 2007). In accordance with that logic, some bodies can be included, while others must be cast out. European states have thus made it increasingly difficult for people to claim asylum in the first place. That, in turn, has led to the tightening of border controls and ultimately to the transformation of the image of the refugee into that of an asylum seeker, and furthermore into that of an illegal immigrant. Within such imagery, it is easy to view refugees and asylum seekers as sovereign-less subjects, victims or perpetrators of the logic of national belonging (see e.g. Zevnik 2009).

For many Europeans – including Finns – Aylan's media image worked as a wake-up call, uncovering the reality and brutality of seeking asylum in Europe. At the same time, however, attitudes towards asylum seekers in general hardened as the number of those seeking refuge in the continent reached the highest number since the Second World War. In Finland, the dead boy's body became, absurdly enough, an instrument for both those advocating more open policies and those emphasising the need for harsher migration policies. In Finland the asylum 'crisis' that began in 2015 led to a heated public debate that juxtaposed the right to seek asylum with citizens' more 'natural' right to receive welfare services and benefits from the state (cf. Squire 2009: 3). Within such an imaginary, citizens represent the 'rightful' political subjects, whereas the asylum seeker comes to represent the 'undeserving' other, a 'welfare surfer', as the grotesque metaphor used in the Finnish political and public debate puts it.

To some degree, the sharp dichotomy between the two opposite views on seeking asylum urged me to look for an alternative approach. More importantly, however, it begged the question of whether it is necessary for scholars to remain with the 'apparent'. It would be easy to stick with familiar categories and frames of interpretation, and explore the world in terms of the conceptual roadmap we have been taught. For me, the image of Aylan was and continues to be deeply disturbing for a number of reasons: for what it stands for, for ethical reasons and for personal reasons, as the mother of three boys who are able to grow up in completely different circumstances. What kind of challenges do we face when we look at the photo, or just lead our lives as European citizens?

The question resonates with the relation between ethics and politics. That might seem a far-fetched point of departure since, as Housni pointed out and as Aylan's faith testifies, the ethics of encountering is not the first thing that comes to mind when looking at what is going on in the world. My choice of focus could even be regarded as a highly insensitive and irresponsible one, considering the overall atmosphere of fear towards asylum seekers that is gaining a foothold in Europe and the desperation with which asylum seekers strive to reach the continent. The choice was not obvious from the beginning. In fact, at first my firm intention was to pursue an Agambenian study of bare life and the camp, as that was what I thought asylum seekers represented as embodiments of sovereignty being enacted. The state inarguably influences our accounts of who we are, who we must be and who we must become as political beings capable of acting in the modern world (see Walker 2009: 57–58). Ultimately, the change of focus resulted from my exposure to the presence of asylum seekers, which made me realise that

xii *Preface*

it was imperative to explore *those relations that the talk about seeking asylum presupposes and on which it rests*. That entails moving beyond sovereignty and opening up ontological space for various hybridities that entwine legacies and interweave peoples and societies (Chen, Hwang & Ling 2009: 744; see also Tickner 2003: 305–307, 323–324).

The international

Even though I do not wish to focus exclusively on the extremely harsh reality which asylum seekers encounter when seeking safety in Europe, I cannot completely ignore it either. Thus, I address asylum seeking as a politico-corporeal struggle that profoundly challenges our thought of political existence. Such a focus frames this work in terms of the senses of the international, its relations and politics, as they unfold in bodies and are unfolded by the body. It is based on engagement and encounters with asylum seekers, migration officers and other professionals in Finland from 2006 onwards. Through empirical insight, the book engages with such themes as sovereignty, mobility and political community. Adopting a corporeal take on those themes enables the exploration of the materiality of the struggle that characterises current European attempts to control borders and the limitations of the political imaginary that lies behind those attempts.

While refugees and asylum seekers are often seen as unfortunate, but somewhat inevitable, products – or victims – of the state system, particular kinds of people with common characteristics (cf. Malkki 1996: 384–387; McNevin 2010: 145), the mobile body is not a passive surface on which sovereign politics writes its saga. Asylum seekers and their bodies give the international a material surface as they articulate political relations as choices, decisions, commitments and engagements (cf. Said 2001: 120). The body, with its multiple strategies, introduces a politics of the body and suggests a sensuous focus on the international. In this work, the international is about the political practices of instituting bodily relations, which are connected to the production of boundaries and hierarchies that classify people into different categories (cf. Mbembe 2003: 25–26). I explore the sensuousness that is always necessarily intertwined with the notion of the international. Accordingly, the international needs to be scrutinised in terms of how it becomes lived, how it becomes formed and the way it resonates through and in the body as well as between bodies.

The international is an eerie concept which has raised plenty of debate, especially in the field of International Relations, the discipline within which I received my scholarly training (see e.g. Bigo & Walker 2007; Darby 2003; Edkins & Zehfuss 2005; Guillaume 2007; Sylvester 2007; Walker 2006b). There is neither a simple way of defining it nor a shared understanding of how the international operates and where its effects can be found. It could be argued that the concept works only at the state and system levels, but that would mean neglecting its wider and far-ranging effects. For me, stories of asylum seeking concern the senses of the international, that is, the politics and relations of the international as they

Preface   xiii

intertwine with the body. Thus understood, a sense of the international can refer either to the *meanings* that asylum seekers give to their experiences, to the *sensory perceptions* that the experience of seeking asylum creates or to the *rationality and logic* according to which sovereign politics upholds a certain state-centred perception of the international.

By engaging with the senses of the international, the present work sets out to explore bodily intersections and relations that come to exist as people move within and across political borders and boundaries. Such an approach does not try to annihilate borders and negate their effects, but rather calls us to consider the struggle that is involved in their operation and maintenance. The central theoretical ambition behind this book is to shed light on the questions of how we have come to think about ourselves as separate (see also Edkins 2005b) and how we might begin to think about togetherness beyond a state-based political community. The present work seeks to reimagine socio-political practices that give rise to a particular understanding of political community, what it can be and where political life occurs. The book explores the contours and conditions of political life, exposing it as it unfolds at multiple fronts and through various strategies that materialise poignantly in the politico-corporeal struggle of seeking asylum.

Relational ethics

Nonetheless, in its explicit focus on asylum seekers, the book underlines the fact that talk of asylum seekers is only possible with regard to their 'other', the citizen/resident. Rather than studying one category in isolation, it is necessary to explore how identities are connected with one another and how their relationship can be conceptualised otherwise. At its core this book addresses the question of political community. The focus stems from my own fieldwork experiences. Studying real people face to face has meant, and continues to mean, that I need to accept my vulnerability to my research participants' reactions and views. I believe that research has to enter into a dialogue with its subjects, the world and the surrounding circumstances. The subject of study, consequently, has influence on what is studied, how it is done and from which perspective the data is analysed. Otherwise there is a risk that research is not valid, omits central dimensions of the researched phenomenon or cannot identify and open up alternative ways of conceptualising familiar issues. In my meetings and interviews with asylum seekers, they challenged me with a fragmentary and yet extremely forceful demand. They called me to reflect upon the unequal positions we were in, the basis for that inequality and its consequences for our lives. There was a strict hierarchy and power relation between us, although I wished and sought to do away with it in my interviews as much as possible. However, those asylum seekers that I interviewed and with whom I interacted did not wish to ignore it.

In short, the demand with which I was presented while researching the topic made me realise that ethical issues can cause significant epistemological challenges to the research process. I feel that migration research can/should never

xiv *Preface*

be free of normative judgment. What I mean by that is that the researcher must acknowledge the research interest that has guided the work, and be constantly aware that the work – no matter how theoretical or conceptual it may be – concerns real and living people. In my case, accommodating the struggle involved in asylum seeking as it was lived, contested and felt by those whom I met in the field with established methodolgy and theoretical traditions was an insurmountable challenge. In order to highlight the complexities of the field, the ambivalence and tensions present in the interviews, I resorted to an alternative ontological approach. Instead of beginning with a fixed and solid theoretical frame, I decided to put the body first. Thus, in my writing I rely on multiple theories concerning agency, mobility and politics. It is not my intention to create a solid frame of analysis, but rather to understand what is at stake in the empirical data that I have collected since 2006.

Collaging research

The ambiguity and lack of solid ground from which to discuss the topic encouraged me to write this book in the form of a collage. A collage, in Christine Sylvester's (2007: 562) terms, basically enables us to look at one thing from different angles, each of which offers a slightly different understanding. While Sylvester has developed the technique of collage in order to combine and juxtapose disparate themes, objects and elements in a single piece of writing and leave the reader/ viewer to relate things together, I do not discuss collage from a methodological point of view. For me, it offered an opportunity to make sense of different perspectives that have an ambiguous relationship with one another and yet are connected. The technique of collage thus allows me to analyse such perspectives and happenings as elements of the politico-corporeal struggle that unfolds in the field of asylum. The struggle is not a uniform effort, but becomes manifest through various acts and events that do not necessarily represent a consious effort towards a particular and definite goal. The creative technique of collage-making enables a focus on happening and evented negotiation around positions and identities. The meanings of being an asylum seeker take shape in and through the body and in responses that people form towards the physical or figural presence of others. This collage seeks to draw together elements and ways in which that eventually happens, and its political consequences.

Making a collage of a tensional and highly politicised issue, and including my personal voice in it, meant an agonising writing process. Instead of separation I wish to look at relationality. That means examining the operation of sovereignty and senses of the international that bodies make visible through their relations, engagements and movement. Throughout the research process I have been at pains to highlight the tensions and multiple relations that are at work whenever the political question of asylum is evoked. Thus, there are two parallel narratives that flow through this book. One tells of sovereign power and practices that intersect with asylum seekers' means of contesting, undermining and resisting the operation of sovereignty and the relevant bureaucratic and institutional processes.

Such a perspective involves exploring the ways in which asylum seekers construct themselves as political beings and take part in political engagements within exclusionary politics. The other is a story of the politics of the body, any body, its means of exceeding and interrupting the state-based body politics and the thus-evoked different political ontology. As a whole this work aspires to reverse the thinking of political community as an entity into which we are born, assimilated, integrated and included or from which we are excluded.

Responsible scholarship

Instead of objectivity, the politics of my research is marked by a sense of responsibility towards the asylum seekers, the professionals, those who worked in my research sites and myself (see Campbell 2005; Doty 2004; Eckl 2008; cf. Chan 2003a). I travel with and am guided by Jean-Luc Nancy's postphenomenological ontology. More specifically, I draw upon his thinking of community, body and philosophy of the political (e.g. Nancy 2003a, 2004a). Nancy's thinking forms the theoretico-methodological ground from which my exploration begins and against which I reflect both the research process and the material collected during that process. Such a take involves interpreting Nancy's thought in rather narrow and selective terms, but my goal has been to explore how it could inform our conceptions of asylum seeking, the reception of asylum seekers and, more theoretically, what political community could become when thought of in terms of always already relational being (see Coward 2009; Puumala 2013; Puumala & Pehkonen 2010).

The main focus of this book is on asylum seekers' engagements with others and their embeddedness in various relations. The book is comprised of Events and Chapters. The Events discuss and present the way in which various engagements during the periods of data collection and fieldwork have shaped my understanding of the topic under scrutiny. Thus, they present evented understandings of state practices and the way those practices take shape and materialise in people's daily lives and their relationships with others. Informed and inspired by an event, each chapter, in turn, adopts a different perspective on the questions of asylum seeking, sovereignty and the senses of the international. Although there are connections between the events and the actual chapters, they can be read separately from and independently of one another. When put together, these internally variant perspectives form complex intersections between theory and the empirical data, the international and the local, the body and politics (cf. Shapiro 2002). With such a research design, I aspired to achieve a politico-philosophical stance, which would depart from dichotomous thinking that characterises political debate around asylum seeking and, instead, open alternative horizons. The choice results from an understanding that our perceptions of others, ourselves and the world are shaped by political constellations put together in particular ways, which are by no means unquestionable or the only possible ways. There is always a possibility to reverse the angle from which one looks. In terms of international relations, that means exploring, besides facts and reason, the tactile and sensuous.

xvi *Preface*

I can only hope that I have managed to relate to people in the manner in which they deserve to be treated, with the accuracy of the ambiguity and multifacetedness of their lives, thoughts and experiences, without claiming to know the absolute truth about them. I have tried not to victimise, demonise, glorify or pity these people, and at the same time I struggled not to do away with the manifold forms of suffering and distress that accompanied the lives of my research participants and asylum seekers more generally. I hope that at least some of that, together with a sense of the incomplete, will transfer to the reader.

Event 1

Ethnographic experiences

Anna, a counsellor at the reception centre, asks if I would help her to clear a room. The Nigerian man who used to live in it was taken into police custody for being a Dublin-hit.[1] This was two days previously, on Tuesday.

We enter the room where the police have already come to collect his personal effects. The first thing that catches my eye is a plate on the table. He did not finish his meal before leaving. The tuna on the plate has dried around the edges. His reading glasses are on the table next to his books, which include the Holy Bible and a prayer book, his shoes lie on the floor, pictures of his loved ones decorate the wall and scattered around the desktop there are letters from and to his family. "*Dear dad, I'm writing you to ask a favour . . .*", "*I hope that you would hold me in your heart until we can be together again . . .*" His CDs lie on the bedside table and some kind of official papers from his home country in the cupboard. Somebody has written the words "**DA BLOOD**" in thick capital letters on the wall. One out of the two cupboards is filled with food. He hadn't planned to leave. My stomach turns when I think about what we are doing and why; the wider political context of our actions. I don't wish to be party to this, but I bite my lips and keep the black rubbish sack open as Anna stuffs his things into it.

We take only things that would go bad, such as opened groceries. Even so the black sack is filled halfway. In the corridor, we pass by a woman from Azerbaijan who sees us at work with rubber gloves, carrying that big black sack. She stands still, does not say a word, but her eyes follow us. Anna notes laconically that the residents will probably have nightmares for the rest of their lives, first of people going missing and then of plastic sacks being carried down the corridors the morning after. Outside, she heaves the sack into a rubbish container.

When we get back to the office, we disinfect our hands – following the general procedure – and Anna phones the police to check whether the remaining personal items could be sent to the man. The police, however, explain that he was returned to Belgium the previous day. Next Anna calls his legal representative, who – as it turns out – is not aware of the situation. The lawyer is outraged by the police action and certain that the return would not have been enforceable in court, because the man has two minor children living in Finland.

2 Ethnographic experiences

I can sense that a certain feeling of resentment begins to rise in me, and I do not like it. I feel tired, hopeless, lost, empty, fed up and angry. I am happy I can return home after the day, and yet the mark of the reception centre does not easily leave me. Its effects stick on my body, they make me sleepy, my limbs get heavy and start aching, and I get easily irritated.

(Research diary, 26th September 2006)

The paths that open out following this event are embedded in the notion that asylum seeking is a struggle. It is a political struggle for control on the one hand, and recognition and response on the other. Furthermore, it is a corporeal struggle to arrive, stay put, move and exist. What the event illustrates is that fieldwork makes it hard to construct and maintain rigid categories. What becomes central is movement in its diverse forms: corporeal and incorporeal, voiced and non-verbal, physical and symbolic. Informed by my bodily experiences, my work argues for the importance of taking note of the manifold bodies and diverse experience-worlds behind administrative and categorical figures. Therewith, fieldwork may challenge not only the composition of the research but also the researching 'I' and the research process altogether. During the period of data collection, I had to reflect carefully upon such questions as: What kind of power was I ready to accept and use in interviewing, undertaking participant observation and writing? What traces does power leave on the body, and what kind of traces do bodies leave on each other? How does the international – as a political project – mark us and how do our daily actions shape notions of the international? Therefore, this work adopts various angles to explore the experience of displacement and the sensuous effects of being out of place.

Even though I began the research process with people and from work in the field, I soon noticed that I was framing and categorising asylum seeking and the complex life experiences that accompany it with disciplinary discussions and paradigms that I had learned during my university training. I was more concerned about establishing my own place within the discipline of International Relations than exploring the issue thoroughly, in a way that would open up new connections and take up emerging insight. At approximately the same time, I also realised that whether I read official statements, guidelines, reports, studies, theories, or political philosophy, I felt increasingly overwhelmed and bewildered. It felt as if I sacrificed the people who made my writing possible in the first place. My field experiences did not go together with the framework I had started to create. In many ways – and on multiple fronts – this work, then, is about struggles. There are my personal struggles within academia, in the field and within myself, and then there are the state's struggle to manage migration and the asylum seeker's struggle for a normal life.

It is fair to state that the overall focus of this work stems from my encounters with asylum seekers, the processes that gained materiality during fieldwork and the personal experience of becoming a subject of evaluation and surveillance in the eyes of both asylum seekers and migration officials. Those ethnographic experiences shook me profoundly and guided my theoretical and methodological choices. Due to them, my research started moving in directions that I had not anticipated at all when I first entered the field in 2006. Situations that I have been engaged in while collecting data have made me reflect on the researcher's role, together with how methodological choices affect what becomes perceived or worth exploring.

My own experiences of the lives that asylum seekers led in reception centres were so overwhelming that finding and maintaining a research position became very difficult, at times impossible. The figure of the objective and securely positioned researcher, who always holds the field at an arm's length, maintains control and comes out untarnished, became a casualty of this process (see Gergen & Gergen 2002). Exactly seven years after I participated in clearing the Nigerian man's room, I found myself sitting at another reception centre. I was meeting with an Iraqi family with whom we were carrying out a photographic project about the ways in which they would like to be portrayed. It was a project based on building and reaffirming positive self-image while waiting for a decision on one's asylum process (see also Chapter 4 and Collage). I had arranged to meet with Nasren, her husband and her daughter in order to look at and discuss the photos we had taken a couple of weeks earlier. Things, however, took a turn:

Nasren[2] looks sad and restless. I ask whether she is ok and she answers in the negative. She explains with her poor English that the family has just received a decision according to which they have to leave Finland and return to France. The Finnish officials have concurred that they will not process the family's application for asylum, as they have earlier resided in France and Italy. There they had received a negative decision with an order to exit the EU area. In France they had lived in Toulouse, undocumented, after which they travelled to Italy, where Nasren gave birth to their daughter. Sahar is now a bit less than 2 years old.

Nasren sits on the sofa and begins to cry. She has taken her veil off, as we will not be taking photos today. Her husband, Farouk, goes out for a smoke, after which he takes their daughter Sahar to bed. Sahar has been observing her mother carefully and seems bewildered to see her cry. I give Nasren a hug and ask her to tell me what is going on in her mind. She repeats the sentences "*What I am going to do now? What about Sahar? What am I going to do with this baby?*" Nasren is seven months pregnant with their second child. "*We have no place to go in France. Where will we live? What are we going to do?*" I have no answers. I can only hold Nasren's hand and encourage them to contact their lawyer.

In the evening I return home and hug my boys. My younger son is the same age as Sahar. I can relate to Nasren's concern as a mother, and yet I cannot imagine the amount of stress the family faces. Again there is the familiar and extremely ambiguous mixture of anger, vulnerability and gratefulness that arises in me. It has to do with the discrepancy of positions, empathy towards Nasren and her family and the multiple privileges that make my life so much easier, safer and more comfortable than Nasren's. Restless thoughts keep me awake the following night.

(Research diary, 26th September 2013)

4 *Ethnographic experiences*

While it was incredibly difficult to get the research process started, it was sometimes far more strenuous to keep up the momentum and to find the will to begin once again the process of data collection. As my research diary from the meeting with Nasren and her family illustrates, years have not made it easier to bear the sorrow or pain of others. Witnessing great anguish and distress, weaving plotlines from bodily experience and conceptualising personal histories in terms of impersonal theories continues to be a point of constant reflection. The first chapter of my collage dwells on these considerations and developments. It begins with the body and from the field, and only through them the chapter moves to connect the topic with sovereignty and mobility studies. This choice results from the personal anxiety that my ethnographic experiences still – after a decade of working with the issue – engender in me, the discontent and difficulties that I experienced in linking autoethnography with stories of asylum seeking and political theories, and the importance of establishing this connection (see Khosravi 2010).

Within academia, I am still occasionally questioned about pushing the limits or outright crossing the line of professional ethics by sympathising with my research participants. My question that has formulated over the years is not how to eradicate sympathy and gain objectivity, but rather *what can be learned from this emotional involvement.*

Notes

1 The provisions of the Dublin Convention introduced a system which assigns exclusive responsibility to contracting EU states for reviewing asylum claims and obliges them to recognise the negative decisions reached in another contracting state as final (also Uçarer 2006: 228).
2 All names are pseudonyms.

1   Exposure

Points of departure

While administrative processes and governmental practices involved in the management and control of migration have received academic attention, studies focusing on asylum seekers' own voices, moves and bodily relations, whether they appear in relation to, in contradiction with or in spite of state practices and asylum policies, remain somewhat less theorised. However, in the fields of anthropology, international political sociology, critical human geography, mobility studies and sociology, the everyday dimensions of state practice and corporeal relations instituted through that practice have received attention (see especially Khosravi 2010; McNevin 2010, 2012; Mountz 2010; Redclift 2013; Rygiel 2011; Squire 2010, 2014). These works have helped in demystifying the idea of the state as a faceless, disembodied entity that operates in ubiquitous spheres, penetrating every aspect of political life and yet existing nowhere. As Alison Mountz (2010: xxiii) claims, the putting into operation of sovereign powers through state practice has material and embodied consequences. That aspect is one element in the politico-corporeal struggle involved in seeking asylum. However, the other and even less theorised question concerns human relations that form and materialise in spite of state practice and the political significance of those relations. From that relationality a whole other take on political community and togetherness arises. Neither of the two exists alone or operates separately; rather there is yet another struggle, this time between two philosophical takes on political existence in the world.

There are no simple solutions, no simple ways of doing research on these struggles in their entirety. Indeed, anyone who has carried out ethnographic data collection or applied reflexive and participatory research methods knows the difficulties in expressing and examining the complexities of human existence. Recording daily life, as it happens, is far from easy. For me the process of data collection changed the whole research set-up. Thus, in order to make the theoretical basis and analytical framework of this work understandable, I first need to address my ethnographic exposure to the politico-corporeal struggle of seeking asylum.

As the chapter reflects my experiences of doing interviews and fieldwork, the narration is quite personal and (auto)ethnographic. In this chapter, I do not aim to present my findings, but sketch a methodologically reflective reproduction or restructuring of my journey into the bodily politics of asylum and where this

6   *Exposure*

search has taken me. It has meant trying to fit together my feelings and thoughts, political theory and philosophy with the expectations, hopes, stories and contradictions that my research participants have presented me with. As a whole, this reflection sets the basis for the rest of the book. It points out that the question of asylum is not one of people needing recognition, but one of having a right to response. Recognition bears the element of inclusion, which is inadmissible – and I might add perhaps only perpetrates certain spatial violence. While responding can, certainly, be just as violent, it also bears an element of relating and a willingness to change or critically engage the self. Through such a take, the chapter suggests approaching asylum seeking by moving beyond the questions of responsibility and hospitality (and their limits) or even rightful presence (e.g. Doty 2006; Rajaram 2013; Squire & Darling 2013). The politics of identification that is also involved in determining and recognising people's right to protection easily fixes us in locked cycles of dominance, retaliation and annihilation. Asylum seekers become sentimentalised and moralised, which silences the violences, violations and injustices that legal and governmental structures perpetrate. (Cf. Agathangelou & Ling 2005: 835). Ultimately, the difference between recognition and response boils down to the question of subaltern existence.

It has been almost 30 years since Gayatri Chakravorty Spivak posed the question "Can the subaltern speak?" (1988). Yet it continues to resonate with contemporary politics. Spivak herself answered in the negative, claiming that the forms of representation that stem from the colonial legacy and the western subject are ill-suited to describe the experiences of people who find themselves at the margins of the political system[1]. Spivak raises the question of the impossibility of a privileged scholar speaking for the marginalised. She believes that such endeavours fall prisoner to a first-world, masculine, privileged, institutionalised discourse that in its analysis reinstitutes the same dominance and erasures it seeks to dismantle. More recently, it has been claimed that the subaltern does speak, but we do not hear or know how to listen (Maggio 2007). My privilege is at the same time my loss. I have to admit that. I also need to give up the quest to frame the phenomenon of asylum seeking around stable concepts and collective loci of identity and agency.

The academic reactions spurred by Spivak's essay seem to rely on an assumption of two rather stable subjects who try to interact with one another. I would claim that Spivak's essay, however, makes room for much more corporeal interpretations, where the body is used as a medium of communication. What would happen if we disregarded the notion of two separate subjects and intact bodies as the starting point for communication? What if instead of a spoken word we would focus on exposure? What if instead of trying to fit asylum seekers' experiences, stories and bodies into the frameworks we have created, we put our own thinking in line?

The field

Before moving on to discuss the actual process of data collection, let me contextualise the empirical work that has been carried out for the book. I have been

Exposure 7

circling around the topic since 2006. I began by examining "failed" asylum seekers' and detainees' ways of enacting political agency and their ways of participating in society. In late 2005–early 2006, there was a heated debate in Finland around the question of temporary residence permits that were issued to asylum seekers who did not meet the standards for international protection, but who could not be returned to their countries of origin either. The permit left its holders in a liminal situation, where they could not access many services and rights in the society. In time the debate over temporary permits grew from an undertone to a cry. Political petitions were made and demonstrations abounded, organised by sympathetic organisations and the permit holders themselves. Ultimately, the Finnish migration officials practically stopped issuing temporary permits for asylum seekers.[2]

At the same time as the debate on temporary residence permits, there was a lot of discussion around the practice of detention in Finland. The detention infrastructure in the country is still in the early stages of development, as the first detention unit was opened only in 2002. In 2014 another specific detention unit was opened. My period of data collection among failed asylum seekers and detainees spans from the time of the growing use of the temporary permit until the peak years when the permit was in active use for the first time. In addition to months of ethnographic observation and interviews with asylum seekers, I interviewed migration officials, health care professionals and social workers who worked with asylum seekers and refugees, as well as asylum seekers' legal representatives. The first dataset was collected between 2006–2008. This particular process of collecting research material forms the starting point for the present chapter.

Another process of data collection was carried out in 2013–2014, among asylum seekers who were waiting for their applications to be processed. That time, instead of focusing on people's lives as asylum seekers, I sought to explore what mattered for them. What was meaningful, important or painful in the lives of my research participants? How did they themselves construct their identities, how would they want to be seen and how did they look at themselves? The second period of ethnographic work lays the ground for the final part of the chapter and paves the way towards the overall focus of the book.[3]

Collecting data involved doing institutional ethnography in the premises of four reception centres for asylum seekers, and in the detention unit. In Finland, asylum seekers are accommodated in reception centres while they wait for their applications to be processed. In the centres they can access social and health care services, and there are organised study and work activities. There is also a continuous element of surveillance and control present, which impacts upon people's lives (see Chapter 4). I studied the rhythm of everyday life in the centres, participated in staff meetings and meetings between asylum seekers and the staff or state officials. I located my participants by presenting my research interests at various meetings in the reception centres. Afterwards I was either contacted directly by interested participants or presented by the staff with a list of asylum seekers who had agreed to meet me. In addition to doing interviews, I spent time in the public spaces of the centres and talked informally with people. I met with most

8 *Exposure*

participants several times and was able to keep track of their lives for months, occasionally even after they had been returned to other countries. Except for one group interview, all were individual interviews conducted in the scarce private places that the centres had to offer. In some cases, however, the person was contacted through the staff. As for the detention unit, all interviews were arranged by the staff in line with the specification I had given: people who have been detained after receiving a negative decision to their asylum application.

The informal chats I had with people in the corridors, group talks, semi-private discussions, debates, emails and phone calls all brought important aspects of living as an asylum seeker to my attention. In addition to the material collected with asylum seekers, I interviewed various policy makers and officials working with asylum seekers in order to contextualise and reflect upon the primary set of interviews with asylum seekers. Among those interviewed there were representatives of the Finnish Ministry of Employment and the Economy, the Finnish Immigration Service, a mental health team from a policlinic for migrants, lawyers from the Refugee Advice Centre, directors of all the centres in which interviews were conducted, social workers in three reception centres and other staff members in the detention unit and reception centres. I also kept a research diary, which addresses the daily life in the centres and my own experiences of carrying out fieldwork. All in all, these ethnographic methods enabled me to form an understanding of the mechanisms of surveillance and choreographies of resistance that materialise in the lives of asylum seekers. As for the second data set, I worked directly with asylum seekers who had agreed to participate in my study based on the information leaflet that the staff of the reception centre had distributed.

Most of my participants have been men, 18–50 years of age, who had arrived alone in Finland; but single women, a female couple, a single mother and whole families have also participated in this research. Mostly my interviews were conducted without (official) interpreters, which obviously limited the number of participants, but on the other hand enabled the creation of an intimate atmosphere and proved to be a trust-building measure. Geographically, the participants have come from Afghanistan, Algeria, Angola, the Dominican Republic, Georgia, Ghana, Iraq, Kurdistan, Lebanon, Nigeria, Nepal, Palestine, Russia, Somalia, Syria and Turkey. But migrant trajectories are rarely, if ever, simple. What is consistent about them is the almost continuous movement between and towards different places. Therefore, besides the country of origin and Finland, people I have met have talked about their lives in and routes in and out of Austria, Benin, Belgium, Burkina Faso, Denmark, Ethiopia, France, Germany, Greece, India, Iran, Italy, Ivory Coast, Kenya, Lithuania, Norway, Pakistan, Russia, Spain, Sweden, Turkey and Yemen. Having said this, I want to emphasise that I am not interested in composing a 'typical' profile of an asylum seeker, tracking down their reasons for leaving or assessing their grounds for asylum.

Even though my empirical work is limited to Finland, the methodological implications as well as the understandings that emerge through the data reach beyond the case study. It has been my ambition to illustrate through methodological reflection and theoretical engagement how the personal and material are connected to the structural and political in terms of both practice and the thought system. The larger question that I wish to address is the philosophico-politico-corporeal connection between the subject, the state/political community and the international. The case study reveals something about the logic of sovereign practice and the senses of the international as they appear in the case of seeking asylum. My interest lies in exploring *how corporeal relations and the body itself mediate our being political in the world, the related senses of the international and the bearings they have on the notions of political community.*

Research motivation

The people that I have met since the early days of my fieldwork are so much more than just asylum seekers. They have had so many other stories to tell and thoughts to share besides the ones related to displacement and vulnerability. People define their identities, positions and actions in their own terms and therefore they challenge the sovereign logic behind border practices. Thus, even though I place the 'asylum seeker' at the centre of my study, I try to move beyond such administrative categorisations, which go against the philosophical framework of this work and my ambitions (cf. Smith 1992). In listening to the experiences, hopes, fears, memories and anxieties that my participants had, I have learned a great deal about myself, about my own prejudices, presuppositions and preconceptions. Furthermore, I have learned a great deal about how my research participants have perceived my presence and how their perceptions have directed their ways of voicing themselves and building separations and connections between us. By showing the fluidity of those categories and concepts on which my writing relies, I hope to avoid incarcerating my participants conceptually (see Soguk 1999: 8) and to allow space for their and my own experiences, however complex and contingent they may be.

Over the years I have had to tackle the following two questions: For whom do we write when we write our academic papers? And for what purposes do we write these texts? (see Doty 2004). In many ways, and on multiple fronts, this work is about political and corporeal struggles; my personal struggle in the discipline, in the field and within myself, the Finnish states's struggle to govern migration and asylum seekers' daily struggles to live with and surpass the ambiguous and yet extremely material effects of sovereign practice.

With the chosen research design and style of discussion, I hope to respect the spirit of the research process, as everything in this work stems from the field. As said, those asylum seekers who have participated in this research guided me with my theoretical choices. They changed the course of my work in directions that I did not realise even existed when I first started this process. They moved my thinking. In the end, that move became the main theme of this work. Writing about asylum began to present itself as an attempt at putting myself, my knowledge practices and my categories of thinking in line. Or, better still, pushing myself out of line into the spaces where people fight their marginalisation (see also Reyes Cruz 2008: 652). This book, by force, is a timid attempt to unlearn

10   *Exposure*

in order to learn anew and to unknow in order to gain insight. My collage seeks to underscore the senses of the international that emerge when sovereign power and state practice are put into operation in the context of seeking asylum. These senses are multiple and take shape in numerous material ways and locations. Besides exposing the vulnerability of people to the idea of political community that materialises in the state, my exploration also exposes the vulnerability of sovereign logic and highlights the transformative political potential that rests in the movements of the body and in the relations the body undertakes. I will discuss the potential of exposure in detail at the end of the chapter, but first it is imperative to ground the move through the demand that asylum seekers presented me with. Years later I realised that the demand represents an event of (ethnographic) exposure.

The demand

EEVA: Can I understand what you tell me, because I have never witnessed war?
NASIR: Well, it's really difficult, I just don't know. I can't say. You should ask someone who himself is in the same position to tell you, so it's really hard. I would say no. I would say no, because many of the refugees have witnessed with their own eyes things which seem or sound really unbelievable, or unimaginable. You can't even imagine those things, which they have even witnessed. I don't want to talk about those very gruesome horrors, because it's, yeah, really nasty. You can . . . There are so many things happening, nasty things happening, that if we talk, you wouldn't believe that this might be happening in Afghanistan. You couldn't understand it.

(Interview with Nasir, March 2007)

Nasir's[4] statement could have signalled the end for my aspirations. His view, however, made me ponder carefully the way in which I was to relate to the accounts that I collected during the fieldwork. After initial bewilderment I decided to follow Brooke Ackerly, Maria Stern and Jacqui True's (2006: 261) idea of "multiple and intersecting workings of power" that encourage the study of "the production of subjectivities and identities, ethics and responsibilities". How do people acquire a legible and visible face, and how does that face always appear in the complex connection between a person's self-conception and him/her being addressed by others (cf. Butler 2001; Edkins 2013)? Face, and the body, are questions of politics. So it is clear that even though I seek to move beyond state-centred narrations about seeking asylum, already my interest in the topic connects my study to a set of sovereign practices that have been instituted to control migration. Yet, embedded in my research there is the intersection between knowledge and power. It concerns the question of studying 'down', which is tricky because the question of 'margins' necessarily evokes questions of power (see Enloe 1999; also Briggs 2002). When the questions of margins and power are raised, questions of political agency, voice and ethics necessarily follow (cf. Dauphinee 2010: 805–813). Who can speak? Whose voice will not be heard? Who can claim knowledge?

Exposure 11

A question of representation arises. As a matter of fact, the people I interviewed were not so eager to accept my authorship in the first place. Often they challenged me openly.

Even though ethnography is sometimes celebrated as a method with emancipatory potential, it is not free from power. In fact, Ruth Behar (2003: 15) draws a close connection between ethnography and colonialism by saying that it began as a method, "which was discovered, perfected, and institutionalised in western centres of power, for telling stories about the marginalised populations of the world". Ethnography as such does not guarantee a way out of colonising other people's experiences and lives (cf. Moreira 2005; Spivak 1988). Power affects the process of data collection and the development of understanding in interviews (cf. Edkins 2005a: 64). While interviewing, I had to constantly reflect on who was to have ethnographic authority in the situation: me with my questions or my interviewees with their accounts (see Clifford 2007; Rosaldo 1986)? Or both of us; me persuading them to answer those things I wished to know, to describe their experiences in ways that I could understand, and them persuading me to discover other stories and the evoked relationalities?

Another pressing question concerned the way in which I would be able to respectfully frame the lived complexities of seeking asylum in relation to academic debates on migration. Furthermore, the accounts I was offered did not have clear plot lines. They were ruptured. There were immense gaps and cracks. The stories were filled with detailed but scattered information, unclear connections and causations. It was impossible to turn the interviews into unitary stories (cf. Sermijn, Devlieger & Loots 2008). In hindsight, there is absolutely nothing surprising in this. It simply points out the multiplicity of sensuous experiences engendered by those state practices that result from the act of crossing a border. Little by little, the constant movement in the accounts and in the daily lives of asylum seekers, together with the refusal of the body to be fixed, started moving my thinking.

> Soran says that he thinks too much, but that he doesn't know how to explain his thoughts to me. He tells me that if I stayed at the centre for a night I would understand, if I went to take a shower there, I would understand, but not even the staff understands, or they do not think about it. When he gets to the point of taking a shower in the centre, I let slip: "I don't want to do that." He looks at me and says, "I know you don't, but then you would understand. How would you feel if you went to Kurdistan, and nobody would help you, talk to you or like you? What would you think?" I tell him I would be sad, angry, bewildered and would want to leave. "Yes, and you could leave. What about me? Why do they take my fingerprints? If I leave, will they delete them? Where can I go?"
>
> (Research diary, 11th September 2006)

Soran considered his status unfair and unjust. In seeking asylum, he had only pleaded for protection. Instead of recognising his claim, the Finnish officials

12   *Exposure*

replied that they had not found a basis for protection or any other ground(s) on the basis of which Soran could be given a residence permit. But as he could not be returned to Iraq, Soran was issued a temporary residence permit for one year. As a result, he encountered a liminal status that contradicted his sense of justice. Soran demanded another kind of response from me. He, when describing being beyond both return and accommodation, needed me to reflect on the relation that had been imposed between us through a political asylum process (also Puumala 2013). Soran did not invite me to elaborate on the private feelings that displacement and 'refugee experience' might create. Rather he pointed out the moral hurt, as well as personal and material relations, that such an experience gives rise to. His protest made me realise that we were not separate subjects, but that in a way I was a complicit in him being categorised as a rejected asylum seeker. We came to be only in relation to one another.

My encounter with Soran, together with other, similar, discussions, affected me profoundly. What shook me was the experience of being exposed to the limits of my being and having to face in the flesh the corporeal consequences of state practice.[5] Tellingly, Soran pointed out my reluctance to change places with him. I am privileged enough to trust in the freedoms and securities that the Finnish state promises. Whether I liked it or not, for the research participants – like Soran – I embodied and enacted a plethora of state practices just by entering the space of the reception centre. It was impossible to claim the position of an objective researcher who merely observes and collects material. Largely, the state structures our accounts of who we are, who we must be and who we must become as political beings capable of acting in the modern world (Walker 2009: 57–58; also Mountz 2010). The state and the system of modern states frame the possibilities of political life. It is therefore obvious that my presence and the way my body was perceived profoundly affected data collection. However, I also realised that, ontologically, my status as a Finnish citizen was just as precarious and without a solid foundation as Soran's condition, although for the moment our situations did not begin to compare.

The process of data collection challenged me to position my own existence in relation to the lives of asylum seekers and to explore their lives in relation to state practices related to seeking asylum. Perhaps Nasir was right in claiming that I cannot understand what it is like to be born and raised in war, to flee from one's country and to live as an unwanted stranger in a society, if understanding refers to the comprehension of the meaning and nature of those experiences. However, Sara Ahmed (2004: 32) suggests that an ethics of responding to feelings and experiences of pain involves an openness to being affected by that which one cannot know or feel. For me, this thought opened an alternative way to write about seeking asylum, the sovereign processes involved in it and the related senses of the international. It enabled me to engage in writing with the demand that Soran presented, which led me to claim that struggle of asylum evokes a different ontology of the political (see also Huynh 2010). First, however, I need to discuss how that demand was reflected in my field practice and the overall politics of my research.

Sensuous scholarship and ethnographic seduction

Paul Stoller (1997; also Denton 2005; Herzfeld 2007) has termed "sensuous scholarship" the type of research in which head and heart mix, and one's being is opened to the world. What is also required from the ethnographer is critical reflection on her roles and positions with regard to the subject studied (see e.g. Marcus 2004; Reyes Cruz 2008). The play of power and politics in the research interviews raised questions of interpretive frameworks and the knowledge-interest that I have had when I planned the various periods of data collection (see Beier 2005; Budgeon 2003; Grovogui 2005; Radhakrishnan 1993). This play also raised questions on the nature of narration prevalent within academia, on the need to enter into a dialogue with another form of narration and bring that within my own discipline of International Relations so as to start thinking about the senses of the international (cf. Chan 2003b: 410). It was, therefore, imperative that my field practice would take note of acts of sharing and the ethics of encountering. In other words, the adopted method must allow room for fluidity in perception and remain responsive to the unexpected turns, like my encounter with Soran, that may change the research focus altogether.

I wanted to learn about asylum seekers' lived, bodily experiences and the sensuous elements of those experiences. I was after stories, feelings and thoughts, not the truth. Instead of doing interviews, I felt the need to respond to asylum seekers' presence. The academically correct term to describe these interactions might be an open-ended interview, but maybe 'conversation', 'talk' or 'discussion' is more true to the nature of our encounters. Still, I use the term interview to stay cognisant of the power hierarchies embedded in the relation. When questions of ethics and epistemology coincide so strongly, as in this case, I decided to use the term "ethnographic seduction" to describe my practice of data collection. It is a term coined by Antonius Robben (1996). Ethnographic seduction entails "a complex dynamic of conscious moves and unconscious defences that may arise in interviews" (Robben 1996: 72). The act of seducing becomes especially relevant in cases where people have high political and personal stakes in legitimising their interpretations. To be precise, ethnographic seduction is not a separate method from 'normal' ethnography, but an inseparable part of doing ethnographic research.

Whereas Robben (1996: 76) ponders how to cope with it, for me ethnographic seduction functioned as a resource. It could take shape in a tone of voice that led to an unexpected story and an opening in which to think the "not-mobilized-yet" (Reyes Cruz 2008: 654). Or it could represent itself in my participant's unwillingness to accept my views or questions, in their emotional outbursts against what my presence embodied for them or in them trying to argue their case through me. None of the above were elements that were intended to become a part of my empirical data. They did so, because they represent articulations, transgressions and enactments of the embodied state on the one hand, and of political existence, on the other. As such, they enable imaging political life and political community beyond notions that rely on citizenship and the dichotomous logic of inside/ outside (cf. Walker 1993, 2009; Weber 2008).

14 *Exposure*

Let me discuss the potential of ethnographic seduction for the research process through the story of Stephen, who was detained at a centre. His narration starts paving the way for the senses of the international, or for the kinds of experiences that the international as a political project sometimes generates. I hope the account tunes the reader's ear to something that cannot be captured by relying solely on the said.

> I ask Stephen why he left Nigeria to seek asylum. "Oh, that's a long story, but I'll tell you," says Stephen, and begins a very detailed explanation of his troubles. (During his story he examines my face as if he is trying to detect whether I believe it.)
>
> Stephen explains that his troubles in Nigeria stem from 'courtism'. 'Courtism' is the practice of setting up secret courts at universities where, as a consequence, the campus is controlled by university students with the power to veto actions, Stephen clarifies. The first of these courts was formed in 1985 by a professor in Nigeria. The group was called the Pirates. In 1989 other groups – called the Black Axe, the Black Eye, the Black Magic – emerged. "If they want to initiate you," Stephen says, "they'll contact you." He was contacted, but he didn't want to get involved. Stephen departs momentarily from his personal narrative to explain the initiation rites to me. He tells me that the initiation takes place at a shrine, which might be located, for example, in the high mountains. It involves beatings, where you are beaten until you fall to the ground. They will then continue, repeatedly beating you until you stand up. Achieving this, you are recognised as a strong man. Then you can perform the rituals, one of which is drinking animal blood.
>
> Stephen returns to his personal story and tells me that one night he was kidnapped from his hostel and taken to a Black Eye gang's shrine. He tells me that he was beaten, and that he thought he would die. Stephen shows me a scar that he got then on his shin; it is quite wide and approximately 15 cm long. They told Stephen that either he became a member or he would be beaten to death. He contends that the police are powerless in the face of these powerful and armed gangs, so that they couldn't have helped him. When he was released from the hospital where he went after the beating, five members of the Black Eye came and took him away. He was made to perform the initiation rituals. Shortly after this, he was told to go to another university where he was to handle some weapons. Stephen, however, ran away, went into hiding in Lagos, and believed that his troubles were over.
>
> Later that year Stephen went to a festival in his old hometown. There was a party one night, where some members of the Black Eye gang spotted him. He explained that there was fighting, and that his brother was killed with a machete. One of the gang members was also killed, along with three others from his town. The police arrived on the scene, and took Stephen into custody. The Black Eye gang members committed a crime near the police station so that ultimately they were put in the same cell with him. "It was dark," explains Stephen, "and you couldn't see anything and the cell was full of people."

Then he felt something in his right arm; an injection. Some days later, Stephen woke up in a hospital. The doctors told him that he had been poisoned.

Soon after that Stephen left Nigeria and moved to Guinea, and from there he went to Germany in 2003. Two years later, in 2005, he was returned to Nigeria. Now he has been "seeking protection for four years. I could have graduated, been somebody. Now I have just been living a hell of a life."

(Interview with Stephen, May 2007)

Let me break into Stephen's story at this point and outline the role of ethnographic seduction to facilitate the reception of his colourful account. Stephen's account continues to remind me why I chose the ethnographic method in the first place. I wished to bring international relations and sovereign politics closer to the ground – manifest the international working in the minutiae – by telling stories of real people in real places. Rather quickly I noticed that people wanted to talk about many things, but in their own ways. The element of seduction in ethnographic research can function as a strategy for interaction and interviewing, and it bears the potential of extending the sense and feel of the interview also to the readers. It gives the politico-corporeal struggle of seeking asylum its flesh and materiality by not relying just on administrative figures or abstractions that emerge through bureucratic practices of the state (cf. Nail 2015).

As a researcher, letting oneself be 'seduced' by the participant's story opens an intervallic space between the researcher and the research participant. The understanding comes close to Jean-Luc Nancy's idea that we are ontologically only together, which means that we come into presence only with others. However, the conversing parties need to share an "affinity of goals" (Harker 2007: 59) or an "embodied involvement" (Sarbin 2004: 18). This brings me to the question of normativity, which is an important dimension in refugee and forced migration studies. The question of the human is, willy-nilly, always also an ethical question. Hence, I fully agree with Norman Denzin (2009: 87) in that "the age of a putative value-free social science appears to be over. Accordingly, [. . .] any discussion of this process must become political, personal, and experiential." To his list I would add also 'experimental' (innovative) in its methodologies and theories (cf. Jutila, Pehkonen & Väyrynen 2008). The act of ethnographic seduction, hence, is a form of relating. All that is needed is time, conversation and "intense intimacy at a close, yet unbreachable distance" (Harker 2007).

Four weeks later, in late June 2007, I return to the detention unit, and find that Stephen is still there. I ask if he would be willing to talk to me again and he agrees. We sit down and start chatting about mundane issues; how he has been, if he has heard from his wife, and if she and the baby are in good health and so on. I tell him that this time I'd like to talk to him about his travels and then his stay in the detention centre, since last time we talked a great deal about his troubles in Nigeria.

I ask how he actually managed to organise his trip to Germany or Finland. Stephen explains that he had another person's passport. "It is very easy, you

16   *Exposure*

know," he states. "There are so few black people in Finland and Europe, that for you we all look the same, and if you have a passport that looks somewhat like you, it is easy. Like me, I know you when you come here, but if I saw you in the street, I might not recognise you, for to me, you all look the same." Stephen tells me that in the passport he used, there were "multiple visas secured." It is easy to find people who will sell you a passport, because it is a rampant form of business in Nigeria. "If you want to travel, they have several passports, and then they'll give you one that is similar looking," says Stephen, "I bought the passport and ticket together, and paid 2.800 dollars." "That's a lot of money," I say. But Stephen says that it depends what you compare it with: "Is it much to save your life?"

Stephen first reached Spain, then France and ultimately Finland. I ask if he was nervous travelling with somebody else's passport. "Nervous, why?" he asks. "It was a look-alike passport. The people tell you not to fear. And, in the worst case, if you are harassed in the airport, you can apply for asylum already there."

I ask Stephen about returning to Nigeria and possible deportation. He says that it would be a death penalty for him. He tells me that he has already sought protection from Germany and Norway, and now he is here. He went to Norway after Germany, but then they told him that his fingerprints had been found and he was sent back to Germany and then to Nigeria again. At this point he reminds me that he has tried living also in Northern Nigeria. Then he found out that his wife had come to Finland, and he decided to join her.

(Interview with Stephen, June 2007)

For Stephen, and others whom I interviewed, ethnographic seduction provided a means to cope with and depart from the framework of the Finnish state practice and its embodied consequences. It comes close to what Sara Ahmed (2004: 179) has termed wonder, which "expands our vision and touch". Importantly enough, there is a link between wonder and learning: "Wonder is about learning to see the world as something that does not have to be, and as something that came to be, over time, and with work" (Ahmed 2004: 180). Furthermore, a link between wonder, movement and politics also exists: "The surprise of wonder is crucial to how it moves bodies. [. . .] The body opens as the world opens up before it; the body unfolds into the unfolding of a world that becomes approached as another body" (Ahmed 2004: 180). Wonder, for Ahmed, potentially energises the hope of transformation, which further evokes the will for politics. This spill-over effect started my journey towards decolonising my own way of knowing (cf. Eckl 2008; Reyes Cruz 2008). I began to look for stories that I did not realise existed, stories that I did not realise I was looking for in the first place, and in the process I tried to leave my suspicions, doubts and theoretical concepts aside (see Behar 2003: 16).

The quest to discover the 'truth' behind people is bound to fail in the sense that the answer one expects will not come, and the received answer will never satisfy completely (see also Chapter 3). In this sense my fieldwork and interviews

Exposure 17

have failed. Instead of receiving neat accounts of identity, I have witnessed life stories filled with movements, shifts and transitions, and views that are based on one's sensuous bodily experience, which does not conform univocally to either sovereign practices or those theories that echoed in my ears when I began this project. In order to succeed, ethnographic seduction requires wondering, and wandering, which might unfold categorical and spatialised identities. Sticking to our learned positions and relying on hegemonic narrations, even if we ultimately wish to challenge them, dispels the bodily experience of wonder. Seduction as an element of ethnographic fieldwork can function as a means to gain insight into the experience-based voices and embodied dimensions of state practice, and shed light also on the senses of the international. Because the stories I heard during fieldwork truly made me wonder, my focus widened from the exploration of the governmental practices related to seeking asylum and their embodied consequences to a will to discover "the deep conjunctures" (Behar 2003: 23) that connect our selves to others and the world. From that viewpoint it is important or interesting not to evaluate the truth-value of what I was told, but to understand that the narratives and reactions appeared for a reason. These narratives now tell me something about what asylum seekers themselves consider to be meaningful, how they relate to others and what kind of relations materialise in their (embodied) narrations.

Shifting strategies of narration and the fluidity of stories function as ways of coping with the situation in which asylum seekers find themselves (cf. Riessman 2002a: 701; also 2002b). After all, refugee life is ripe with rumour (Moorehead 2006: 136). It is a life that depends on stories that would entitle them to protection. Should it be any wonder that stories circulate? Why should that circulation be unacceptable or illegitimate from any other perspective than the state's, as it struggles to institute networked practices of governance and surveillance to control migration? According to Caroline Moorehead, stories are exchanged "among people terrified that their own real story is not powerful enough" (2006: 136). How easy and natural – and I might add how humane – it is to shape the past in such a way that it provides more hope of a better future. I do not mean, however, that all refugee stories are invented. In the narrative construction of the self, positions are taken and explored for the purposes of self and world construction (see Bamberg 2004: 137; Chapter 2 on positionalities). Hence, narratives – whether verbal or embodied – are situated actions, and in the case of seeking asylum they need to be listened to and read in relation to the situation these people find themselves in, not as avenues to speakers' minds and identities (e.g. Denzin 1994). In fact, both the identity 'we say we are' and the narratives about 'what happened' are always more than, less than or other than what we 'really' are and what 'really' happened (see Gergen 2004: 270; also Richardson 1994; Solis 2004). The excess and opacity of our existence and experience-world falls outside the terms of identity (Butler 2001: 28).

As the exploration into the intersections between Soran's demand, Stephen's story and research literature illustrates, seeking asylum represents a politico-corporeal struggle to which I am a party due to embodying a particular political

18 *Exposure*

and gendered subjectivity. At first I had no intention of including myself in the picture. Yet, while doing fieldwork, the idea of in-betweenness implied by ethnographic seduction formulated a methodological tool with which it is possible to tap into sensuous bodily experiences that raise a different relationality between variously categorised people (cf. Ellis & Berger 2002; Osella & Osella 1998: 198; Tanggaard 2009). Thus, in the end it was obvious that I could not leave myself out of the collage. In taking note of the variety of registers, voices, visions, desires, materialities and positionalities, ethnography restores the complexity of human existence to knowledge production (see Chen, Hwang & Ling 2009: 745, 763). The entwinements that emerge when we, as human beings, sense and respond to asylum seekers' presence is an example of political life taking shape through relational events and corporeal exposures (cf. Grayson 2010; Inayatullah & Blaney 2004; Jenkins 2010).

While I was doing fieldwork, the narratives of hopelessness, helplessness and haplessness that are often used to characterise the lives of asylum seekers and refugees began to deeply trouble me. That was due to the fact that those narratives often present people more favourably positioned as capable of empowering asylum-seeking others and with the authority to include them in the space of citizenship. It is as if there is a need to justify asylum seekers as legitimate and acceptable actors, while the ground of the rationality that gives rise to prevailing understanding of legitimacy, agency and politics remains unquestioned. But how is the focus or the mind-set behind asylum politics to be moved? How was I to convince the reader that the interviewed asylum seekers spoke beyond their own immediate experience (cf. Agier 2008; Huynh 2007), and that they actually presented our thinking with both a practical and philosophical challenge that needs to be taken seriously?

Lines of life

> *"We need to talk to you. We have been looking for you." That is how we got started. The TV with an Indian film on is muted. I leave my shoes in the company of four pairs of flip-flops. How can they wear those at this time of the year, I wonder. Almost everybody does, though. Flip-flops in the snow. "A glass of tea?" As a guest: as in an ordinary visit to a friend's house. In the centre, their home. Photos on the shelves, a small and lonely-looking red chair in the doorway, next to a dustbin from which an empty carton of milk sticks out. I bury my toes in the thick, soft carpets that cover the floor as they question my motives and intentions. These five men and me, learning to be with one another, negotiating the space of what might appear. It took us four weeks, five emails, three talks and four cancellations to get here. For them the journey has been longer still.*

Oruzgān, Sar-e, Ghaznī, Kabul:
Afghanistan.
We all have it.
The B.
Unjust.
Unjust and unwise.

Exposure 19

Finland has never been an attractive
country for refugees.

When they interview, they point out flaws
and they make their decisions but they
don't bother (to) ask you again
or allow you to come and appear
before the judge in the court
to explain why those flaws exist, you have reasons for them
sometimes there isn't any contradiction, but they think there is.

In the interviews
we
only answer the questions asked.
Most of them not really important.
Not relevant.
Most of the time silly questions
"Why you came to Finland?
What if we send you back?"
Questions that are in their interest.
Being (as a) police, or being (as) an official.
Try to show off – being efficient, doing their job well.

Under the Taliban regime, well
(silence)
It was, yeah . . .
Chopping off someone's hands
Stoning someone   until death
Blow his brains off,
with stones
Mujahedin were even worse.
The same, now in power
slaughtered   in the district of Afshar,
south-west of Kabul
8.000 men, women and children.
Cut off their breasts,
cut off their heads,
and yeah,
so babies . . .
                    [Nausea. Chills.
                    I don't want to know.
                    Afraid of what might come next.]

"We should work to remove the dictators,
to remove the threat."
In theory it sounds really   good.
Really fancy,
and yeah.

20   *Exposure*

(silence)
Why are you not doing what you say? So,
this is the irony.   [A very harsh irony.]
Yeah, bitter.

[Can I understand what you tell me?]
I just don't know I can't say
I would say   no
things seem or sound really
unbelievable or unimaginable. I don't want to
talk about those very gruesome things
because it's,
yeah, really nasty.

[Are you comfortable talking about this?]
They involve your family.
Persecute and punish
the whole family. And you know
that there are, these families
close, big families, living together:
brothers, uncles, aunts.
Everyone suffers.
This is a problem for everyone
who gets into some kind of problems.
So,
we should not go into personal things.
                [Remembered the note
                taped on his chest:
                "Better to die suddenly,
                than to die
                little by little."
                It all happened not too long ago.]

[This, I'm not comfortable asking.]
Many people have died
after they have survived in their own country.
Could not survive on the way   to a safe place.
Died on their way.
To some safe place.
People have,
yeah,   drowned.
In rivers, in oceans. People have
come with those
balloon-boats, yeah?
People have crossed the sea with those boats,
Balloon-boats

Exposure   21

Almost . . . many.
From Turkey to Italy or Greece.
Just imagine.
And they would pump it with their own mouth.
From Turkey to Italy on those boats.
Very few reach safely.
          [On the shelf, yellow narcissuses, made of plastic;
          and a statue of a naked white woman.
          Toothbrush and toothpaste.
          A big, white box of medicine.]

They said the district I came from,
it is safe
and you can return.
And, I wondered.
I don't care if it's safe or unsafe it is not
safe for me I have problems there.
I have talked to you about
my problems and you
are telling me it is
safe who the hell cares!?
Where ever they would return me,
once you are there in Afghanistan, yeah.
You're dead.

They don't even think
for a second that
they could be wrong. Incorrect.
Or that we could also be right.
We could also be
telling the truth.

Family.
The most important thing.
Your safety. Their safety.
And that you have a,   yeah,
a normal life a peaceful life
a career.
All of us have one thing in common,
we all strive to live a normal life.
And I guess we have
a right to have a normal life. Just like
any other person.

Being a refugee or
having been born and raised in war,

22   *Exposure*

these two things
can't be explained in words. I'm trying my best,
but I can't.
So many, so many things.
This stress, mental stress.
You are away from your family.
Uncertain about your future.
Your safety.
And yeah, that people
look at you with a different kind of,   you know.
(silence)
This feeling of powerlessness.
That someone else
has your destiny in his hands.
And he can do whatever he wants to.
He can . . . If he wanted,
he could give you that opportunity.
Give you that life,
normal life. Give you your only dream.
And if he wanted,
he could destroy and finish everything.

[A sleepless night]

The writing 'I'

What I found, got involved in, during my fieldwork was seemingly a completely different world. Yet, that world was not separate from mine. For me, the reception centres and detention unit materialised a world in which, in Moorehead's (2006: 147) words, "nothing is what it seems, and nothing stays the same". It took me time to understand it, but from early on the stories I heard, the things I witnessed, the people I touched and who touched me, and the smell of that world affected me. A good deal of the emotional discomfort came from learning to see at a close distance the connections between myself and the asylum-seeking 'other'. Their stories were stories of lives torn apart, of dislocation and grief. Much of those stories involved the practices related to the process of seeking asylum in Finland. The distance between the world in which my participants lived and the world in which I lived was non-existent and yet insurmountable. My response was emotional: one of discomfort, rage and extreme vulnerability. The stories hit me hard: unbelievable, too possible, inconceivable and yet so concretely there (also Ahmed 2004: 35–36; Behar 1996). What presented itself before me was a world which had a very dark side, and I was almost swallowed by that darkness. However, it was not a world without any light. It was a world with slender distinctions, and yet a world which represented sovereign practices and border control very concretely in flesh. The stories that I was told did not fit with the stories familiar to me, on which I had relied. I encountered the problem where what I experienced, felt and began to grasp, did not go together with either my existing experience-world or the conceptual world of academic international relations (see Moreira 2005: 53). How was I to represent that world in writing? Instead of simply reporting my findings and presenting the empirical data, the problems of representation and authority of knowledge meant that I needed to develop a writing strategy.

Writing is not only purposive but also, according to Laurel Richardson (2004: 516), a way of knowing, "a method of discovery and analysis". In and through writing, academics find new perspectives on their topics and work their relationship with these topics. For Richardson, form and content cannot be separated in writing, which again connects writing to ethics. For me, in addition to serving as a method, a tool for data collection, ethnography plays a central role in developing the analytical framework and writing up research. I will go further and argue that ethnography can, through the notion of exposure, be also conceptualised as ontologically potent. In political studies and International Relations, ethnography can make a difference to how we conceive the international and the world (see Brigg & Bleiker 2008, 2010; Jackson 2008; Rancatore 2010; Vrasti 2008, 2010; Wedeen 2010; also Cerwonka & Malkki 2007; Humpreys 2010). Ethnography can present us with a deeper understanding of sovereign practices and the multiple senses of the international that the politico-corporeal struggle involved in seeking asylum evokes (Puumala 2013; see also Jenkins 2010: 86; Jutila, Pehkonen & Väyrynen 2008).

The element of struggle makes not only listening to and interpreting but also representing the experiences of asylum seekers hard because "no textual staging is ever innocent" (Richardson 2002: 879). In representation we take part in a wide range of social and political practices, which – as Paul Rabinow claims (1986: 240) – "constitute the modern world, with its distinctive concerns with order, truth and the subject". Academic writing is not free from these limitations. Where was I to search and find meanings? How to frame my argument? How to do justice to feelings and corporealities of being marginalised; living at the edge and beyond border's grip? How to write without victimising my research participants regarding the 'culture' of self-harm, mental disturbance and grief so prevalent in the situation of asylum seekers? How to tell about their multidirectional stories, which defy any simple, straightforward interpretation, without demonising and adding suspicion or contempt towards asylum seekers? (see also Smith 2002: 461). It is incredibly easy to lose the fragmented nature of their stories, and thus also that 'extra' of the stories. To lose that 'extra' would also mean the incapacity to transcend the status and the effects of sovereign politics. In my writing I am not, then, analysing what was explicitly said or intended. That, however, makes it imperative to openly acknowledge my own role in constructing meaning and to challenge both myself and you, the reader, to look for alternative interpretations (cf. Wright 2009: 629–630). My writing strategy changed as I was blown away by the plurality of the voices, finesses, sensualities and emotionalities present in the empirical data (see Ellis & Berger 2002; Hill 2005; Richardson 1994; Rosenblatt 2002; Smith, P. 1999).

24 *Exposure*

The effects of sovereign practice and the senses of the international are articulated through a plurality of meanings and feelings, senses and touches that are embodied and corporeally expressed. Thus, an alternative style of writing can function as an alternative way of knowing and acting. I took refuge in poetic representation. Poetry enabled me to reflect on the corporeal and embodied experiences of seeking asylum and doing research on the topic. In the end, it paved the way for constructing the book as a collage, in which different events and chapters reflect the multiple relations, practices, sets of institutions and networks of governance that are evoked in the politico-corporeal struggle of seeking asylum (see e.g. Newland 2010). As both the state and the international are enacted in daily life, they are simultaneously both reinforced and undermined by people's movement and the relations people take up. Poetic representation was my first attempt to include in the research text, besides what was voiced, the sensuousness, corporeal and material elements present in the data.

In academic writing, poetry has been approached as a method embracing feelings and embodiment. As such, it is in line with my experiences of doing fieldwork and composing research. Constructing this book as a collage means that I am trying to push myself beyond conceiving the categories of the subject and object, fact and fiction, truth and make-belief as dichotomous. Poetry bridges the gap between the Cartesian division of body and mind.[6] It is (at least) two-directional, reaching both to the concrete, sensual outer world and to the mental interior world (see Brady 2004: 631; also Poindexter 2002). By resorting to poetry, I hope to illustrate the way in which, in the interviews, the question of representation was actually a question of power (see Brinkmann 2009; Kvale 2006: 487). In the interviews there was always a "muffled subtext" (Mazzei 2003) present.

According to Laurel Richardson (2002: 879), "the body responds to poetry". Thus conceived, poetry and ultimately the choice of collagic writing are my ways of opening my interpretations up for scrutiny (see Pugliese 2004: 27; Threadgold 1997: 1). My elaboration concerning the representation of the interviews is actually an effort to develop an ethical relationship towards not only my research participants but also readers. Altering the language of representation, claims Ivan Brady (2004: 628), changes the analytic game itself.

In composing the poem *Lines of life* from a group interview with five Afghan men, I was not only writing the other, but also "relieving emotional pressure" (Richardson 2002) and "rewriting myself" (Richardson 1992) and my relations to the asylum seekers *and* the academic community (cf. Richardson 1998). The poem allowed me to write my presence into the narrative, and allowed the appearance of multiple voices – shifting *I*s, *you*s, *they*s and *we*s – which blur the notion of a single, stable and sovereign subject. Poetic representation is a form of resistance to dominant interpretations and ways of interpreting, just as shifting and changing stories can be understood as my research participants practising resistance and acting beyond the conditioning effects of sovereign power (cf. Abu-Lughod 1985). Poetry grounded my further explorations. It was a point of departure. Poetic representation made me feel comfortable with myself and enabled me to find my position in this research. It made me understand that the methods used in scientific writing imply particular kinds of transactions and engagements with the world (see Atkinson & Coffey 2002: 807). It was my first step in my attempt to answer the demand that, at a later stage, after years of elaboration, became the focus of this collage.

To an extent, the present work is an autoethnography of borders and sovereign practice. In this genre it is, however, different from, for example, Shahram Khosravi's (2010) take. While Khosravi draws insight from his own experiences of seeking refuge in Sweden, my personal take is limited to being exposed to such experiences and stories. Thus, rather than reflecting on the value of first-hand experience as a source of insight and information, I emphasise the aspect of relationality that autoethnography involves. Autoethnography is an approach that acknowledges the inherently relational character of knowledge and leaves some room for the subaltern to adopt various agentive roles and positions (cf. Didur & Heffernan 2003: 2).

While in anthropology the self has been a legitimate source of knowledge for a long time, in International Relations it is less so (see however Cohn 1987; Dauphinee 2013; Doty 1997, 2010; Huynh 2007, 2010; Löwenheim 2010; Neumann 2010). In fact, as Morgan Brigg and Roland Bleiker (2010: 782–784) point out, confirming Wanda Vrasti's (2010) perception, most efforts within the discipline are headstrong in writing the self out, rather than in. One reason for this is that the international and personal are regarded as separate spheres. Another possible point of concern is that by 'bringing the self in', research becomes not only 'biased', but also self-absorbed. These concerns, however, miss the mark and lose the potential of autoethnographic writing. First, as much as state practice, international relations is of this world, and as such it cannot be – or must not become – separate from the question and place of the human being (this includes the researcher). Second, autoethnography is not ethnography of only or even mainly the self, but a relational practice evoking a certain understanding of knowledge. The writing 'I' becomes an important piece of the research puzzle.

A hermeneutics of the ontologically potent body

Asylum seekers seek to negotiate and transform their daily lives and identities, which are often overshadowed by official definitions or material limitations created through networks of governance and sets of institutions that operationalise sovereign power on a daily basis (Puumala & Pehkonen 2010). Stories similar to the ones presented in this work abound among those seeking asylum in Finland, and they are not rare in other parts of the world either (e.g. Evans 2003; Moorehead 2006; Nyers 2008; Pugliese 2002, 2004; Solomin 2005). These stories raise the broader questions of political agency and community. The demand that we face through asylum seekers' stories and experiences is not only a methodological or theoretical one, but also a philosophical one. All of us are presented with it.

Through my reflection on data collection, research encounters and writing, I have tried to illustrate that ethnography can function as an epistemological attitude, or even an ontological practice. For me the promise of ethnography lies in

26   *Exposure*

its potential to expose international relations – and the international – as a set of culturally and historically situated accounts of people and their political place in the world. In the poem *Lines of life*, the men could not verbally express the meanings of being a refugee or being born and raised in war. A form of narration that included seeming contradictions and the silences within the account enabled them to articulate and negotiate spaces and relations. That negotiation lies also in mundane acts – like wearing flip-flops in the snow. Those seemingly meaningless details can evoke feelings of home and familiarity, but even more so they (re)construct the multiple ways of enacting the political. The absent words and silences in the interviews, or my research participants telling me that I asked things that could not be described in words, provided valuable insight into the senses of the international.

Soran's demand, Stephen's free-flowing story and Nasir's frustrated attempt to make me understand what was at stake in the struggle they were involved in ultimately turned into a necessity to rethink "the meaning of the tie, the bond, the alliance, the relation, as they are imagined and lived" (Butler 2003a: 29). It needs to be remembered that accounts of seeking asylum do not aim to present an identity, but tell about the processes of making oneself and being made by others, as well as the possibilities of becoming. My ethnographic adventures into the 'world' of seeking asylum gestured a turn towards the body and its relations to other bodies. In order to understand how the body is being foregrounded in the chosen approach, we need to investigate the notion of exposure. A focus on exposure helps me to remain true to those reasons for which I wanted to study the topic in the first place: real people in real places (Behar 2003). The following conceptual development already begins to pave the way for a discussion of the potential of Nancian politics that begins and ends with bodies within political and mobility studies.[7]

Exposure, and events of becoming exposed, form the wider framework through which the politico-corporeal struggle involved in seeking asylum is conceptualised in this work. Exposure repeats Nancy's (e.g. 2000) thought that identities are shared between people. The body requires others to become a body. It is not enough to think of an individual subjectivity when we think about the body and bodies, since the body never exists alone (see also Manning 2007: 160). Exposure does not allow room for a clear-cut or pre-existing idea of a subject. Rather, it is movement between bodies, in relation to, towards and away from other bodies. Such a take offers a different kind of understanding of political existence, one in which the asylum seeker is not only an object of and a figure in sovereign politics, but also a moving agent of their own making – even if not unconditionally (for a critical reflection see Chapter 2). It requires rethinking the place and space for the sensing, moving and experiencing body, and also the spaces, places and relations that the body creates through its movements and gestures.

The asylum regime in the EU can be understood to play a critical role in confining more inclusive notions of political community and political life. Its focus on bureaucratic processes and the underlying administrative logic easily reduces asylum seekers to speechlessness and invisibility. The whole question of asylum, from a statist perspective, thus becomes a question of knowledge-making that bases political subjectivity on the state (Kynsilehto & Puumala 2013; Puumala & Kynsilehto 2015; Rajaram 2013: 694). Nancy offers the notion of exposure as a method of thinking about political community beyond state-centred governance (see also Puumala 2013; Rajaram 2013). It becomes central to take note of the evented nature of our selves, our bodies, and the political, which allows us to pose important questions about the practices of bordering and the categorisation of human bodies.

In many discussions of migratory movement and borders, the body is mentioned only when it is subjected to practices of control, evaluation and surveillance. Why is it that the body is worth mentioning there, but not in contexts which would study the way the body matters from the point of view of the moving person and the way that their own body bears meaning for them? The latter focus would help us understand the feelings, behaviours and practices that are most meaningful in the daily lives of asylum seekers and how the politics of borders that is necessarily related to asylum seeking *matters* in people's daily lives. According to Vinciane Despret (2013: 55), the study of how something matters goes beyond a semiotic query. It involves seeking to understand the other's perspective and the fact that some things are more meaningful than others. That, in turn, is a question of affective value, sensuousness, which cannot be separated from the body and its relations with, connections to and separations from others. Thinking through exposure involves theorising bodies as 'growing' multiples in diverse practices and relationships. The shift of focus is not merely epistemological, but, much more importantly, it is political and ontological (cf. Coole 2005).

Exposure is onto-politically potent as it relates the body to the world and to others, and either determines or changes the conditions through which we sense the world and the presence of others (Nancy 2008; also Kearney 2015; Panagia 2009: 7). It allows for conceiving of the body as a site of the political where sense and meaning take place (Nancy 2008; also Manning 2007: 20). The body – as Nancy fathoms it – is constructed neither within discourse or a social symbolic order, nor as the material and physiological object of medical science. The body discloses existence in *an interrelation between discourse and matter*. The corporeal represents a rupture or fracture of national space (see James 2006: 131). Exposure can, therefore, be fathomed as an existential relation that we all live on a daily basis, in ways that transcend hierarchies and discriminations between subjectivities and political positions. It poses both a philosophical and a praxical challenge to a particularly constituted political reality that bases itself on sovereignty. By applying the notion of exposure, the various pieces of this collage will present a nuanced understanding of political existence, as well as of the happening of the political in concrete encounters.

From a personal perspective, the uncomfortable experience of exposure made me question the identity that I was seen to represent, along with the political community where I 'belonged', its basis and its ultimately lacking foundations. It required me to think about the political as a lived and imagined relation that not only ends with a body, but also begins with the body. The political community that is thus formed is not a place for expectations and substances. Instead, community in Nancy's thinking

28   *Exposure*

is a place for the happening of bodies, where happening is a central characteristic of that space. The event of exposure forms the essence of community. In the end, my ethnographic experiences were experiences of sensing originary togetherness, violent connections between me and my research participants and mutual – although by no means equal – vulnerability to the presence of the other.

Notes

1 Spivak herself talks in her essay not about refugees and asylum seekers, but about the postcolonial subject and, more precisely, women of colour. She has expressed concern over generalising her argument to cover all marginalised subjectivities (see Didur & Heffernan 2003).

2 In 2015 this practice was revived, and most recently when the Finnish Alien's Act was tightened in 2016, the B permit is no longer issued to asylum seekers who cannot be removed from the country after receiving a negative decision.

3 In addition to the data gathered with asylum seekers, I carried out extensive data collection with Finnish migration officials in 2011 and 2014–2015. As the present chapter focuses on insight gained through ethnography, the institutional process of data collection will be introduced in detail in chapter 3. Methods used in the institutional research include a qualitative web survey, interaction analysis from video recordings of asylum interviews and document analysis of asylum decisions.

4 'Nasir' is a composite voice based on a group interview with five men living with a temporary residence permit. The reason for choosing to present the group interview under one pseudonym is that one of the men interpreted the views and answers of the others in a manner that constructed them as one subject with a unified message. Although I am aware of the ethical and epistemological problems related to constructing this composite, I find it impossible to differentiate between the speakers, who picked up where the other had left off and weaved views and perceptions into one another's stories. One of them translated my questions to the others and their answers to me, and instead of word for word translations he participated in the discussion and presented his views as a part of the others' answers.

5 On many occasions people asked me to help: to intervene in the asylum process, give them a place to live, prevent them being returned or organise contacts with the media, which put me in a difficult situation. In the end, I tried to help as I best saw fit, by giving people advice such as which NGOs to contact if they wanted to publicise their stories, how the asylum process proceeded in Finland and asking the legal representatives' advice on specific concerns related to the process. However, I made it clear at the beginning of each interview that participating in my research would not affect the asylum process and the decision they would receive, or change the decision they already had been given. If people still wanted to tell their stories to me, I was more than happy to listen. Most asylum seekers wished to contribute in order to increase the knowledge of what it was to seek asylum and to make their 'case' useful in developing better practices in the asylum process.

6 The questioning of this division lies also at the heart of Nancy's work, which is why I resort to his writings so strongly in the later parts of this work. Nancy's ontological thinking of the body opens a theoretical and philosophical framework to reconceptualise political existence and community together with the way we are always connected to other bodies that live in this world.

7 The next chapter will further discuss the importance of Jean-Luc Nancy's thought regarding the notions of political community and sovereignty.

Event 2

Political lives, professional ethics, and sovereign practices

Soran contends that the centre is not good, that I cannot possibly understand. "Not everybody is the same. We are not the same. Or what do you think?" I answer him that "in principle we are all the same, but . . ." Soran cuts in: "What does that 'but' mean?" I tell that the difference that most bluntly separates us is my living somewhere else and him being accommodated in the centre. I cannot pretend that we are in a similar position. This is one aspect where I rise higher; where the benefit is on my side. Soran nods and we agree that we are not quite the same.

The inequality of our positions is also reflected in our capacity to take control of our daily lives. Soran is well aware of that: "If I ask somebody here a question, they don't answer, my lawyer doesn't answer. They just say that the culture is different. I don't think that." He needs me to answer him; to hear me say that I do not have the answers or that there are no ultimate justifications, no proper reasons to be given.

(Research diary, 11th September 2006)

I see Hussein standing in the hall and decide to ask, if he still wants to talk with me. "No," he says, "there is nothing to talk about now." He smiles, but is not happy or even content. I feel inadequate in my roles, work, and being there, for there is nothing that I can do to ease the sorrow, hopelessness, anger or frustration that he is going through. The thought of his pain being a building block of my professional career is hard to confront. I can only listen, offer an ear, and be there, but not really help. The things he desires are not big, but rather simple ones, and yet so unobtainable to him and out of my control/power.

I don't know what to say when Hussein suddenly exclaims "*B, mikä vitun B?* [The B, what fucking B?] Everybody goes crazy here." I cannot promise that everything will get better, that his current state goes with the fact that he is an asylum seeker. I cannot look him in the eye and say that. Hussein says something in Arabic, looks at me and asks "*mitä tarkoittaa?*" [What does it mean?] I tell him that as he knows, I don't understand. He smiles and says that it meant that it would be better if everybody died. How am I supposed to react?

(Research diary, 14th November 2006)

30   *Political lives, professional ethics*

The claim for authority and the right to control one's life that come through Soran's and Hussein's frustration and anger is strong (see Benhabib 2004: 49–69; Moulin & Nyers 2007; Squire 2009: cf. Bleiker & Kay 2007; Burke 2002; also Chapter 5). Their voices are closely linked to the Finnish politics of asylum, but do not acquiesce to it. The political becomes exposed through the sensuous experiences that waiting and constant uncertainty bring to bear on the body. The political relationality that arises from both Soran's and Hussein's accounts cannot be unambiguously categorised or contained. The more I talked with people and observed what was going on around me, the more the aspect of struggle and the way in which the body was involved in the struggle started intriguing and interesting me. In the end, the interviews made it imperative for me to reflect upon the space for politics and the possibilities of political life – possibilities that for some are self-evident and for others unattainable (cf. Rajaram & Grundy-Warr 2004; Walters 2006). The disparity between people's possibilities of enacting themselves politically necessitates developing a theoretical stance that distances itself from the accounts of sovereignty and the sovereign subject. The logic that founds these concepts does not leave space to account for the multiple expressions of political existence that asylum seekers, for instance, enact.

Yet, it is not possible to speak and write about seeking asylum without addressing sovereign practice, its embodied and material effects and the associated bureaucratic processes. This became all the more obvious as I realised that my body was by no means unaffected by the networked practices of sovereign power:

> "I'm worried about your professional ethics," says the director and looks poignantly at me. I have been called to a meeting with the director of a reception centre concerning my research practices. The director's worry about me crossing ethical limits was caused by the fact that I had informed the centre's staff about a person's wish to change lawyers, as they had requested me to do because I was fluent in Finnish. The director is utterly annoyed by my actions. She tells me off for intervening in the asylum process, something that had been explicitly forbidden as a condition of my data collection. I then ask whether it is not possible for the asylum seekers to change their lawyer anymore. "No, that happens all the time, but it has to go through us. They need to contact the staff themselves," the director explains. I reply by saying that I had merely passed the request to the staff, explained the basis for that request, and asked the 'client' to contact the office in the centre in order to take the matter further. And yes, I did express understanding for the person's concern. "You are not supposed to intervene in the process in any way!" I'm told. "The process must not be intervened! If the fact that there is someone here in this centre intervening in the process reaches the ears of the Immigration Service, we will lose all our credibility. Don't you understand that people's lives are at stake here? For the love of God, don't take responsibility for someone else's life on your shoulders!" I listen quietly. And I start to wonder. Ultimately we reach an agreement that my violations have not been grave enough to put the functioning of the centre in question. I point out

that I will adhere to my own professional ethics and face the consequences should I cross the line. We find a compromise and the director allows me to carry on with my fieldwork.

(Research diary, 2nd October 2013)

Both my research participants' and my personal struggles to find a position and maintain an image of ourselves as authorities within our lives, whether personal or professional, are concrete examples of the corporeal and material consequences of state practice. The question of sovereignty and sovereign practices reaches well beyond the state's borders. Other than at geographical borders, sovereignty is enforced in the course of our daily lives. Furthermore, as the excerpts from my research diary show, the body is one register of state power, but sovereign politics cannot totally own it. The body exceeds totality in all forms; total control, total freedom, total submission and total knowing.

The framework that begins to take shape through the events presented here necessitates that the political is theorised and thought about in terms of exposure, relations and practices. It requires – not necessarily coherently and intentionally, but in a scattered and incomplete way – that we think of the asylum seeker's presence in terms of an expression of the 'real' of the world that cannot be reduced to essential identities (see also Nancy 2000). Such a reality, as Soran's and Hussein's voices and my personal experiences suggest, emerges from a sense (of place) that takes us into the continuous oscillation between presentation and withdrawal and that exposes us to one another as singular plural beings. During my fieldwork, I have become increasingly aware of the ways in which the enactment of sovereignty shapes lives, and that in some places its effects are physical, spatial, corporeal and sensuous all at the same time (see also Moon 1991). I have also become aware of the fact that sovereign practices are far from being concerned only with the moving body, and that enforcement practices not only bear embodied, corporeal consequences, but also come with a human face.

In order to scrutinise what actually is at stake with our exposure to others, the following chapter examines the conceptual relations between sovereignty, mobility and the body. Instead of remaining with a purely governmental frame of analysis, I will introduce the potential of the ontology of the body that Nancy has developed. It enables studying these relations without remaining captive to the dichotomous logic of sameness versus alterity, identity versus otherness and inside versus outside that characterises at least the political and public debates around seeking asylum. In order to depart from that logic, I start my shift into rethinking politics as a bond as that bond is lived and imagined (see Butler 2003a; Cavarero 2002: 519–520). Sometimes engagements with asylum seekers expose sovereign politics uncomfortably close to those of us leading 'normal lives', apparently untouched by either sovereign control or the troubles of the world.

2 Sovereignty, mobility, the body

In search of solid ground

The faceless movement of people.
Mobility studies, border studies, anthropology of the state
critical security studies, autonomy of migration tradition.
Theories trying to grasp movement.
Border patrols, bureaucratic processes and policies in action.
Practices trying to control movement.
Their promise falls short.

When one looks at the phenomenon of seeking asylum, it is hard to concur with the studies that have declared the death of the state or the loss of its significance in politics. In the field of human mobility, the state continues to play an important role (e.g. Mountz 2010; Puumala 2013). In their efforts to govern, regulate and control increased mobilities, states have introduced a wide range of new technologies at the border and in the processment of claims for residence (e.g. Ceyhan & Tsoukala 2002; Walters 2006). People's rights are put on hold, restricted or limited in various spaces or states of exception (e.g. Agamben 2005; Bigo 2007; Dauphinee & Masters 2006; Nyers 2003). In order to fully appreciate these developments, we need to take a look at the state and the networked practices of governance and discipline that are put into operation to control migration and the human body. Sovereign power is dispersed in daily practices that intersect and entwine with one another. Such practices, whether disciplinary, bureaucratic or expressed through mundane relations, uphold and reinforce the state apparatus. At the same time, however, they can be studied in order to undermine the notion of the state as 'structural', beyond people's control and a unitary disembodied entity.

The idea of the international and the state as a unit upon which the world has been politically organised is being challenged 'from below'. The founding distinction of sovereignty between inside and outside is facing dissolution, made visible by the asylum seeker (see also Squire 2009). State practices and the principle of sovereignty are increasingly incapable of coming to terms with the growing number of asylum seekers, as the current situation in Europe illustrates. Despite the efforts to control and enforce sovereignty, the idea of the state is in trouble. The present conceptual puzzlement not only demonstrates the datedness of the

34   *Sovereignty, mobility, the body*

categories of the nation-state, but also calls for a rethinking of political theory (e.g. Cavarero 2002: 512; also Brown 2002; Doty 1999). That also necessitates reconsidering what politics is.

> I think about Asad, an eager fan of Bayern München
> No Mercy. People in Europe feel no mercy, said he.
> The ink letters on his wrist would always remind him of that.
> A plea
> One that falls from the lips of all refugees, as Nancy put it in *Being Singular Plural.*
> A struggle –
> multiple entwined struggles.
> The question touches everyone.
> It is not a question of a body, but of the body.
> Of bodies multiple.

We face an ontological challenge to that understanding of the international that lies at the heart of the whole system of political asylum. That system has been built on an idea of "ontological belonging" (Agnew 2007), where the political existence of the body is connected to the state. Asylum must be sought and can be received only in a state that is not one's own, and only for reasons of facing persecution in one's own country. Seeking asylum is also a question of life and death – concrete existence. In 2015, Europe faced the biggest refugee crisis since the Second World War. It seems that alternatives for how to live and how to envisage human life are called for now more than ever, but there are limited options in sight.

> I think about Nasren and her newborn son Ismael.
> I think about Soran harming himself and Farzad who missed his mother deeply.
> The play of representation, perception and withdrawal.
> There is a face, many faces.
> I owe a response.

The demand with which asylum seekers presented me, involving thinking about the senses and meanings of how our beings are connected, founds the theoretical ambition in this work. I will try to create a theoretical basis that would allow taking account of the body as both a target and consequence of sovereign practices and a concrete example of an alternative ontology of the political. This chapter will draw connections between such an ambition, the framework of asylum politics, mobility studies and the notion of sovereignty. In the end, I will introduce in depth the connections between my take on the issue and the emerging senses of the international as a basis for thinking about new politically relevant relationalities. Throughout the discussion I will reflect on how the political and theoretical frameworks resonate with empirical evidence.

Sovereignty, mobility, the body 35

The adopted frame has evolved over the course of the years as a scholarly response to the ethical demand that people whose lives, agencies and connections I have traced and researched presented to me. It has transformed from a way to seek solace into a methodological attitude and, further yet, a philosophical stance.

Sovereign control and the body

Within International Relations the principle of sovereignty, to put it crudely, seeks to solve the problem of 'otherness'. In a political imaginary based on sovereignty, stability and social order are products of social conformity and homogeneity, situated within a state or possibly within another form of sovereign authority. Sovereignty presumes human commonality and claims that such commonality must be created (Inayatullah & Blaney 2004: 95).

The European efforts to control migration and curb the arrival of asylum seekers resonate closely with Giorgio Agamben's (1998) claim that the original activity of sovereign politics is to give form to life, which turns the body into a target and question of state practice. One way of control and governance is the inscription of categorical identities to bodies, which makes them appear conquered, disciplined and organised into spatially constrained imaginaries (see also Ahmed 1999: 99; Calhoun 2003: 548; Foucault 1979; Parr 2001; Smith 1992: 495; Vidler 1993). Concurrently, asylum seekers are easily assumed to form a unitary and problematic population that needs to be re-situated within the statist imagination. And yet, borders, boundaries and limitations are not purely 'national' projects, but are orchestrated within the international (see Walker 2009: 2). A move from the national towards the international means that the idea of sovereign borders needs to be decoupled from the idea of sovereign territory, as borders are much more than mere geographical markers. They are upheld and constituted with a network of intersecting practices, strategies of governance, institutions and bureaucratic processes. Such an understanding allows room for thinking about the concrete corporeal and sensuous effects that state practices have on people.

According to Agamben (1998: 148), in the logic of sovereign politics that concerns the body, "the biological given is as such immediately political, and the political is as such immediately the biological given". The body is deeply, sensuously and materially caught in the deployment of power. This notion relates closely to feminist debates where the focus has been on thinking not only about the skin, but also with or through the skin (e.g. Ahmed & Stacey 2001; Manning 2007). These contributions explore how skin becomes meaningful by being read, and how readings produce different skins (see also Butler 2004: 26). Seeking asylum represents one instance where a particular type of skin/body is produced through a bureaucratic process and a variety of other measures of control. These measures illustrate the way in which a particular political imaginary is enacted at various sites and sensed at a very intimate level, as, for instance, a concrete touch of sovereign power in the interaction between border officers and asylum seekers (see e.g. Salter 2006). Charlotte Epstein (2007: 150) has described this touch in the following manner: "Felt [. . .] right at the fingertips; the experience is of an encounter with power, of

36 *Sovereignty, mobility, the body*

a new kind: immediate and sensory, and yet harmless – at least physically". When the state seeks to come to terms with the problem of never knowing the truth of, yet trying to solve the problem of, the border-crossing body, it resorts to regulative practices and biopolitical techniques of surveillance and governance:

EEVA: Did you come with a fake passport or somebody else's?
BENJAMIN: Somebody else's passport.
EEVA: Somebody else's.
BENJAMIN: Yeah, it's a Portuguese passport.
EEVA: Okay.
BENJAMIN: Yeah. So, I come with it, [. . .] and they [the Finnish Immigration Service] told me that they can't grant me [a residence permit]. I said "fine, I have a chance to appeal." [. . .] So, we are here to see what God would do, because they said they have to prepare my documents to turn me back. And now after you hear my story finish, you are preparing to send me back, to my destiny. So that means [that] even if I go and die, it's not your problem.

(Interview with Benjamin, June 2007)

Benjamin's story makes concrete the limiting effects of European asylum policies on asylum seekers' options for entering Europe and seeking protection. When safe and legal routes do not exist, people resort to human smugglers or travel with fake documents. As Benjamin's account further illustrates, crossing a political border puts the identity of the asylum seeker under suspicion. Unclear identity, that is lack of certain knowledge from the state's perspective, creates space for a struggle over the meanings of the asylum seeker's body. As a result, Benjamin was detained. He had crossed the Finnish border, but did not manage to move *across* it, as his body was symbolically placed between state territories in the act of detention (see Haddad 2008; also Doty 1999: 597; Nevins 2008: 27–28). The spatial practices involved in the reception of asylum seekers define the places in which these abject bodies can exist (see Perera 2002; Rajaram & Grundy-Warr 2004, 2007): reception and detention centres, waiting zones and refugee camps. Those are the "mezzanine spaces of sovereignty" (Nyers 2003: 1080) – spaces which are in-between the inside and outside of the state, yet tightly within sovereign control, and which give a specific materiality for the asylum seeking body in terms of the bureaucratic process (see also Chapters 3 and 4).

As in Benjamin's account, the EU stipulations on human migration in effect transform the asylum seeker's body into a form of luggage stored in the mezzanine spaces of sovereignty or transported between countries by "the international police of aliens" (Walters 2002). In fact, the desire to manage and control migration has lead in the (western) states to the creation of what Peter Nyers (2003) has termed "deportspora" – an abject diaspora – where the sovereign's decision on life can suddenly turn into a decision about death, as Benjamin pointed out in his account (see also de Genova 2002, 2004, 2007; Norris 2000b; Masters

Sovereignty, mobility, the body 37

2006). Indeed, as Benjamin implied, while sovereign politics directly concerns the human body, it effectively outsources the ethical dimension of asylum. After the bureaucratic process has reached its conclusion and the asylum seeker's case is closed, the officials can contend that what happens to the person afterwards is no longer their problem. The minimum requirements that the Finnish state is required to fulfil have been met, and no ethical concerns about the destiny of the person are necessary.

The politico-corporeal struggle involved in seeking asylum relates to the operation of sovereign power at the level of the individual body, affecting its movements, actions and possibilities (cf. Norris 2000b: 49–50; Pugliese 2002). The state is able to decide who will be provided with protection, which, as Nyers (2003) points out, represents a claim to monopolise the political. Sovereignty, hence, is not merely a spatial construct. It represents a form of authority that relates to community formation, as it gives communities a sense of continuity and enables the development of narratives of belonging and home. Sovereignty is perhaps best conceptualised as a process that authorises distinctions and separations and seeks to maintain and enforce them.

The act of seeking political asylum not only represents a procedural or bureaucratic issue, but also poses fundamental questions about how a society is formed and bordered (see Chapter 4; also Rajaram 2013: esp. 695; Walker 2009). Sovereign territory emerges as a moral and political form, as certain relationships are made out to have connections (Rajaram 2013: 682–683). In other words, the idea of a state that forms a political home for a close-knit community established and maintained through sovereign practices connects place, history and identity together. The possibilities of conceiving human existence are ontologically connected to the state, in/to a particular and determinate place and sense of history (see Agnew 1999, 2007; cf. Gustafson Scott 2004; Massey 2004). Within the sovereign imaginary, life and the body are inscribed in the sovereign political order. Unarguably, it would be easy to conceptualise asylum seekers like Benjamin as sovereign-less subjects who are yet firmly situated in the sphere of sovereign decision, included through their exclusion (see Agamben 1998, 2005; also Huysmans 2008). The ontological privilege given to sovereignty can be utilised to deny some people full subjectivity, rights and agency (see e.g. Nayak & Selbin 2010: 29). From the perspective of the moving person, this would suggest that becoming uprooted from a national community would automatically signal the loss of one's identity, traditions and culture (see Malkki 1995). My empirical explorations do not support that notion, although seeking asylum is clearly a disruptive experience:

AYAN: They say: "You are not Somali." If I'm not Somali, what am I? I don't know, really.
EEVA: They said you are not Somali . . .
AYAN: Yeah, "we don't know if you are Somali. You only tell all these things." They asked me where I lived, and I told. They said "it's not true." Now they are rejecting my application, and saying that we don't know if you really are what you say you are. . . . And now that I have my [alien's]

38 *Sovereignty, mobility, the body*

> passport, they wrote it there that we can't identify this person, really. [Ayan goes through her things in her hand bag and finally pulls her passport out.] Here, it's here, you see.
>
> EEVA: Ah, "it has proved impossible to verify the identity of the holder."
>
> AYAN: And they write it there, that we can't verify your nationality, if you are a national of Somalia. I say: "If I am not a Somali, what am I?"
>
> (Interview with Ayan, October 2006)

> Abuukar reads aloud the sentence "it has been impossible to verify the identity of the holder," and asks if he can ask the police to change this. Abuukar recounts that he has provided the police with his driver's licence and all the other ID papers that he had got from Somalia. He tells me that his documents are genuine and that he has never had this problem before. "I have an identity," he says, seemingly nettled.
>
> (Research diary, 1st March 2007)

As Ayan's and Abuukar's accounts illustrate, it is not the case that asylum seekers have lost their identities. Rather, asylum seeking is an example of people finding themselves limited by the role that they encounter and feeling that the role is restrictive or oppressive, or, more radically, alien to them (see also Gagnon 1992: 235). Articulating and expressing oneself is an act of self-creation, a claim to authority that enables the subject to define him or herself through the power derived from experience. Hence, although the asylum seeker's body is deeply affected, it is not completely overtaken by the functioning of sovereign power (see e.g. Agier 2008; Blom Hansen & Stepputat 2005; Edkins 2000; Edkins & Pin-Fat 2005; Squire 2009). In particular, Michel Agier (2008: 65) has claimed that conceiving asylum seekers' existence merely in terms of sovereign politics annihilates any political space on shared speech and obstructs "a world of relationships that tends [. . .] to recreate this". The mezzanine spaces of sovereignty are filled with the tension that exists between the voiceless victim and the subject, which starts to form again as soon as a contact between different subjectivities is re-established (see also Agier 2008).

Approaching asylum through exposure

It has become common to claim that self and other are not antagonistic, but rather co-existential: the self cannot be, come to exist, without the other (e.g. Agathangelou & Ling 2005; Ashley 1989; Darby 2003; Kristeva 1991; Radhakrishnan 1993; Walker 1993). This has become more or less a normative statement, a question of political correctness in doing research on the self and the other. I have come to wonder what it could mean in practice. The philosophical challenge of that notion, I would claim, remains to a great extent unanswered, as co-existence does not simply imply relations between two or more sovereign subjects. It implies a willingness and courage to expose oneself to another being, to not insist on one's views being more correct or authentic than those of an other. And it is still more.

It requires an ontological explorarion into what being 'us' means, and a negotiation of one's existence in relation to, with, one another. A concretisation of the ontology of being-with – co-existence – can emerge in bodily encounters, varying in nature and kind by those acting and creating the space in their meeting. It represents a communal and felt way of being in the world.

For me, meetings and discussions with asylum seekers materialised the idea of identities unfolding in relation to one another in encounters. When they explicitly addressed the disparity of our positions, my research participants enticed me to imagine what it would be like to live in the material surroundings of a reception centre. Being an asylum seeker affects one's daily life in multiple ways; it is reflected in the body, its physical surroundings and possibilities and in one's relations within the society. In many ways, seeking asylum is an extremely intimate and sensuous experience. For example, when Soran (see Chapter 1) suggested that I should spend the night or take a shower in the reception centre, I thought of rooms that accommodated six to eight people with little or no privacy, the typical restless soundscape, the poor (or non-existent) air conditioning and resulting odours, the unhygienic kitchens and the overall non-functional change that the building had gone through, from being an envelope factory to a temporary home for those seeking protection. I thought about what it was like to live in a place where people's private lives turn into public performances, objects of professional practice and supervision. I thought of the element of surveillance that was involved in living there. The multitude of encounters like the one with Soran changed my perception of how identities are necessarily relational and how that relationality – shared exposure – both unfolds and is formed here and now, whenever bodies come together.

Approaching the relation between bodies, borders and sovereignty through exposure shifts the analytical focus. Instead of defining the act of seeking asylum and political subjectivity through a territorial imaginary, the idea of exposure puts notions of space in flux and encourages us to think about space in terms of the interval. For Nancy, the interval is the place between bodies where existence happens (see also Heikkilä 2007). It is marked by the event of exposure, which means that space is not an extant framework for action, but is articulated through the body. Exposure allows us to think of space that resides in bodies, rather than vice versa. Furthermore, in privileging the body, exposure disrupts speech and narrative as the main forms of political expression and allows for a more nuanced understanding of the political and of the questions of who constitutes a political being and how a community of political beings is formed and articulated.

Exposure offers a way to tap into the complex experience of existence (see also Sylvester 2013; Väyrynen & Puumala 2015), even though discussing experiences of seeking asylum is not a straightforward task. According to Nevzat Soguk (1999: 4), there is no common refugee experience, beyond the immediate experience of displacement, that can be found. That underscores the element of struggle involved in asylum seeking, and, at the same time, the necessity to think about our own existential and concrete involvement in that struggle. The meanings and sense of the struggle are negotiated not only in terms of, but also in relation and

40   *Sovereignty, mobility, the body*

in difference to, state practices. Often both theorisations of and policies related to asylum seeking fail to take note of their human dimension and thus they leave the mobile person without a face and a name – as a figure in statistics, a mere drop in the wider flow of her/his kind. However, the fact remains that sovereign imaginaries are ultimately played out on people's bodies. (Cf. Butalia 1998; Perera 2006; Shapiro 2003). Despite their severely disadvantaged positions, asylum seekers' ways of engagement and presence materialise the challenge that current political debate and thought face (see also Doty 2001 on putting statecraft in peril).

As stated earlier, my thinking on existence and the body relies on Nancy's work. For him the world is finite and contingent, fragmentary and resistant to any totalisation. It is a place of material bodies that come-into-presence with one another (see James 2006: 151). Nancy goes so far as to claim that consciousness occurs only in the rupturing of self-identity, in events and contacts in which a secure ground for knowledge and thinking presents and withdraws itself at the same time (see James 2002: 46, 226). Such an understanding makes Nancy's notion of exposure indispensable in thinking about political life. Exposure is a demand to think of 'being' as existence that does not allow any references to an overarching unity, commonality or totality. This makes it both "*an ethos* and *a praxis*" (Nancy 2000: 65; also Norris 2000a; Schwarzmantel 2007; Wagner 2006; cf. however Caygill 1997; Critchley 1993; Elliott 2011; Fraser 1984). According to Nancy (1999), we – each and every one of us – must at all times be able to answer for our existence through how we respond to others and communicate through these responses. It is our ethical and existential responsibility to one another. However, it is exactly this that the spatiotemporal logic of sovereignty prohibits us from doing by seeking to frame our rights and liberties in terms of our political situatedness in the state. If we, then, wish to come to terms with this existential responsibility, we must resort to a different ontological order, a different status of what is (see Devisch 2011: 6; Nancy 2000: 179).

The notion of exposure suggests that we should understand ourselves as beings who become intelligible to each other only within a social context (see also Librett 1997). Singular beings emerge together from the beginning, which means that community takes place as compearance in a shared space (see Dallmayr 1997: 181). Thus, the community that arises from Nancy's thought exceeds discussions about intersubjectivity. Indeed, as Fred Dallmayr (1997: 181–182) points out, Nancian community is not constituted or constructed, nor is it a matter of intersubjective bonding. It does not emerge among already given subjects; rather it is a form of 'being singular plural' (Nancy 2000; also Kellogg 2005: 340). In the end, community, to put it very simply, implies exposure. Hence, adopting a Nancian lens requires that we approach seeking asylum as a politico-corporeal struggle that calls for an ontological understanding of the body and existence as singular-plural.

Because of the limitations embedded in the principle of sovereignty, I need to go further than inquiring after the effects or practices of resistance and struggle among asylum seekers. Exposure allows a deeper questioning of sovereignty as a founding ontological principle of the international and as a basis of political life. Nancy (2000: 36) invites us to think about "what becomes of sovereignty when it

Sovereignty, mobility, the body   41

is revealed that it is nothing but a singularly plural spacing" (see also Motha 2002; van der Walt 2005). Fathoming sovereignty through exposure demands us to think how we are 'us' among us (Nancy 2000: 26; also Devisch 2011; Motha 2002). This task exceeds notions of foundational identity and difference, and it deconstructs the identity of national community as a collective subject situated in the state (see Matteo 2005: 316). The ethos and praxis of exposure might work as a political and corporeal art of facing, understanding and addressing difference (on the need for such an art see Inayatullah & Blaney 2004: 94–95, 123; cf. Jackson & Nexon 2009). The asylum seeker is not an anomaly within the political order, but their presence concretises an ethical and existential demand to think about the possible forms of political life (see also Chapters 4 and 5).

A politics of voice, the politics of the body

Interest in studying 'the politics of mobility', namely migrant agencies and the multiple practices through which borders and states are instituted in modern politics, has increased among critical scholars (on the latter see Mezzadra & Neilson 2012; Mountz 2010; Walters 2015). My approach comes close to the autonomy of migration tradition (see Mezzadra 2010), in which the aim is not merely to look at the practices of the state, but to adopt a perspective that prioritises the subjective practices, experiences and engagement of migrants themselves, without forgetting the context within which movement occurs. The focus is on the struggle that goes on in the field of migration (see also McNevin 2012; Rygiel 2011; Squire 2009). In that tradition, migrants do not simply stake a claim to obtain formal citizenship, but enact citizenship in their daily lives and thus make a claim for rightful presence (e.g. Isin & Neilson 2008; Squire & Darling 2013). Migrants' agencies are not, however, romanticised, but conceived in terms of a multifarious, contingent and contradicting field. What most closely connects my take on the issue to the autonomy of migration tradition is a focus on the element of struggle that is involved in seeking asylum. Nonetheless, there are some important differences that set this book apart from that tradition.

Instead of focusing primarily on the migrants' subjectivity, I wish to explore the interdependency of political identities outlined by asylum seeking and citizenship, and their mutual vulnerability to one another (although not parity thereof). The practices of the state, within such an approach, lose their mystical and disembodied qualities, and their effects are also exposed in mundane encounters and daily life. One subjectivity is not privileged above another. The existential exposure of all identity categories calls us to think about the nature and qualities of political community thus far fathomed in terms of sovereignty. This moves the focus from citizenship to the political as a bond that is lived and that exists in relations. Furthermore, through Nancy's philosophy, there is a heavy emphasis on the corporeal and the body in this work. Even the most critical works on mobility neglect the body as an important register of the political, and prioritise voice and narratives. I do not suggest neglecting the verbal realm totally, but rather wish to explore voice as one, although not necessarily the most important, element of

42 *Sovereignty, mobility, the body*

political expression. My take on the body is not materialistic as such, although it draws on the material dimension of existence (cf. Coole & Frost 2010; Squire 2014, 2015).

Asylum seekers, when lodging their claim, encounter not a state or a society, but a bureaucratic system of processes, procedures, forms and sequences that, as Prem Kumar Rajaram persuasively claims (2013: 685), fragments their political subjectivity and separates them from the sphere of political life *within* the society. Rajaram considers that an example of the territorialisation of space around the sovereign state. Furthermore, contemporary political life is largely based on the privileging of language and narrative as a means to make political claims and in order to constitute oneself as a political being. Davide Panagia (2009: 12–13) has termed this narratocracy, by which he means that narratives function as a standard for the expression of ideas and for the rules that determine what is and is not valuable action, speech and thought. Narratocracy and the territorialisation of space feed into the sovereign imaginary, as they constitute a particular type of political subject: the literary citizen (see e.g. Vuori & Hirsiaho 2012). Asylum seekers are not figured as political beings or agents prima facie.

As Spivak's (1988) famous essay on the subaltern's capacity to speak and make him/herself understood suggests, language, voice and speech are not free from the effects of power. In fact, any view that considers language as a privileged means for political expression constitutes some identities as pre-eminently and prominently political, also erases certain bodies from the realm of politics. In her feminist exploration of the relation between ethics, power and corporeality, Moira Gatens (1996: 23–27) has claimed that, in political theory, the idea of a unified body politics has restricted the political vocabulary to one voice only. This voice can speak of one body, one reason and one ethic. At different times, different bodies have been delineated to a space where they are practically excluded from political and ethical relations. This makes it imperative to search for alternative expressions of political life (e.g. Puumala 2012, 2013; Puumala, Väyrynen, Kynsilehto & Pehkonen 2011; see Chapters 4 and 5).

My solution to cope with this exclusion and silencing resulted in looking at voice and verbal communication as parts of the embodied exchange that takes place in a shared space, a 'we-world' (see Nancy 2000). In the we-world, the value of the story depends on to whom, where and how it is told, as well as, but not exclusively, on the other's reception of it. For Nancy, argues Diane Perpich (2005: 77), this we-world, of which meaning is inextricably a part, is a socially constructed and maintained space. This shared space, however, is never homogeneous, totalising or monolithic. In this world, interaction requires mutual transformation, not just opening up a space for different voices. Meaning is always shared or divided between bodies, formed in the interval. Hence, it is important to take a wider glance at how meaning travels and how it is affected and changed depending on who the parties sharing the story are. Within such a framework, voice and verbal narrations represent one modality of exposure, that is, the act or event of exposing oneself in front of and in relation to the other or becoming exposed to the other.

Sovereignty, mobility, the body 43

Sharing reflects Nancy's idea of identity and how its possibility is necessarily related to multiple others and to the world (see also Perpich 2005). Different positions need to face one another, engage with their differences and become altered/ moved by the interaction (see Muldoon 2001: 52). Addressing the senses of the international involves exploring how both the community within the state and the one between states are enacted and inhabited by bodies that represent various nationalities, statuses and positions, but that are yet joined together by their singular plural condition. Each of those bodies is equally political and capable of politics, even though their ways of engagement and articulation may differ. Within such a frame, the politics of voice is not opposed to or separate from the politics of the body, but rather voice and body are inseparable.

The approach differs quite a bit from discussing the speaking political subject and his/her identity (Smith 1992; Teleky 2001; see Agathangelou & Ling 2004). Instead of the subject and voice, the body and space gain prominence. For Nancy, space and spatiality are not measurable and three-dimensional, but thinkable in terms of exteriority and 'extension', which make distinctions between mind/body, sensible/intelligible, transcendent/immanent meaningless (see James 2006: 60). For Nancy, an 'I' presents and withdraws itself at the same time. This 'I' can never coincide with the subject of discourse produced in a fable of a stable national community, in the production of which the bureaucratic asylum process participates. Subjectivity comes to represent the giving of being in terms of a bodily instance, in which singularities expose themselves to each other (James 2006: 61–62). Exposure exceeds the logic of the sovereign subject.

In line with this kind of notion of subjectivity, I approach speaking as a kind of sonorous touching. Asylum seekers' voices and the sensuousness they evoke carnalise language, making me apprehend its bodily immediacy (see also Chapter 3). According to Nancy (1993a: 234–247), voice actually has nothing to do with speech. There is no speech without voice, but there can be voice without speech. Each voice is unique; there is no singular voice that can speak for asylum seekers. Instead, each of them has several possible voices and thus also several ways of articulating themselves politically in relation to others. Like meaning, voice, for Nancy, is always shared. Theorising voice comes down to an understanding "that being is not a subject, but that it is an open existence spanned by ejection, an existence ejected into the world" (Nancy 1993a: 239). A voice, contrary to an account or a story, cannot be challenged, for it is an imprint of a body's presence. It calls the other to come out in one's own voice, as a singular-plural (Nancy 1993a: 245).

The body becomes – *is* – a question of politics that materialises a particular regime of power and governmentality and simultaneously withdraws from them (see also Edkins 2013: 539). In engaging with the body and the politics that emerges from the body, I wish to explore whether there is also something beyond or other than language – perhaps an other of language – that is used to express what words cannot represent properly. Namely, I am interested in *whether and how the body might be thought of as a means of political expression or as an event of the political.*

44 *Sovereignty, mobility, the body*

Events of the political represent articulations of a "different kind of inhabitance" (Ahmed 2004: 39), which makes it possible to think of the body as a site of political and communal exchange. The way in which agency, speech, political space and community are deeply entrenched with the political project of sovereignty necessitates that we seek to disrupt the implicit and learned connections between these notions. In order to critically examine the questions of social belonging, agency and participation that such a focus brings to forth, I will use the prism of exposure. Therewith I seek to open space for the asylum seeker to articulate and identify his/her being and body through alternative means, instead of using primarily (or solely) the categories made available by international law and the bureaucratic practice of asylum procedures (see Mountz 2010; Rajaram 2013: 694; Zetter 1991). The chosen perspective refuses to take the state as the natural basis of political subjectivity. Instead it seeks to rethink the relation between the body and politics. Otherwise, disrupting the ordering principles and the basis for divisions that form the social fabric of political communities is not possible.

The ontological body

The body is a site where both the modern political agent and modern society take form, which makes it imperative to explore how (political) life is being corporeally performed. Through the body it is possible to scrutinise "the boundaries of what it means to touch and be touched, to live together, to live apart, to belong, to communicate, to exclude" (Manning 2007: 9; also Ahmed & Stacey 2001). Although both ethnographies of asylum seekers' experiences and state practices exist, it is typical of the works to address merely one of these aspects. However, an exploration of experiences easily grants an air of mythical qualities and uniform strategies of governance to the state. Ethnographically grounded analyses of state practice, in turn, reveal the networked nature of governance and the multiplicity of bureaucratic practices that are at work when sovereignty is enacted (e.g. Kynsilehto & Puumala 2013; Mountz 2010; Puumala & Kynsilehto 2015). Both of these approaches have succeeded in making visible the resistance and negotiation that state practices evoke in asylum seekers and the effects that practices of governance have on individual bodies. But what if the body is not 'individual' in the sense that it contains and belongs to a subject, to an 'I'? What if the body is not merely a matter of politics, but ontological, and as such an ethical question of existence and a concrete example of the taking place of the political?

Talking of a politics and ontology of the body signals that the body is a thread in the larger story of political existence (see Coker 2004: 22; Kleinman 1989). The body is not a neutral, asocial and apolitical place, but one where both the modern political agent and the modern society take form (see Epstein 2010: 332; also Foucault 1978, 1979, 1982). In the politics of the body, the political emanates from the experiencing body. The questions that my exposure to asylum seekers' presence and demand brought to the fore are: How exactly does the body shape and articulate the ways in which people understand their place in the world? Can the asylum seeker's body be ontologically potential, so that it opens a ground in

Sovereignty, mobility, the body 45

which the role of the body becomes explicit in a way that would remain unnoticed in a society that remains securely tied to its institutions, history and geography? And if so, how?

As my thinking of the body relies on Nancy's philosophy, the body is not fathomed either as a biological given or as being produced through practices of governance or in discourse. For Nancy, the body is a place of existence that is characterised by openness. He claims that "the body never happens, least of all when it's named and convoked" (see Chapter 3; also Said 1978: esp. 49–73). Our being and bodies resist exhaustive telling and knowing. Therefore, the body never makes sense, but is a sense in action: always on the edge, at the extreme limit, "about to leave, on the verge of a movement, a fall, a gap, a dislocation" (Nancy 2008: 33). The refusal to firmly situate the body in a place, historical narrative or identity makes Nancy's thought intriguing in the context of asylum seeking, in which the body is by notion mobile and unstable in the sense that instead of staying put, it is prone to movement, be it voluntary or initiated by the governing practices that enact sovereignty (see Chapter 4). In Nancy's thought the body signifies that what is outside, next to, against, nearby, with a(n) (other) body; it is an opening and an exposure (see Nancy 2008: esp. 5, 15–17, 33). Such an understanding of the body is ontological. Ultimately, the 'taking place' of bodies is a matter of the creation of a shared world, which in turn is a question of community (James 2006: 143; see also Nancy & Connor 1993; Morin 2009: 44–46). In fact, Nancy thinks of community as a space left empty by the withdrawal of a foundation, which would guarantee forms of political organisation or historical becoming (see James 2010: 173; Nancy 2004a). The demand to think about how we are 'us' among us exceeds notions of foundational identity and difference, and it deconstructs the identity of national community as a collective subject situated in the state.

The question of the political in the body is related to the physical expression of culture, tradition and self that is often thought to be lost in the existential condition of the refugee/asylum seeker. Although, as Ayan's and Abuukar's accounts illustrated, the self is not lost, seeking asylum is a chaotic experience in the sense that it represents social and political breakdown, which further repeats itself in the breakdown of language (see Coker 2004: 33). Some elements of that experience, as in the experience of being born and raised in war discussed in Nasir's interview, are beyond verbal description, at least in a way that would make sense. Yet, the experience is sensed concretely. The gap between verbal testimony and the representation of sense requires thinking of political agency in terms of 'the political'. The sensuous body can redefine what counts as political and what is the space of politics. A focus on the politics of the body does not, however, suggest that we should disregard the politics of voice. Rather, it is imperative to understand that voice is always connected to a body, but body is always something more than or other than what emerges in discourse.

In engaging with the body in its materiality and physical situatedness, Nancy's ontology of the body poses 'being' as a movement of sense, which is always bodily (see James 2006: 103). A Nancian lens allows me to utilise my field experiences as an important point of insight into the challenge that the presence of

46 *Sovereignty, mobility, the body*

asylum seekers introduced to my thinking and being. It urges me to question the foundations of being (political) and my ways of knowing (see also Hewett 2004). Nancy's thought enables us to transcend the play of identity and difference, sameness and otherness, and allows – or perhaps even demands – an examination of the possibilities of political life within the international through exposure. In eluding stable ideas of selves and others, asylum seekers potentially destabilise the logic of inside/outside that pervades international relations and structures the spatio-temporal framing of politics within its spheres (cf. Inayatullah & Blaney 2004: e.g. 96, 105, 120; Nayak & Selbin 2010; Walker 2009: ch. 4; also Tickner 2003). Besides representing a political project, the international, in the course of my work, takes shape as a political process which should not be univocally coincided with the material world. Thus, ontological descriptions of exposure and the politics of the body are not contemplations of the status quo of the world, but lead to a much deeper exploration of the problems confronting our time (see Devisch 2011: 7–13; also Matteo 2005: 323–324). The scholar is called to move beyond the apparent.

Compearance – beyond essentialist politics

The ontology of the body conceives the body in terms of a place where politics both begins and ends. The body is inscribed with various meanings, but it always also incessantly exscribes itself and exceeds both the marks imposed on it and the lines drawn to control its moves. A focus on either dominance or resistance, hence, misses the ambiguity and mobility of social and political relations, which materialises in the daily lives of asylum seekers (see Campbell & Heyman 2007; Darby 2004; Joseph 2010; Takhar 2007; Walker 2009: 44). If we, nonetheless, choose to speak of resistance with regard to the struggle of asylum, this resistance belongs to another world; asylum seekers resist the appropriation of their bodies within an essentialist politics (see Nancy 2004a: xli). It is extremely difficult – if not impossible – to illustrate the vulnerability of the asylum seeker to state practice and vice versa with a focus on just one; we must take into account the entanglement of these vulnerabilities. Neither would exist without the other. Once more, we are faced with the notion of ontological exposure, which makes it imperative to address Nancian interpretations of the political and community in more detail.

According to Nancy, the very notion of the state testifies to the necessity of discovering a principle of grounding and of solidity, where such an absolute foundation is definitively lacking (Nancy 2007: 9; cf. Ahrens 2005). He argues that political longing for a community of people joined by identity and background is just another name for nationalisms and sub-national forms of identification, which lead to conflicts (Nancy 2000: 101–143; cf. Shapiro 1997; also Olsson 2007). The raison d'être of the statist community has tragically failed its (unachievable) promise – a stable territorial/ethnic community – and the amount of human suffering caused by politics driven by sovereign body political idea(l)s has become too great to ignore (see Nancy 1993b). So, instead of problematising movement and the moving body as such, the notion of political community built on sovereign

Sovereignty, mobility, the body 47

imagination begins to seem unstable. Nancy suggests that human existence is a question of compearance: we come to presence – happen – only with one another. Being unfolds when bodies come together and 'the political' begins to take form on the surface of the body, arousing feelings and sensations. Furthermore, the ontology that arises from the notion of compearance places emphasis on punctuations, encounters and crossings (Fischer 1997: 34). 'The political', thus understood, marks the ways in which the body exceeds the question of both sovereign authority and subjectivity, and the ways in which the singular plural body always comes into being with other bodies.

But how to go about the ethico-political challenge to think being (political) in terms of the sharing of existence? Nancy's answer is simple and yet incredibly demanding. He suggests that we should understand ourselves as beings who only become intelligible to each other socially, but that this sociality is never a way of common being but a form of being singular plural (Nancy 2000, 2004b; also Kellogg 2005: 340). In a Nancian understanding of community, claims Catherine Kellogg (2005: 351; also Nancy 2000, 2004a), community does not, cannot and should not guarantee meaning or that there is only one meaning, which is given the place of the truth. If the statist or national community is understood as a guarantor of meaning of being political in a modern world, we essentialise it. If we suggest that displacement also involves the loss of one's identity, culture and tradition, we essentialise the sovereign state. That, again, signals the closure of the space of the political, because it assigns a common, or general, being to community. Furthermore, it marks the loss of the in, between and with of being.

Nancy makes a fine but significant distinction between politics (*la politique*) and the political (*le politique*) (see Lacoue-Labarthe & Nancy 1997). In Nancy's philosophy, 'politics' refers to empirical action, praxis, which takes place within the sphere of normalised order, in processes of governance. The political cannot be reduced to governmental rationality or the composition and dynamics of power, for it indicates philosophy, a system of meaning/intelligibility within which politics manifests itself. (Puumala 2013; Puumala & Pehkonen 2010; see also Dikeç 2005: 185; Norris 2000b: 54). The political is something that occurs when bodies come together and relate to one another. It emerges from relations rather than precedes them (see e.g. Lacoue-Labarthe & Nancy 1997: 133). For Nancy the political is our ontological state and situation – a question of the nature of our existence (see Lacoue-Labarthe & Nancy 1997: 110). Not only does this elaboration suggest that the body has a central role in politics, but, even further, it implies that the body is inseparable from the political. It also implies fathoming the body as ontological, which privileges the processes of *exscription* and events of *exposure* that mark the body's capacity to articulate a relational politics. In a manner of speaking, then, politics denotes various ways of actualising the political and putting it into practice. In my thinking, politics represents a project of organising human existence and a struggle over that existence. The political, again, takes form through humane restlessness brought about by a process of becoming, which remains open and subject to change and which the experiencing bodies consider lacking (Puumala & Pehkonen 2010: 56; also Puumala, Väyrynen, Kynsilehto & Pehkonen 2011).

48 *Sovereignty, mobility, the body*

According to Nancy, even our being occurs between us or, in other words, we *are* not, but we *come-into-presence*. Our being and bodies resist exhaustive telling and knowing. Even the relation between 'us' cannot be named beforehand as it has no specific shape; rather, it is "a movement of withdrawal from any substance" (Caygill 1997: 23). Conceiving the political in terms of relation results in the disposition of community as such. Indeed, the sharing of the community and the political can stand as synonyms for one another (Dallmayr 1997: 182). Hence, the openness of 'the political' demands rethinking the structuring principles of community, or thinking of community in terms of "the destination of its sharing" (Nancy 2003a; Nancy 2004a: 40; cf. Edkins 1999: esp. 125–146). This means thinking of political community as something that is not related or equivalent to a state, an ideology or a political orientation (see also Fynsk 2004; Panelli & Welch 2005, 2007). This approach disposes of not only the nation-state and the system of states, but also, and most importantly, the sovereign subject. It requires engagement with the political potential that the inherent withness of being exposes. Community thus fathomed, claims Howard Caygill (1997: 23), provides radical reconceptions of freedom, ethics and the political. It frames politics in terms of ethics and ethics as a politics.

Exploring the event of exposure

Trying to understand the value of Nancy's work in an empirical context is not without caveats. Nancy himself offers no insight into how the way in which he re-treats some of the key concepts that shape our understandings of politics, community and identity could be put into operation. In fact, he refuses to be addressed as a political thinker, and identifies his work as a thinking of the political (see Lacoue-Labarthe & Nancy 1997). The fact that Nancy himself refuses to envision what the kinds of understandings of the body, politics and community could mean in terms of actuality does not signal that they would have no value. For me, personally, his thinking offered a means to both distance myself from the debates and discourses in terms of which asylum seeking is addressed and a way to try to understand being political as it unfolds relationally, through events and acts (see Chapter 1). I am not suggesting that we should conceive the body as an esoteric series of material events that merely appears as it comes together with others. Whenever we come in the presence of another being, we tend to address him/her in terms of markers such as status, nationality, ethnicity and gender. Thus, a critical reflection on Nancy's thought in relation to the processes of forming positions and identities seems to be in order.

The question of the subject is profoundly linked with the principle of sovereignty, posits Rob Walker (2009: 193, 206–208), as this principle claims to express a form of subjectivity that is potentially universal. Yet this form always finds its home in a specific place, be it a territory, an institution or a body. The subject becomes the foundation without foundation on which our conceptions of the possibilities and limits of political life are built. Nancy's way of approaching existence and the political, through events, puts the principle of sovereignty in

Sovereignty, mobility, the body 49

flux. It frames exposure as the taking place of the crisis of foundational thinking. Nancy suggests a different ontology and offers an alternative way of treating the question of human existence. It needs to be stressed that Nancy does not aspire to establish the body as ontological in the sense of a concrete category of being (cf. Manning 2007: xxi). There is no foundation upon which existence is; for Nancy, "there is only the 'with' – proximity and its distancing – the strange familiarity of all the worlds in the world" (Nancy 2000: 187). In this sense, the concept of ontology might not be the most suitable one to describe what he seeks to emphasise, namely, *the event of becoming as the essence of being-with.*

Can Nancy's refusal to engage with politics as empirical action and his position as a quasi-transcendental analyst of the political (see Caygill 1997: 26–29; Lacoue-Labarthe & Nancy 1997) be conceived as an advantage? For me, Nancy's choice to privilege the political, which indicates philosophy, results in him not taking into account the operation of governmental rationality or the dynamics of power that are active, for instance, in the process of seeking asylum. This could be taken as a considerable failure, which in itself could be a reason to discard his thinking altogether in any work that tries to understand the struggle that unfolds between people and states. Yet, the determination to transcend actuality enables Nancy to form a different way of thinking about human existence and community. In the politics of the body, identity is positioned in difference and the radical (im)possibility of identity as an essential and substantive category is articulated (see Librett 1997, also Nancy 2004a). This frames the principle of sovereignty as a spatiotemporal project that constrains our notions of politics and political life, where they can be found and what forms they might take. Nancy's thinking functions as a means to put my own thinking in line, and to explore the politico-corporeal struggle that asylum seeking unfolds in terms of events of exposure that put our way of organising the world in flux.

It is obvious that Nancy's refusal is not merely an advantage. His writings about the body are far too abstract for them to function as analytical tools. How to think about exposure as it takes shape through bodily events? What kind of elements and dimensions of the body are relevant for an empirical analysis of exposure? Clearly it is not possible to ignore the various networks and dynamics of power that condition and limit people's possibilities of articulating themselves and constructing themselves as political beings (see also Hamacher 1997). If the body needs others to become a body, there are multiple stereotypes and perceptions with which it needs to negotiate in order to make us receive rather than perceive its presence. How does the asylum-seeking body, for instance, challenge our perceptions of itself and ourselves? Thus, whereas for Nancy the demand to think about plurality and sharing is a philosophical one, I approach that demand as a political one, trying to fathom its political consequences.

The body performs – or perhaps gives a materiality to – different positionalities, according to which it is perceived and categorised. These categories are not free from the operation of power, but imply a situational hierarchy. Several scholars inspired by feminist and intersectional analyses have underscored the need to understand the dynamics that are at play in subject production and with

50 *Sovereignty, mobility, the body*

regard to the multiple enunciative positions that a person can adopt in the performance of his or her identity (see e.g. Bürkner 2011; Choo & Ferree 2010; Kynsilehto 2011). Exploring the actual empirical event of exposure necessitates that the body, voice as a part of the body and sense are all understood as multiples. Thus, there are numerous ways in which the event of exposure can take place and several channels through which it can be articulated, even in the condition of seeking asylum.

Nancy's thought about exposure, sense and sharing is a move against a notion of politics that founds itself upon the principle of sovereignty and the dichotomy it suggests between interiority/exteriority and self/other. Although these concepts have conventionally been fathomed as mutually exclusive, I think of them in terms of happening and events. Hence, they are categories that take shape only when people come together. The asylum-seeking body articulates itself by invoking different, intersectional positionalities which resonate with different ways in which subjectivities are constructed (see e.g. Kynsilehto 2011). It bears the potential to illustrate the inherent and ontologically relational constitution of thinking where nobody exists alone, but the idea of being somebody is always related to the process of differentiation. Thus, identity lies in difference. In evoking exposure, the body puts into flux the whole principle of sovereignty, not just its political manifestations such as the state and political subjecthood based on the state.

An empirical analysis of exposure necessitates that, besides political positions, the way in which asylum seekers mobilise e.g. gendered, ethnic, sexual, cultural and religious positions, is accounted for. Exposure as an ontological notion refuses to locate identity in any location that would give substance to identity. It withdraws from all fixed categories that represent totalising narrations of being and existing. The event of exposure between bodies becomes possible when the body manages or happens to put our perception of itself in flux, when it disrupts learned ways of thinking and distorts them in a way that makes us receive its presence as that presence unfolds then and there.

Exposure does not imply intentionality or involve a conscious effort; it can also be evoked when something that no one has anticipated happens and enters into how people position themselves in relation to one another and how they relate to one another afterwards. Thus, although concepts such as gender, ethnicity, sexuality, culture and religion appear in my writing, it is not my goal to explore how these matter in people's lives. Neither is it possible to offer a critical reflection on these concepts, although none of them are self-evident. This is not to say that such an approach would not be valuable, but it falls outside the scope of this book and what I wish to accomplish. Instead of being categories of analysis for me, these concepts offer an analytical prism into how exposure is articulated in order to gain a deeper and more refined empirical understanding of the precise arenas and ways in which asylum seekers' politico-corporeal struggle unfolds in relation to sovereign power and other subjectivities. In addition, they allow fathoming what kind of stereotypes, hierarchical positions and practices are mobilised as the sovereign power struggles to reinstate itself. Finally, they enable an understanding of the rich variety of senses that can be discussed when the ways in which the international enters into people's lives is under scrutiny.

Exposure, when its is analysed through the actual channels through which it happens and the positionalities that are mobilised in the process, can illustrate the political potentiality of the body and the value in engaging with the politics of the body vis-à-vis sovereign power. In an asylum seeker we encounter the "exposed nerve of humanity" (see Huynh 2010). The politics of the body represents an attempt to articulate relations between bodies that are simultaneously both ambivalently scattered and tightly located within the spheres of the international. Thus, the context from which asylum seekers articulate their presence is that of a "potential politics-to-come" (Manning 2007: 2). Asylum seekers' bodies, articulations and movements require us to get involved at least philosophically with the bloody and dirty business of international relations. Staying clean and distant is not an option.

Towards the senses of the international

As a way of organising political existence within the international, sovereignty affects people's capacity to take up political acts and constitute themselves as political agents. Within this frame of interpretation, the body is a property of politics, where a political identity results from the person's relationship to the state. But a second frame of interpretation is also possible, as regards the place and role of the body within politics. In my attempt to better understand the ways in which sovereign power falls short in determining the body – a notion that stems from my empirical work – I have relied on Nancy's writings, which I have found almost painfully beautiful and capable of opening something within my scholarly self. For Nancy, the body is both a point of departure and an end. The kind of Nancian interpretation that I have adopted introduces what a politics that begins and ends with the body might mean for the international. I am curious about the ways in which the body's political agency, that is, its expressions of a singular plural condition, can highlight such aspects of political community that have been virtually absent from political science thus far (cf. Edkins 2005b; Vaughan-Williams 2007). There is a definite difference between these two takes on the body: the first implies a different epistemology, the latter a different ontology. Yet the frames intertwine as the body and sovereign politics unfold each other constantly, through various relations and corporeal strategies, and expose the senses of the international.

The struggle that materialises in the act of seeking asylum concerns both sovereignty and political existence; both a way of governance and life. Furthermore, it is a struggle that during 2015 became extremely loaded politically in Europe. If it is as Cynthia Weber (2008) has claimed, and the modern liberal citizenship is a failing design, we need to pay closer attention to the structural and political logic that links the international and the body through the framework of the sovereign state (see also Walker 2009: 47). The demand that asylum seekers present

52 *Sovereignty, mobility, the body*

affects understandings of the limits of citizenship and political community, and also raises different forms of political life within the international (cf. Doty 2001: 526; Soguk 1999: 28–29). The force of this demand is becoming greater as the number of people on the move grows. Yet, the demand is not explicit; rather, it is expressed through the presence of the asylum seeker.

A focus on the political that emanates from the body enables the creative study of the possibilities of political life within the international. The demand that asylum seekers present is in their movement and ways of engagement and relating with various others. It is in their sensuous reactions to the touch and effects of asylum politics on their bodies and to the relations that the politics institutes between their bodies and the society. That turns my attention to the political relevance of sense. The final verse of the poem that I composed from the interview with Nasir (see Chapter 1: *Lines of life*) illustrates the necessity to engage with sense better than any academic formulation:

> Being a refugee or
> having been born and raised in war,
> these two things
> can't be explained in words. I'm trying my best,
> but I can't.
> So many, so many things.
> This stress, mental stress.
> You are away from your family.
> Uncertain about your future.
> Your safety.
> And yeah, that people
> look at you with a different kind of, you know.
> (silence)
> This feeling of powerlessness.
> That someone else
> has your destiny in his hands.
> And he can do whatever he wants to.
> He can . . . If he wanted,
> he could give you that opportunity.
> Give you that life,
> normal life. Give you your only dream.
> And if he wanted,
> he could destroy and finish everything.

It would be misleading to claim that Nasir and the rest of my research participants were simply presenting personal stories of seeking asylum. Rather, their accounts, together with their embodied and sensuous responses to their condition, connect the body to sovereign power in legal, technological, and political terms in multiple ways. Stories of seeking asylum resonate within the sphere of the international because, as I have highlighted in this chapter, the political institution of asylum

Sovereignty, mobility, the body   53

evokes a relationship between a sovereign state and a system of states. Moreover, these accounts are stories of the international, its politics and relations, and the ways they and the body intertwine. The sensuous experiences of persecution and seeking asylum, in fact, evoke a sense of a history that cannot be totally owned up to by or reduced to an individual subject. Yet, as Nasir's account illustrates, the body concretely resonates with these experiences and materialises the political relations that are related to and born out of them.

The spatiotemporal practices of sovereignty are constantly enacted, lived, contested and exceeded in the politics of asylum. When we look at, for instance, the struggle in Europe that began to unfold in 2015 and the related attempts to respond to the growing numbers of asylum seekers, it is obvious that the mobility of people causes a flux in policies. Any responses to the arrival of asylum seekers are reactive rather than proactive. These policies can never anticipate the scope and direction of bodily movement. Such an understanding allows us to conceive both the sovereign state and the international in terms of particularly enacted political projects that aim to produce a particular political order in the world. This project carries very concrete material and corporeal consequences for people's lives, as we can sense from Nasir's account.

When approached through the prism of exposure and the related understanding of compearance, the international takes form as a process that – unlike a project – has no specific end-goal or scope. This means that the international can be conceptualised otherwise, and it is always prone to change. The hope of transformation, and the related hope of seeing a different political project of the international, involves regarding political displacement as something that is not inevitable and that resonates with a notion of political belonging that came to be over time and with effort (cf. Ahmed 2004: 180). The international is not something waiting to be found and recorded, but as much a social and political product as the asylum seeker. In this sense, the question of the international is also a politico-corporeal struggle fought on multiple fronts, with varied strategies and means, in the bodily relations between people. A focus on asylum seekers, their bodies, and the political illustrates the international in terms of an uneven and pitted process which is transformed and shaped with various means, even by people often considered its shadow bodies or those who have no part in its politics and relations. My engagement with asylum seekers has made me realise that in people's lives there is no singular strategy or common identity on which agency is built and from which it arises. Instead, there are complex relations between people. The agency of the asylum seeker and the socio-political structures that shape and are shaped by that agency are closely connected.

As Nasir stated, the experience of being born and raised in war cannot be accurately described in words, which immediately connects the experiences of persecution and seeking asylum to the need to think about the political relevance of the sensuous. The examination of the senses of the international involves thinking of the political in terms of an ontological relation between singularities, whose being always already signals togetherness. In this particular ontology, politics emanates from the acting, sensing and experiencing body. Sometimes it resonates with sovereign power, but at others exceeds it and puts forward an understanding of the

54　*Sovereignty, mobility, the body*

political that every body is. Asylum seekers are affected by political and social circumstances that they cannot change, even more so than those of us who belong within the "national order of things" (Malkki 1995). Their life strategies, however, are also directed towards the everyday and normal, and ultimately towards survival in the face of removal from the country. The shapes that these strategies take vary to a great extent, but they are not totally conditioned by how the body politics of asylum, administrative logic or political representations give these people away to be known. This signals a move from sovereign power towards an ontological understanding of the body and Nancian 'body politic'.

Nancy's thinking of existence, exposure and compearance allow us to fathom political community as an expression of every body's singular plural condition. This means examining agencies and the political that are made visible through the relations and movement that the body enacts and in which it engages. The senses of the international materialise in the ways in which (inter)national politics effects, constrains and moves the body, and, simultaneously, how the body can contest, affect and exceed sovereign politics and state practices.

Event 3

Asylum, a monologist narrative of the state?

EEVA: Do you think that questions presented in the asylum interview are the most important ones?

NASIR: Most of them are not really important. Not really *relevant*.

EEVA: Hmm, can you give me an example?

NASIR: Well, the questions . . . The [officers] spend most of the time asking silly questions like why did you come to Finland, what if we send you back and sometimes they concentrate on very little things.

EEVA: Like detailed information?

NASIR: No, no, no, no. Not detailed information, when it comes to detailed information, which is important for *us*, they just [move] on. That is because there is no time left for any detailed discussion about *our* case. Things that are in *our* interest. They ask questions that are in their interest. Being as (a) police, or being as an official of the *Maahanmuuttovirasto* [Immigration Service], and they try to show off, try to show that they are efficient and they do their job very well. And things that relate to our problems [are addressed] very briefly.

(Interview with Nasir, March 2007)

The bureaucratic asylum process was not a subject of interest for me when I first started exploring the multiple manifestations of the political in the condition of asylum seeking. Like my own exposure to the asylum seeker's presence, the whole question of the process emerged as a result of doing fieldwork. In my experience, no matter at what phase of the process the asylum seeker is in, the question of asylum interviews is taken up. Most often, like in Nasir's case, this is related to an experience of not being properly heard or listened to in the interview, of not being understood or of being asked irrelevant questions. It is not uncommon to hear asylum seekers complain about the officer showing clear distrust towards their accounts, which they felt compromised their capacity to articulate their cases as convincingly as possible. For some, the grounds of the decision-making process were utterly clear but they had not understood *how* they should present the experience-based evidence for their claims. It was, anyhow, clear that the determination process shapes the asylum seeker's perception of him/herself, affecting adopted agentive strategies and the ways in which they make political claims, constitute their presence in the receiving society and relate to others.

56 *Asylum, a monologist narrative of the state?*

The international that arises from the logic of sovereignty and from a strict division between inside and outside is not only about organising political power, but also a political way of organising people (Haddad 2008: 48; see also Agamben 1998: 6; Epstein 2007; Nevins 2008; Walker 2009: 47). Finland, for instance, has sought to keep as close a record of the population as possible, including migrants, in order to provide some kind of welfare services to the population. At the same time, it has upheld policies that are intended to make Finland look like a non-desirable country to seek international protection, one where migration policies are efficiently put into practice (also Kynsilehto & Puumala 2016). Besides the sovereign aspiration to attain a monopoly over violence, the state claims a monopoly of the political in its desire to manage and control migration (Nyers 2003; see also Bartelson 1995; Squire 2009). With regard to the multiple restrictions that follow from statuses and categories, asylum seekers are, in a manner of speaking, banned from the sphere of political life within the state (see also Agamben 1998, 2005; Bigo 2002, 2007; Walker 2006b). In fact, the asylum process actualises concrete spatial and embodied relations, as asylum applicants cannot freely choose their place of residence. They are confined to reception centres or the detention unit (see Perera 2002; Rajaram & Grundy-Warr 2004, 2007; cf. Edkins 2005a; also Chapter 4).

The profound discontent that asylum seekers presented towards the determination process urged me to take a closer look at it. It is clear that asylum seekers most often do not imagine their identities and presence in the terms of asylum policies and the categories and statuses that are produced through those policies. Yet, the representatives of the state – the migration officers, the police and the employees of the reception centre – have to picture and carry out their work in terms of categorical, institutional statuses outlined in international treaties and through a range of policies. That task is far from simple, as I was to find out when I started to explore the quotidian practices of producing categories through which people are placed within the larger national body politic. I decided to hear what the migration officers thought about what happens in the asylum interview and how positions are situationally articulated:

> If the applicant does not want to talk or reply, or if for example despite continuous advice, s/he interrupts the interpreter [. . .], or if I've advised that s/he should tell about personal experiences, not about the overall situation in the country, but the applicant continues to refer to others instead of him/herself, my frustration shows. Then the questions become more poignant, so the applicants have to reply to what I asked.
>
> (Migration officer, survey response, 2011)

> Naturally the applicant's fear or aggression affects the atmosphere of the interview. . . . If the applicant's body language shows disrespect or contempt, I'll use body language that shows that I'm in an authoritative position. Usually that is enough to settle the situation.
>
> (Migration officer, survey response, 2011)

Asylum, a monologist narrative of the state? 57

When the applicant's and the migration officers' views regarding the asylum interview as a central part of the asylum determination process are combined, the locality, intimacy and corporeal negotiations that are related to sovereignty become evident. Both parties describe in their own ways the dynamic negotiation of positions and the struggle over knowledge that unfolds in the interview. These views deconstruct the monologist narrative of the state and articulate the human and corporeal dimensions of state practice. The sovereign state and the system of sovereign states – that is, both the national and the international – are constituted within social relations where power and knowledge are negotiated in a physical encounter. It needs to be asked: what space can the asylum-seeking body occupy in the face of sovereign practice, and what kind of senses of the international thus emerge (cf. Mbembe 2003: 12)?

While the perspectives of the officer and the applicant on the asylum interview may be profoundly different, it is rather clear that the process involves a multiplicity of practices and (subjective) evaluations before the status of the applicant is determined. The idea of the state as a unified decision-maker and the related idea of political community built on the state begin to erode when the empirical practices of sovereignty are scrutinised. Borders take shape as concrete walls only occasionally in practice, as in the case of building fences and walls to curb the arrival of asylum seekers in various parts of Europe. It is much more common for borders to be enforced, through various practices, by civil servants and employees in the field of migration in a variety of locations. This enforcement relates to the strategic putting into operation of sovereignty, where different responses are enacted to create distinct categories and protection statuses (see also Mountz 2010). This realisation initiated my journey into exploring the asylum interview as a corporeal encounter where knowledge about the body is produced and where political existence is communicated and negotiated.

3 A struggle over the body

Contestation and connection

The sovereign state plays an important role in constituting political life and its manifestations. In the fields of migration control and management, identities of the mobile body are scripted in numerous ways by those involved in immigration governance. In the asylum determination process the applicant's claims of displacement for political reasons and suffering from a well-founded fear of persecution are examined. It is also assessed whether the applicant is likely to be persecuted upon return to the country of origin. If these conditions are fulfilled, the applicant is granted refugee status. In the Finnish context, all other grounds upon which the applicant could receive a residence permit are also examined.

When so much is at stake, it is understandable that the determination process represents an anxious encounter between a representative of the state and an asylum seeker. If we are to understand the corporeal strategies through which the asylum seeking person negotiates and transcends the logic of sovereignty, it is imperative that we first pay attention to the embodied exchange that later on comes to limit and condition asylum seekers' agency in their daily lives. The asylum process is not an impersonal matter of bureaucratic practice, but culminates in the concrete encounter between the interviewing officer and the applicant. How are identities performed, scripted and positioned against one another during the process and in the course of the actual asylum interview? What are the struggles that become evident in the daily work of asylum officers and bring forth the political nature of determining the right to asylum?

Studies of the link between the institutional logic of the assessment of asylum applications and body politics do exist (see, for example, Bögner, Brewin & Herlihy 2010; Bohmer & Shuman 2007; Eades 2009; Shuman & Bohmer 2004; Wettergren & Wikström 2014; Wikström 2014). However, most of these studies either focus on the experiences of asylum seekers or rely on analysing verdicts or adjudication procedures, omitting the dynamics that lies at the core of the evaluation process (however see Coutin 2001; Granhag, Strömvall & Hartwig 2005; Kynsilehto & Puumala 2013; Puumala & Kynsilehto 2015). Because there is a stark hierarchy between the parties in the asylum process, it is important to bring forth the agentive capacities embedded in marginalised conditions in order to

60 *A struggle over the body*

avoid reductive and victimising interpretations of the ways in which the mobile body enacts itself politically.

Asylum seekers are not in control of what happens to them as a result of the asylum process. Thus it is not an overstatement to claim that their bodies and lives belong to a multitude of others that represent the state in a variety of ways: bureaucratically, administratively and politically. As a result of the asylum process, the applicant's position in the Finnish society is determined. The process is not based only on the applicant's personal account and the officer's estimation of their truthfulness, but also on 'country of origin information' and other 'objective information', to put it in administrative terms. Through the process, asylum claimants are inscribed into the national, and also international, body political imaginaries, but yet they are not reducible to completely sovereignless subjects even during the process. They cannot escape the effects that the process and resulting categorisation have, and thus their agency and political potential are not solely about freedom of action or self-control. Their agency is easily reduced to frustration and anger, if it is interpreted in the light of sovereign power and practices.

The present chapter engages with the asylum determination process by exploring the corporeal and political struggle that is involved in it. Of particular interest are the concrete ways in which that struggle takes shape in face to face encounters between asylum applicants and the representatives of the state. It argues for sensory ways of knowing that are inherently corporeal and that can promote an understanding of the international and the state as something that are enacted, lived and contested in relational mundane practices. The modus operandi of sovereignty is not solely systemic, but also embodied and interactional. Thus, there is always a subjective dimension to the determination process that aims to be objective and impersonal by nature. The state and the enactments of sovereignty can, within that approach, be conceived as institutionally arranged social practices. According to Alison Mountz (2010: xxv), migration officers have the potential to be subversive in their daily work and make profound changes within the state. When the scripted identities are not fixed and essentialised, what kind of dynamic negotiations take place in the encounters of asylum applicants and migration officers? With that question in mind, this chapter explores the body as a site of both contestation and political connection (see also Chapter 1).

Gaping discord

The element of struggle in asylum seeking involves differences in perception that result from two very different angles on the issue. The representatives of the state look at the question of seeking asylum from a politico-governmental perspective, while the asylum applicants are involved in a personal struggle. In a manner of speaking, then, the asylum process is about the gap between knowledge and experience, or, more precisely, turning experience into knowledge. The gap between the two 'mentalities' at work is an opening, in that through the gap a space opens for discussing the ways in which agency, the international and the political come together in the body.

The flux and changes in migration policies evoke responses among asylum seekers, who would like to have a say in the policies through which their futures are shaped. These responses are emotionally loaded, and the applicants' quest for agency in the context of asylum interviews is extremely strong. Yet, asylum applicants often express discontent towards the asylum interview and their possibilities of presenting their cases in a satisfactory manner (see also Event 3). However, asylum seekers cannot openly confront the asylum officer's interpretations of their presence in the receiving society and claim a response from them. Before engaging with a more theoretical argument and the actual asylum interview, I will briefly discuss the gap that separates the two conversing parties using an empirical example, where the dynamics between state practices and applicants and the dynamism of the asylum seekers comes through. Through the example, it is possible to see what the consequences are, if the interlocutors lock themselves and each other in strict positions and address one another through them.

While I was doing fieldwork in a reception centre in 2007, a group of temporary residence permit (the B permit) holders asked for a meeting with the Finnish Immigration Service. The migration officials had just updated their estimation of the security situation in Afghanistan, which meant that an effective return policy could begin to be enforced. This caused restlessness in Afghan B permit holders especially, as the grounds for the B permit were re-estimated each year and if the conditions that had prohibited return had yielded, the permit would not be renewed. The Immigration Service replied to the asylum seekers' plea to be heard, and a meeting was organised concerning the planned changes in return policy. At the time, the officials were exploring the possibility of enforcing an effective return policy covering not just Afghanistan but parts of Somalia and the Kurd areas in Iraq as well, as these regions were considered safe enough. A similar development took place again in 2015, when Finnish officials started planning returning Iraqi, Afghan and Somalian asylum seekers to their home countries. In the latter instance, the idea was to curb the arrival of asylum seekers from these regions to Finland, as other EU countries had adopted stricter policies towards applicants from Somalia and Iraq.

The meeting that took place in late February 2007 was set to discuss policy developments with the affected individuals. The situation was unique. Its actualisation created a sense of establishing dialogue and communication with Finnish asylum officers. Among asylum seekers who resided in the reception centre, the meeting was seen to openly recognise them as capable of taking political action and reveal their views as being as legitimate as those adopted by the officers. The objective of the meeting was to enhance communication between involved parties, as well as explain existing norms and changes in the Finnish asylum system to the holders of a temporary residence permit. Two police officers and representatives from other relevant institutions were also present at the meeting. It was the first time that a representative from the Finnish Immigration Service (FIS) came to meet asylum seekers and answer their questions. The Immigration Service is responsible for determining the applicant's (A) right to asylum, while at that time the police or border patrol officers conducted the first interview when the asylum claim was lodged. All in all, 88 people were present at the meeting, 68 of whom

62   *A struggle over the body*

were residents in the reception centre. The other 20 participants were migration officers, policemen, nurses, staff from the centre, interpreters and myself. The director of the reception centre chaired the meeting.

FIS: Apparently most of you have been given a temporary residence permit in line with clause 51 of the Aliens Act, and it most likely has been justified by that. Due to a technical hindrance you haven't been able to be returned to your home country, but otherwise you haven't had any grounds for receiving a residence permit, so that you could stay in Finland. And after that, it is so . . . [*general restlessness in the audience, talk*]

Ok, I haven't finished yet. I'm still continuing! So, after one year your situation is reconsidered and then it is still possible that you'll get a temporary permit for another year, and then again the situation is re-assessed. This legislative situation has not changed at all.

In the Immigration Service country profiles are made. And the one concerning Afghanistan has been updated. And, in practice that means that we no longer consider there to be technical hindrances to enforcing returns to Afghanistan. So, if a person has no grounds for a residence permit here in Finland, s/he can be deported or returned to Afghanistan. However, this does not mean group deportations or returnings, but each situation is individually examined. [. . .]

A: How do you know that the situation in Afghanistan has ameliorated? Don't you know that the officers have reported in the media, that the year 2006 was the worst year in Afghanistan, since 4,000 ordinary people were killed? And people are still suffering from hunger and thirst. Why are we being returned, if we will still have trouble and problems there and the war is still going on?

FIS: There is a country unit in the Immigration Service that follows the situation of each state very closely. And we also have our own researcher, who has done a so-called fact finding trip to Afghanistan. We should have very up-to-date and reliable information about the situation in Afghanistan. [. . .] And over 4 million refugees have voluntarily returned to Afghanistan.

A: So as to Afghans there is a possibility technically and otherwise, since the situation has calmed down, to return us or deport us to our home country. This means that you think we are lying about everything we have told you. . . . Nobody has come to Finland, just to get married or to work; it is a question of security and every one of the Afghans came here because their lives were threatened. Actually *you* are lying when you say that there's peace in Afghanistan and all kinds of possibilities, you are lying. Believe that you are not right!

FIS: If you have a negative decision to your application, first we examine if you have any other reasons to stay in Finland, working, other bonds, etc. Every situation is individually considered. And then we also see from which parts of Afghanistan you are, and if you could return and what would be your future possibilities there.

A struggle over the body 63

> [*The fuzz among Afghan asylum seekers is growing.*]
>
> FIS: If you get a negative decision, you can appeal to the Administrative Court. [*It has become virtually impossible to hear anything.*]
>
> FIS: This whole process will take approximately one year, so you don't have to fear, nobody will be leaving, at least not immediately. I'm not finished yet! [*in a raised voice*]
>
> CHAIR: [*ordering in vain the audience to be silent*]
>
> A: [*In a raised voice, almost shouting*] I want to know what is happening, she's not answering!
>
> FIS: I will just say that when the moment of deportation comes, we will check the situation in the country. It is always checked, if returning is possible on that day. Police will see into that. Nobody can be turned back to areas in which their lives are in danger.

> The Afghans who have been present at the meeting stand up one by one excitedly, speaking in a heated tone and gesturing vividly. Chairs fall over when they jump on their feet. At that point, the meeting has gone on about 45 minutes. After the meeting the policeman tells us that he has phoned the police station so that if any rebellion breaks out in the reception centre, several patrols will arrive without delay. According to him, there was obvious aggression in the air during the meeting.
>
> (Research diary, 6th February 2007)

The encounter between the asylum claimants and the migration officer illustrates that a narrative construction and presentation of the self meets limitations in the condition of seeking asylum. Speech and narrative are often connected with a person being able to achieve catharsis and to restore their position as a political agent/being. In the context of seeking asylum, the requirement to narrate and give verbal evidence of persecution is a question of the politics of asylum. Furthermore, it is a question of the limitations of the politics of voice as the main avenue into a person's mind and experience-world. The categorisation that is done through the asylum determination process represents a type of politics of visibility, which positions subjects in particular ways in relation to the state. The process is not only bureaucratic, but also an integral practice in securing sovereign imaginaries such as the nation-state and national community.

The politics involved in narration aims at creating a narrative self that finds itself a stable place within the narrative structure of the society (see e.g. Howell 2011; Kearney 2007). As becomes evident in the above exchange between the asylum applicants and the migration officer, the politics of voice that is at play in seeking asylum regards the questions on whose terms experiences of persecution need to be voiced and whose political lexicon should be used in the process. There are severe restrictions in the communication between 'the subaltern' asylum seeker/refugee and the (western) witness or civil servant. The western emphasis on verbal testimony, suggests Edward Mallot (2006), actually ignores other critical modes of remembering and disclosure. It leaves out ways in which the human body can retain and reveal individual and collective memory, and thus function

64 *A struggle over the body*

as a means of political expression (see Chapter 5). In the meeting, the asylum seekers exposed the officer to the political capacity of their bodies by leaving as an act of protest when they felt that no fruitful communication was possible. The act revealed the gaping discord between the conversing parties, although it by no means – as the police officer's reaction indicates – managed to establish them as equally exposed to one another.

Through the asylum determination process the "national order of things" (Malkki 1995) is inscribed in/onto the applicant's body. Gaping discord emerges when 'stories' and the body, which both belong to the domain of experience, are transformed into 'cases', categorised, and thus placed in the domain of knowledge and reason (cf. Zetter 1991: 44). Living with a categorical and essentialised identity is always and at all times extremely political, dynamic and ambiguous. This identity gains multiple significances and can function as a potential source of agency that exceeds the limits of national body politics and the narratives of the state, as people rarely, if ever, view their identities in the terms set by the state. Rather, in their struggle they seek to open up, occupy and claim spaces and positions between and beyond categories, policies and international treaties (see also Mountz 2010: 26).

The we-talk in the meeting sought to establish asylum seekers as legitimate actors with valid interests. As Carolina Moulin and Peter Nyers (2007: 365) argue, international treaties are filled with references to a 'we' that allocates to state authorities the ability of defining 'their people'. When the asylum seekers claimed knowledge in their own right, they sought to challenge the hierarchical power relationship imposed between people during and as a result of the asylum process. Leaving the meeting as a group marked a moment of exscription as the asylum-seeking body moved away from the presence of migration officers in order to question the power relation between the bodies in the asylum determination process. The protest was not necessarily intended to change the policy, but it questioned the grounds upon which that policy was premised (see also Edkins & Pin-Fat 2005: 21).

The gaping discord that took shape and materialised in the meeting did not permit deliberative exhange of ideas. No consensus was reached. The representative of the Finnish Immigration Service talked about knowledge obtained through the asylum interview and the so-called objective data, while the asylum seekers voiced a claim for knowledge based on their experiences. The discord that appeared in the discussion concerns the authority of knowledge and the inequal positions between asylum officers and applicants. When the representative of the Immigration Service stated that people sitting in front of her had no legitimate reasons for being in Finland, the focus of the meeting shifted from dialogue to a kind of confrontation that cannot surface and be openly addressed in the official asylum interview.

The representative's approach in effect denied the applicants a status in the debates about asylum and deportation. Her statement that the people were allowed to stay in the country only because of technical impediments constructed them as culpable subjects. That, in turn, put the criticism that the participants presented towards Finnish asylum politics beyond political debate (cf. Squire 2009: 60). In the meeting, the representative of the Immigration Service monopolised speech acts about asylum policies and also about everyday life in Afghanistan. As a result the Immigration Service claimed a position as a source of authentic knowledge through a monologist narrative of the state (cf. Moulin & Nyers 2007: 369–370; Mountz 2010).

Ultimately, the asylum determination process represents an encounter between sovereign practice and individual lives. As the vignette from the meeting illustrated, these encounters are not without frictions and tensions that take shape both verbally and through the body (see also Nancy & Connor 1993). The process is not exhaustive in producing knowledge about the applicant's body. Nasir, in my interview with him, elaborated on what happened between the Afghan asylum seekers and the migration officer in the following manner:

> We wanted [that meeting] because we disagreed with the policy concerning the B permit. We were going to talk about the B and everything. [We] wanted to question and we wanted to hear from her, and unfortunately she didn't seize that opportunity. You don't insult a group of people that way. Maybe we don't have our own homes in Finland, but we have our dignity, our self-respect, all people have that. We are no less, or worse than normal [people], neither superior nor inferior. And we are not idiots.
>
> (Interview with Nasir, March 2007)

A profound discrepancy, or even an ontological gap, emerges through the data.

Equal discontent towards the process

EEVA: Do you experience pressure in the process of applying asylum? And if so, how would you describe it?

NASIR: Yeah, that that pressure, that frustration, it's strange. You can't really describe how. I don't know, maybe I can't describe, maybe some really, yeah, some professor or some scholar will do, but I am not so good in explaining. And some of the refugees are illiterate they have never been to school. It is they [migration officials] who decide and unfortunately they think in a different way. Their mentality and how they approach, these things, . . . these . . ., our cases, is really different. It's really different.

(Interview with Nasir, March 2007)

Nasir's answer to my question reveals that the asylum process represents dispute over the right to construct knowledge and the possibilities to claim authority of knowledge. His description of the different perspectives through which the central actors in the process approach the issue reflects the divide between mind and body, knowledge and experience. Furthermore, seeking asylum relates to a contemporary view of political life and subjectivity that is contained in the state (cf. Walker 2009: 23). The bureaucratic asylum determination process is designed to re-establish the monologist narrative of the state about political community, the ontological functioning of which the asylum seeker disrupts.

66   *A struggle over the body*

As Nasir's account illustrates, the applicant's incapacity to speak the 'language' that the asylum officer expects leaves them in a vulnerable situation. The words with which the applicant is expected to characterise their experience might not correspond to the lived reality which they inhabit. Furthermore, some words may carry connotations and references that one is not willing to accept or that make the story seem contradictory (see also Chambers 1994). Nasir was not ignorant of the different 'mentalities' at work. Instead, he directly addressed the role of professionals in translating the body of an asylum seeker to others. In its quest for knowledge and truth, asylum has become the realm of scientists, doctors and other professionals, which leaves the applicant without an audible and understandable voice.

The gap that separates the applicants and the migration officers concerns the ways in which existence and knowledge about the asylum-seeking body are supposed to be constituted and communicated. Despite the profound consequences of the process for themselves, the applicants do not care about bureaucracy and policies as such. The asylum-seeking body does not equal to a status, but it constantly exposes itself with multiple means, at various fronts, with other bodies. This exposure reaches well beyond the politics of voice, as it seems to belong to a different register than verbal testimony, or the narratocratic practices of sovereignty and monologist narratives of the state. The way in which the interlocutors position themselves in relation to one another does not exhaust asylum seekers' possibilities for agency. In the course of their asylum interviews, applicants can articulate their cases and presence through alternative strategies that do not acquiesce to the bureaucratic logic of the process. The enunciative positions that the applicant assumes and the officer's perception of the applicant's being can, even in the course of the asylum determination process, be an opening for contesting, interrupting and exceeding the principle of sovereignty. Furthermore, the relational process of negotiating their roles and positions represents asylum seekers' attempt to overcome their separation from others and the related demand to rethink politics.

It might not be surprising that asylum applicants express discontent towards the process. What makes that notion interesting is that the officers show similar discontent, which enables questioning of the underlying rationale behind the determination process. The breakdown of communication in the meeting between asylum applicants and the migration officer urged me to explore the asylum determination process through the perspective of a state. In order to accomplish that, I carried out a qualitative web survey in 2011 with those migration officers who conducted asylum interviews in Finland. The survey was designed to chart the interpersonal dynamics that become enacted and take shape during the asylum interview and their potential ramifications for the evaluation of the applicant's account and the ultimate decision-making process. Furthermore, the asylum officers were asked to elaborate on their views of their own attitudes, presuppositions and presence in the whole of the process. The link to the survey form was sent out by email to all officers who at the time conducted asylum interviews in Finland (N = 52). Fifty-two percent of the officers filled out and returned the questionnaire. It comprised 24 open questions. The responses led me to think that the asylum interview exemplifies a case where the problems of politics have turned into problems in administration.

The incapacity to articulate one's experiences, to which Nasir in his elaboration referred, appears especially problematic when it is contrasted with the migration officers' perception of the applicant's responsibilities and role in the determination process (see also Kynsilehto & Puumala 2013):

> I explain what the relevant aspects with regard to international protection are and ask the applicant to stick to those. If he or she begins to tell lots of irrelevant things, I will intervene and say that there is no need to talk about such issues. I often tell the applicants that we have knowledge of the situation in their home country and thus there is no need to talk about the general context of the country. Often, the applicants also ask about this.
>
> (Migration officer, survey response, 2011)

> I stress that this is the situation in which the applicant must give all the reasons why he or she is applying for asylum in such a way that I understand them. I underline the importance of including even the smallest detail. I stress that it is the applicant's responsibility to speak for him or herself, to take the initiative and talk about all the grounds for asylum, as the officer may not necessarily know sufficiently about the situation to ask about the right things, to ask about the things that he or she does not know. I try to make the applicants understand their own responsibility in the interview.
>
> (Migration officer, survey response, 2011)

In order to explore the gap between different voices and positions, the migration officers were asked to elaborate on the methods they used to introduce the scope of the interview to the asylum claimant. As the two quotes illustrate, interesting and differing methods of interviewing arose together with telling categorisations of knowledge and non-knowledge (see Kynsilehto & Puumala 2013). In the first quote, the officer presents herself as a holder of knowledge about the applicant's home country. This reflects an understanding that there is only one way to talk about a country's history and the general political context of the country. The task of the officer in this case is to fit the applicant's experiences to the general context that can be read from various reports and estimated in the light of the European Asylum Support Office (EASO) training module that concerns evidence assessment. In the latter quote, the officer emphasises that he does not have and cannot possess the kind of knowledge about the applicant's situation and cultural background that enables him to ask the right kind of questions. In other words, the asylum claimant is constituted as the subject of knowledge, but, rather problematically, it is expected that he or she knows what is relevant for the officer and knows how to communicate that in an understandable way.

There seems to be no solid understanding of what constitutes knowledge and how the 'right' kind of information is reached in the asylum interview. Instead,

68   *A struggle over the body*

the interview is an encounter full of tension that concerns shifting positionalities, ways of (re)presentation and knowledge. Although the migration officers highlighted their role as objective professionals who make the decisions on the basis of knowledge, their responses to the survey clearly bring to light the role of subjective estimation and 'gut feeling'. There is an interesting dynamic at play between the officer's suspicion (experience) and how this suspicion needs to be clarified in order to arrive at certainty (knowledge). The following quote illustrates the way in which an experience of the truthfulness of or suspicion towards the applicant's narrative is related to the creation of knowledge and objectivity:

> If the applicant's narration seems completely truthful, perhaps I can see that there is no point in asking unnecessary questions. Let's stick with the necessary questions, if there is no need to ask too precise questions about the truth value of the narrative. If I feel that the narrative is untrustworthy, then naturally I ask plenty of further questions. [. . .] If I begin to suspect something that the applicant says (for example, I know otherwise based on country information), then I try to ask more detailed and exact questions and guide the interview in that direction.
>
> (Migration officer, survey response, 2011)

A focus on the politics of voice leads into a bleak notion according to which the asylum determination process, which is based on the logic of "selective opposition" (Squire 2009), deprives the applicant of the right to determine what counts in his or her own story (see also Bohmer & Shuman 2007; Good 2004). The asylum interviews concentrate on getting the facts right, on "both what happened in a particular country and about a particular individual's role in that political scene" (Bohmer & Shuman 2007: 609). Without question, these interviews are laden with tensions, which unfold with unequal consequences in the communication between the asylum applicant and the migration official. The legal right to seek asylum is by no means countered by the state's obligation to grant refugee status. The discrepancy of the rights of a person vis-à-vis the state represents the international as a political way of organising people and the world (Haddad 2008: 48; also Epstein 2007; Nevins 2008).

In their responses to the survey, many officers mentioned the challenges that the language barrier poses to their work. Mostly they were concerned whether there were equivalent terms for notions like persecution in all languages, or whether some other term was used. A few respondents also mentioned the difficulties that cultural differences in perception can cause to the asylum interview. In particular, they reflected on culturally differing notions of time and distance between asylum claimants and themselves. However, some replies addressed explicitly the gap between the two perspectives that come together in the asylum interview:

> The applicant's and the officer's conceptions are too far apart, which makes communication between them extremely difficult. In Finnish, there may

A struggle over the body 69

not be proper concepts to describe the nature and background of a conflict between different groups in Africa.

(Migration officer, survey response, 2011)

I guess there are some cultural differences in description. Also, for the applicant, the asylum interview is a one-of-a-kind situation. It is rare in life that you are expected to describe something in particular. So the interviewing officer should take a look in the mirror and ask how well the hearing went and whether what is expected from the applicants has been clarified to them.

(Migration officer, survey response, 2011)

Furthermore, one respondent explicitly suggested that the whole way of posing questions should be altered, because the terminology used in asylum interviews is profoundly unfamiliar to applicants. The officers' experienced difficulties in conducting asylum interviews reveal that sovereignty is not a monolithic construction, but a dynamic practice that puts both interviewing officers and asylum applicants in impossible positions. Even though individual officers can in their daily work adopt practices that disrupt sovereign imaginaries, they cannot escape their position as representatives of the state. The discord between the applicants and officers gives shape to a political dilemma that concerns the exclusion of asylum seekers, who are affected by the consequences of the process but who do not have a say in the criteria of their exclusion (Benhabib 2004: 15, 112; also Munro 2007: 458). The ontological gap between the parties concerns the kinds of hierarchies that are at play in both representation and interaction. Migration officers' responses revealed clearly that the monologist narrative of the state is not immune to the politics that begins with and emerges through the body. Even though the role of ambiguity and subjective judgment in the asylum determination process may be undermined, migration officers do acknowledge their existence in and effects on the asylum determination process.

[I evaluate] the overall story, how the interview has been, how the applicant has behaved; whether s/he has been in a hurry to leave; whether s/he has been restless, because the story has been hard to tell. Usually [after telling a difficult story], the applicant is totally drained after the interview, even if s/he has been restless during the interview. I also pay attention to the applicant's gestures, reactions, ruptures in the story (not in the case of traumatized, truly depressed applicants). Small details; colours, neighbours' names, the makes of cars etc. The way in which s/he replies to more detailed questions, whether s/he can specify answers instead of just repeating what s/he has already said, or stating that s/he does not know. What kind of noteworthy corrections s/he wishes to make when we go through the interview script and how s/he adds detail to the story . . .

(Migration officer, survey response, 2011)

Many respondents recognised the difficulty in 'knowing' whether the applicant has told 'the truth' as required by the administrative regulations and brought

70   *A struggle over the body*

forward all aspects that attest to the applicant's right to receive refugee status. Furthermore, they struggled with the necessity stated in law to make an equitable decision on the case. Professional duty, as well as learning to discern the truth in applicants' stories, was regarded as part of becoming a professional (also Kynsilehto & Puumala 2013). Migration officers' views lead to an understanding that the body, embodied communication and subjective responses are not insignificant in the asylum interview. In order to explore the meanings of the body in the context of the interview, I will resort to a notion of mutuality of address according to which speaking bodies open tensions. The notion derives from Nancian thought, where communication is not primarily about verbality, but about the articulation of (corporeal) existence which gives itself to be felt (Nancy 2010). The body introduces a sensuous politics, upon which different ethics, claims and agencies emerge.

Representation and articulation

The equal discontent that is detectable from both asylum applicants' and officers' views concerning the asylum determination process requires that the connection between representation and articulation is scrutinised more closely. Once again, I take a cue from Nancy, for whom representation is a matter of the intensification of presence, intense presence, that is received (rather than perceived) by the other (Nancy 2010). The intensification of presence, which grounds my conception of asylum seekers' political agency, concerns exposure, which is the condition of all bodies, an inseparable part of existence. This means that we *are* not without others. According to Nancy, the speaking body presents itself by opening itself, which means that it *exposes* itself to others, projects something out of itself in front of itself. The kind of Nancian understanding that I propose is reflected through Nasir's view on the pressure that characterises the asylum interview and the claim made by one migration officer that the whole way of asking questions should be altered. These views serve as a warning not to concentrate exclusively on semantics, on the spoken word and its meaning. There are different ways of structuring the world at play in the asylum determination process, ways that make contemporary conceptions of political space and organisation fluid. These ways undermine the functioning and even the very grounds on which the monologist narrative of the state has been built.

Difficulties embedded in the gap that concerns differences in perceiving the whole question of asylum might arise before the actual asylum interview has even begun. What is important for the asylum officer might not be so important at that particular time for the applicant, who might be preoccupied with a whole other set of questions:

> "The [asylum] interview was weak. I just talked about my children. I did not understand clearly the meaning of the interview, and did not state my problems – just talked about my children. My decision says that I had no problems in Somalia, and I got a B." I asked Abdi if he complained about the

decision. "Yes, I also got a doctor's report after showing my scars [points at his legs, arms and stomach] and explained my situation in Somalia."

I meet with Abdi a couple of weeks after my first interview with him. He invites me to have a talk with him in his own room. We talk about how he is and what has happened since our last talk. Abdi stands up, goes to one of his suitcases, opens it and pulls out an envelope. It is the decision of the Administrative Court on his appeal. He asks me to read it and tell him what it says. The paper is in Finnish. It presents Abdi's personal history from 1991 to 2005. In conclusion, the court thinks that the applicant is entitled to asylum either because of the need for protection or for personal, humane reasons. The court thinks that now the new evidence that Abdi has presented in his appeal to the Court can, and should, lead to a positive decision.

(Research diary and interview with Abdi, August 2006)

When I received the B permit, I appealed after a month. The process took some 13 months. Then they called me that I need to come to court. And then I went there and . . . I went to court like, was it 16th November year 2006. Then it took three months after which I got a positive decision. [. . .] I can recall when I received the B decision and there it said that you're lying. [. . .] It was very difficult for me to accept this answer [. . .] It was really difficult, terribly difficult. But luckily that time has passed. It passed, but was really difficult. [. . .] They asked maybe 40 times, in different ways, the same thing, although there is but one answer. I remember, when I was interviewed, it was some 13 times he asked and I answered. [. . .] And then my representative, he said: "You can't, when the question is so obviously similar [to the previous one]."

(Interview with Tahir, April 2007)

In Abdi's case the misunderstanding of the scope of the interview stemmed from his concern for his family that he had left in Somalia. Together, Abdi's and Tahir's accounts illustrate that asylum applicants are interviewed in order to answer the question of what, rather than who, one is. By this, I mean that a person's account is examined in relation to the characteristics set for international protection based on a well-founded fear of persecution in one's own country. Thus, the asylum interview is not interested in the person as him/herself, but as a potential representative of a certain political status. Yet, the applicants articulate their whonness in these interviews and, as in Abdi's case, do not necessarily understand that actually their whatness is under examination. Furthermore, the vignettes illustrate the embodied, sensuous and material consequences of the gap that separates the communicating parties in the asylum interview. In Abdi's case, he and the interviewing officer actually talked past one another. One question was asked, and a different one answered. Yet it is the applicant, as made evident by both Abdi's and Tahir's accounts, who has to live with the consequences of the gap. In the end, both Abdi and Tahir were granted residence permits based on their need for international protection.

72   *A struggle over the body*

It is imperative to grasp the amount of pressure that the applicant experiences during the asylum determination process, which puts one's account under tight scrutiny, aiming to spot any inconsistencies within it. In addition, Tahir's account manifests the stress that the applicant feels during the asylum interview. The pressure intensifies when the applicant begins to understand through the officer's questions that every word or mismatching detail can potentially be considered as a sign of 'false' pretences. A different answer, a minor change in detail, perhaps even a change of terminology, can potentially have a negative impact on one's application and be taken as a sign of fabrication. Considering the element of subjective estimation in the interview, it may not be surprising that the migration officers' responses to the survey revealed that aspects that enhanced the credibility of an account for some officers decreased it for others. While a couple of migration officers mentioned in their responses to the survey that the lack of details decreased credibility, for others credibility was decreased by too many details (cf. Khosravi 2010: 33–35, 112; also Kynsilehto & Puumala 2013).

The mutual sense of suspicion, distrust and incoherence that characterises the communication between the parties in asylum interviews demands that attention be paid to the ontological principles upon which the whole process is based. The ontological backdrop is connected with the international governance of asylum and the political organisation of the world into a system of sovereign states (see Puumala 2013; also Robinson 2011: 859). In their articulations that open tensions, asylum claimants expose interviewing officers to the impossible task of imposing order on movement that is not subject to that order. Indeed, asylum seekers may very well tie their accounts to "different ontological stuff" and constitute "their anchor chains [. . .] from different identity principles" (Olsson 1991: 73–76) than those interviewing them. They represent a different political imaginary, one that does not fall under the logic of sovereignty upon which contemporary notions of political belonging are founded (see Epstein 2010; Khosravi 2010). Thus, when a decision over the applicant's right to asylum is made, it may be made according to radically different ontological presuppositions and identity principles than those according to which it was articulated in the first place. Such an understanding calls for an ontological understanding of the political that is articulated through the body (see also Chapter 2).

In the framework of the politics of the body, voice represents a carnal and corporeal relation, a point of contact between bodies and bodily surfaces: a plea draws closer, suspicion drives apart and a hand can gesture both towards and away. Articulation represents the world, as the articulate body gives sense to the world by being exposed to the world (see Kellogg 2005). In my approach, language and verbal testimony are not to be confused with voice. Rather, for Nancy (2000: 3), voice is world-making, as "the speaker speaks for the world, which means the speaker speaks to it, on behalf of it, in order to make it a 'world'". The speaker occurs in anticipation of the world, "before it, exposed to it as to its own most intimate consideration". The possibility of exploring the senses of the international begins to take shape in the space that opens at the moment when an asylum application is presented. In the gap between the applicant and the migration officer, the sovereign logic of organising political existence is susceptible to alternative interpretations (also Puumala & Kynsilehto 2015). The potential in such a subversive reading of the asylum determination process lies in the body being exposed and exposing itself as capable of voicing and 'speaking' for/against/of the international, to its relations and on behalf of a different world.

The body as a point of reflection

The asylum interviews are characterised by an assumption that language is the primary and objectively most reliable avenue for communication, as it is usually considered as belonging to the field of rationality and logic (see Puumala & Kynsilehto 2015; also Damasio 2005; Neocosmos 2012). The assumption is problematic, as illustrated through both the applicants' discontent and the migration officers' responses, which concerned the interactional dynamics of the interviews. During the asylum determination process, complex experiences are translated into "endistic narratives" (Sylvester 2007: 565–566; cf. Sermijn, Devlieger & Loots 2008). These determination processes are often theorised as bureaucratic and impersonal practices that are thought to operate along a particular logic (see Bohmer & Shuman 2007; also Event 2).

From the migration officers' perspective, the introduction of the scope of the asylum interview was regarded as decisive in shaping interaction. It was considered as an option to open up room for discussion, relieve the applicant's pressure and chart if there was something that might affect the applicant's capacity to articulate their condition (personal communication, 19th May 2011). The underlying assumption that precedes the interview is based on the notion of the sovereign subject and his or her autonomous and free agency (cf. Frost 2010; Grosz 2010). Philosophically speaking, the process aims to solve the question of a person's "ontological belonging" (Agnew 2007: 141). It reflects the reconstruction and reinstitution of the territorial political community, secured by a sovereign state through exclusionary relations of governance and belonging (see also Squire 2009: 21). Resultedly, a plethora of statuses and temporary protections emerge, which effectively restrict access to refugee status and conceal the political agenda and ontology that give rise to it (see Zetter 2007). However, the process culminates in the coming together of people, most notably the migration officer and the asylum claimant. Thus, the role of the body and non-verbal communication in the context of asylum interviews merits closer scrutiny.

In the context of asylum determination processes, attention is most often paid to the ways in which the applicant's body matters in the evaluation of the asylum claim. According to Suvendrini Perera (2006: 638), the applicant finds his or herself in a position between modalities of bearing witness and giving evidence. The credibility of the applicant's story can be evaluated with a language test with which it is possible to determine whether his or her accent matches the accent of the region from which he or she claims to come. It is also possible to perform other tests on the body, such as different types of bone examinations, to determine his or her age, as minors are rarely returned. This biopolitical process, through

74 *A struggle over the body*

which it is eventually determined whether the applicant is entitled to receive a residence permit in Finland, makes it clear that the applicant's body plays a role as a source of information and as a piece of evidence. That is, the applicant's body is systematically evaluated and subjected to medical tests and the information thus gathered is contrasted against his or her verbal account in the actual asylum interview (see also Puumala & Kynsilehto 2015). Biopolitical practices form an integral part of sovereign politics in the field of migration. The practices and processes of evaluation are not necessarily spectacular or grandiose, but take shape as observation in the course of the asylum interview, as the following quote illustrates:

> Gestures and body language can reveal if a question makes the applicant uncomfortable. Depending on the situation, one can try to clarify what is going on, or if the question was related to a traumatic experience, maybe a change of perspective is in order. Emotional states can strengthen the credibility of the applicant's account or then not. Often people cry at the interview. Often genuinely, sometimes less so. If the applicant seems aggressive, the interviewer must be especially careful. . . .
>
> (Migration officer, survey response, 2011)

The applicant's cultural background, level of education, gender and personality affect the officer's behaviour and approach during the asylum interview. Furthermore, the officers reported using applicant's bodily reactions and emotional expressions as evidence and as a point of reflection in the process of evaluating the verbal account presented. It is especially noteworthy that the emotional reactions of the interviewing officer also take a corporeal and gestural shape. As one officer stated: "If the applicant's body language shows disrespect or contempt, I'll use body language that shows that I'm in an authoritative position" (see Event 3). The survey responses reveal that communication and the officers' ways of responding to an applicant's account are inherently corporeal and intertwined with subjective interpretation:

> I think, for example, if the applicant is emotional when telling about his/her family's situation, that the emotional state supports the account. You can also detect credibility from the applicant's gestures in the sense that at points it feels that the applicant's eyes are sparkling with excitement when s/he recounts about pleasurable and positive situations that one can assume to be true. When that is compared to the applicant's state of mind when s/he talks about the reasons for applying for asylum, it is possible to interpret the truthfulness of the applicant's narrative.
>
> (Migration officer, survey response, 2011)

The emotional states of the applicant play no role in the assessment of credibility in my case, because different cultures express emotions in different

A struggle over the body 75

ways, or not at all. In some cases, spontaneous emotional reactions can be significant: e.g. the applicant told about a building that used to be near his/her home. At the end of the interview, I showed the applicant pictures of this city. As the applicant saw a picture of the building that s/he had described, s/he became seemingly excited and explained it being the building s/he had mentioned earlier. The reaction supported the estimation of credibility concerning the applicant's place of origin.

(Migration officer, survey response, 2011)

The excerpts above illustrate some of the diversity in reading applicants' corporeal presence. For some respondents, the difficulty in interpreting emotional states and the applicant's gestures constituted a reason to disregard them, not the insignificance of the corporeal as such. The second response at first downplays the importance of the applicant's behaviour completely, but then elaborates on a particular situation where the applicant's emotional response during the interview did contribute to the assessment of the account. These examples were by no means the only ones where respondents acknowledged that the body and interpretations of the corporeal play a role in the interview. In fact, in their responses almost all migration officers reported having trouble and struggling with how precisely to interpret the applicant's behaviour and what to make of corporeal interaction in the interview. During the asylum interview the applicant's body is constantly evaluated against or in the light of the verbal narrative. Yet, it is not solely one body that is in line and under scrutiny in the interview, but *the* body as an ontological concept.

An exclusive focus on the applicant and his/her body – due to the disparity of positions and the unequal power relations – easily hides from view that also the officer's body is dynamically present in the situation. Yet, the migration officers' responses make it clear that their bodily reactions and gestures also serve as a point of reflection. Moreover, officers' differing methods of detecting the applicant's behaviour illustrate well that in the context of asylum interviews, it is crucial to pay attention to the power and hierarchy that are inevitably present in this form of communication (cf. Robinson 2011: 846). The officer's interpretation of the applicant's gestures and emotional expressions is a part of the interaction between the parties, which makes it meaningful to explore the political being expressed through the body. Furthermore, it suggests theorising gestures as acts and events of the political that, however, do not fall into the sphere of rational, reflective agency and intention (see also Neocosmos 2012: 541–542). Any suspicion and discontent from the officer's part are perceivable to the applicant and begin to play a role in how the asylum interview unfolds (also Puumala & Kynsilehto 2015). Furthermore, an interpreter and a legal representative are also present in the interview and play an active role in the interaction and in the construction of an asylum narrative. The corporeal dynamics of asylum interviews are a lot more complex than one would initially assume, and that affects the interaction.

The dynamics of asylum interviews

It can be concluded that the data that I collected from migration officers reflects a similar problem to the one that I encountered when interviewing asylum seekers (see Chapter 1). The problem concerns the role of the body in bridging the gap between representing and understanding those things one does not know or feel personally. The question increasingly haunted me to a point where it became imperative to begin yet another process of data collection. In 2012, I approached the Finnish Immigration Service with a research permit request to video actual asylum interviews in order to explore the communicative dynamics and the way in which the unspoken and corporeal may affect the ultimate decision on asylum. In addition to the interviews, I requested permission to access the written interview records and the ultimate asylum decisions. After a long and complicated permit process with several actors – the Immigration Service, legal advisors, interpreters, the reception centre and the Department of Social Services and Healthcare, which administered the reception centre – I was ultimately given permission to take a first step, which involved identifying suitable participants. Following this I was required to obtain the consent of all parties who would be present at the asylum interview before my data collection could go ahead. Six interviews were recorded between July 2014 and January 2015. The videoed interviews lasted between 3.5 hours and 5 hours 15 minutes[1]. In looking at the data, I am interested in how the ontologically understood body takes shape and matters in the ambivalent dynamics of asylum interviews and what kind of corporeal practices are involved and play a role in the situation.

It cannot be denied that, besides being to some extent ambivalent, culturally relative and gender-dependent, gestures and body language are also impossible to know in advance, as they always take place and are acted out in relation to others (cf. McNay 2008: 279). Despite the difficulties in using body language and the senses as sources of knowledge and conceptualising them as politically relevant, the officers' answers clearly point out that they do give direction to interaction in asylum interviews. Thus, it is necessary to address spoken, embodied or imaginatively gestured messages as a precondition for speaking to and being heard by the other (see also Spivak 1998: 824). The data points towards an understanding that the asylum interview involves interactional and bodily elements that support the notion of politics happening between people, or the political becoming manifested in events. Thus, a wider focus on the political meanings and senses of the body in politics is required.

The migration officers' survey responses regarding the uncertainties of and their personal reflections on the practices of interviewing illustrate that migration policies are not solid entities that are interpreted and simply put into operation during the asylum determination process. Rather, the asylum interview entails moments of negotiation that are not exclusively based on reason, logic and narrativity, but are bodily, gestural and emotional (see also Damasio 2000, 2005). Identifications and categorisations are relationally (re)constituted between the parties during the interviews. They are not qualities of sovereign subjects with a certain political status in reference to the state. Indeed, the capacity of the body to expose the other to its presence makes the interview situation highly volatile. The continuous reflection that a migration officer has to undergo illustrates that our identities are constructed only as we present ourselves – appear – to the other and as the other receives and responds to that act or event of appearance. The asylum interview, hence, is an event through which sovereignty is enacted and sovereign imaginaries are enforced on people's bodies and movement. The processes of distinguishing between selves and others, insides and outsides, are extremely ambiguous moments of sovereign practice.

The following vignette from one asylum interview illustrates that the applicant and the officer perceive possibilities and practices in a different way. The interacting parties are the interviewing migration officer (OFF), the interpreter (INT) and an asylum applicant (APP)[2].

OFF: yea:ah (.) eum (.) we:ll (.) I still specify about your being in Turkey so when you went to Turkey so did you reg- register there at the UN refugee agency so were you there as a refugee registered by them
INT: [((translates, looks at the applicant and gestures with his right hand))
APP: [((looks at the interpreter))
    (.)
APP: ((sighs and answers, lifts his right index finger))
INT: ((talks to the applicant and leans towards him))
APP: ((talks and lifts his index finger))
INT: ((repeats a word that the applicant said))
APP: ((repeats the word said))
INT: a-ha ((writes down))
APP: ((talks, nods and points forward))
INT: mm (.) mm ((nods, looks at the applicant and writes down))
APP: ((talks, gestures with his right index finger))
INT: aah ((nods))
APP: ((talks, gestures with his right index finger))
INT: okay
APP: ((talks, gestures with his right index finger))
INT: okay
APP: ((talks))
INT: mm (.) there was in some corner there euh outsi outside euh some off- euh office an own office
OFF: mm
APP: ((looks at the officer))
INT: and soon however there euh Turkish [police euh (.) he like arbitrarily
APP: [((glances momentarily the interpreter and then looks again at the officer))
INT: he chose certain people that e euh and sent euh them back ee across the border ((gestures with his hand))
OFF: mm-m
INT: [to Iraq

78 *A struggle over the body*

APP: [((talks, lifts his finger and looks at the interpreter))
INT: and this happened in front of this UN office
APP: mm-m
INT: in [place]
OFF: mm-m ((types continuously))

In the vignette, the interviewing officer wishes to find out whether the applicant registered as a UNHCR refugee while he resided in Turkey. The applicant does not give a direct answer to the question, but begins a detailed account about the corruption within the Turkish police forces and the way they mistreated refugees in the vicinity of the UNHCR office. The applicant pays close attention to the officer's behaviour; while she is typing the applicant's account, he looks at her and leans slightly forward so as to see what she actually is doing at the computer. His eyes are on the officer while the interpreter translates what the applicant just told him about how it was in Turkey. Three things are noteworthy here. First, the intensity with which the applicant looks at the officer, what she is doing and how she receives his account (cf. Goodwin 1981: 30; Kendon 1990); and second, the way in which he perceives the officer's question in the first place and relates that to the situation he is in. Finally, it is worth noting that interaction takes place mostly between the interpreter and the applicant, who organise and formulate the reply between themselves without the officer interfering in any other way than giving minimal feedback.

Interaction is always contextual, which does not intend that it is merely shaped by a particular context, but that it can seek to shape and negotiate the context (see e.g. Heritage 1996: 278–279). Instead of replying in the negative to the officer's question, the applicant felt compelled to position his final negative answer with regard to the general context of action in Turkey so as to explain why he has behaved in a particular manner. By doing so, he illustrated a gap between how he, from the officer's perspective, was expected to act, and how the reality that he encountered resulted in him choosing otherwise and living as an undocumented migrant in Turkey. The applicant's answer was dependent on his interpretation of the situation and of what was happening in the interview (see e.g. Heritage 1996: 156–157). In the next vignette this is reflected in the extent to which the applicant describes and reiterates the behaviour of the police and his resulting reluctance to register at the UNHCR office. He articulates his case through both verbal account and topical gestures (see Bavelas 1994 on topical gestures).

APP: ((talks and gestures with his hands, making first a pulling gesture and then
      spreading his arms))
INT: okay okay
APP: [((talks, looks at the interpreter and gestures with his hands))
INT: [so I wanted euh to say that even though the the distance ((gestures distance
      with his hands))
APP: krhmh [((coughs))
INT: [ju: UN office it was only it was only 50 metres

OFF: m[m
INT:　[but still
APP: mm ((looks at the officer))
INT: they they or when they had (.) a full power to do what they want
OFF: mm-m
INT: >or when or< in front of the UN (.) in front of the place
OFF: mm-m
APP: ((talks, looks at the interpreter, shakes his head and makes a tearing gesture
　　　and after that a throwing gesture))
INT: mm
APP: [((talks and makes a tearing gesture and after that a throwing gesture))
INT: [((talks))
APP: ((talks and makes a throwing gesture across his shoulder))
INT: ((nods))
APP: ((talks and gestures throwing))
INT: and some like euh Tur- euh Turkish police tear ((makes a tearing gesture))
　　　those asylum seekers ee some ee some ee documents and
OFF: mm
INT: put them in the rubbish bin
OFF: mm
INT: just just there
OFF: mm-m
INT: in public
OFF: mm ((typing continuously, focus on the computer))

The vignette illustrates that the asylum-seeking body is located in the ambivalent space between discourse and matter. It is both inscribed with meanings and categorised through sovereign practices, but it exscribes itself out of those meanings as it does not belong to the sovereign order. Hence, in Nancian philosophy, the body represents the dynamics of our existential responsibility, which makes it imperative to focus on the evented nature of the political as it unfolds through moments in which subjectivities are exposed to one another (see Nancy 2000, 2008). Nancy's philosophy takes note of the marks and effects of power, and the functioning of processes of inscription, on the body. Yet, it moves beyond mere embodiment by engaging with exscription and exposure, which function alongside inscriptive practices. They mark the capacity of a body to contest the practices of inscription, its capacity to withdraw from them and articulate a form of politics embedded in the relation or 'with-being'. The withdrawal moves the body from the sphere of politics to the sphere of the political.

In terms of doing research, the move from politics to the political enables me to overcome inutile bickering about who is right and who is wrong in the struggle of seeking asylum. In the adopted framework, agency arises from the event of exposure, from the tension that materialises when people meet and that in the context of asylum interview signals the coming together of politics with the political. In order to explore how vulnerability, inequality and resistance unfold through

80 *A struggle over the body*

interaction, between bodies, the corporeal dynamics of asylum interviews merits exploration. That would underscore the conceptual and philosophical challenges that the body and senses present to sovereign politics and its practices (Puumala & Kynsilehto 2015).

Evented positionalities

Both experience and knowledge are made, remade, and negotiated at boundaries that – as Rob Walker (2009) persuasively argues – are extremely active sites, moments and practices that produce specific political possibilities and necessities on either side. The whole notion of 'well-founded fear' of persecution becomes a negotiable designator during the asylum interview (see Kynsilehto & Puumala 2013; cf. also Berard 2006: 237; Connolly 2010: 182–183). The asylum interview represents a boundary or a threshold, as it marks the moment of decision on whether a person can access the national space and what the rights of that person with regard to the state are. Far more attention should be paid to the multiple and ambiguous ways in which political existence and corporeal communication affect the process through which individuals can be identified as 'legitimate' asylum seekers. Otherwise, there is a risk that we make wrong assumptions about which experiences are relevant and which terms, gestures and emotions are appropriate to express people's histories and relations in the context of asylum seeking (cf. Berard 2006: 245). But how should we think of and make sense of the body, if the body is ultimately formed only when it comes together with other bodies?

Such an endeavour might begin with an exploration of the political as an element in the act of presentation, not a condition for it. The sharedness of the political – Nancy uses the French term *partage* to emphasise the simultaneous act of sharing and dividing – can no longer be seen solely as a question of politics, as the putting of an ideology into operation. Rather, it represents the constant interplay between politics and the political as the essence of our existence. The political takes shape and comes into presence through events. Not all acts or events are political, but they bear the potential to become political. Whether an act – a gesture, a move or speech – becomes an event of the political depends on its reception and whether it changes the dynamics of interaction. The political unfolds, in the course of asylum interviews, in terms of both deconstructive acts and phenomenological events (see Nancy 2000, 2008; Watkin 2009).

OFF: and then a couple of questions about your identity so your identity card from Iraq has been investigated and proven forged by the National Bureau of Investigation (.) do you want to comment on this issue
INT: ((translates))
APP: ((speaks and nods))
INT: ((talks to the applicant and nods))
APP: mm ((nods))
INT: [((talks to the applicant))
APP: [((nods)) mm

A struggle over the body   81

INT: ((talks to the applicant))
APP: ((nods))
INT: ((talks to the applicant))
APP: ((answers))
INT: impossible ((shakes his head)) it's impossible
APP: ((talks and shakes her head))
OFF: ((has been observing the interaction between the applicant and the inter-
      preter during their conversation, now turns her gaze at the computer and
      begins to type))
INT: ((smiles to the applicant and nods))
      (0.5)
OFF: well then what about that on your Iraqi identity card and Iraqi certificate of
      nationality there are different years of birth (.) how so
INT: ((translates and [gestures with his hands))
OFF: [((looks at the interpreter
APP: ((talks and points towards herself))
INT: we- so my year of birth
OFF: yes ((nods)) in the other it says 74 ((looks at the applicant)) in the other 72
      ((looks at the interpreter))
      (2.5)
INT: ((translates and gestures with his [hands))
APP: [mm ((shakes her head and looks at the
                                         interpreter))
INT: ((talks))
APP: ((talks and shakes her head))
INT: th- no: no impossible to be so (1.0) wh
      (3.5)
      ((The officer turns back towards the computer, starts typing and lifts her left
      eyebrow))

In the vignette, the asylum officer makes a strong claim for the authority of knowledge. She does not explain to the applicant what is wrong with her identity documents in the first place, but merely offers her a possibility to comment on the issue.
She supposes that the applicant has intentionally given incorrect information about
her identity. The vignette illustrates that emotions and bodily reactions emerge
through practice, which includes the power dynamics between the parties but
which deviates from stable power relations. The officer assumes a distancing professional role when she addresses the applicant formally and presents the questions
to the interpreter instead of turning towards the applicant. Only when the interpreter
translates and the applicant answers the inquiry does the officer pay attention to
the interaction between them, and looks keenly at the applicant (see e.g. Bavelas
1994: 205). The questioning of the applicant's story and her identity cause her to
react strongly by shaking her head, pulling back from the table and opening her
eyes wide open. She refuses the officer's perception of her documents being forged.

The applicant, after asking to see the documents herself and scrutinising
them closely, admits that her year of birth is poorly written in her certificate of

82   *A struggle over the body*

nationality. That put her identity under suspicion in the eyes of the Finnish officials. The officer at that point does not ask the applicant to clarify why that is so, but moves on to explain that now her identity cannot be considered valid, which can make it difficult to, for instance, open a bank account in Finland. The applicant reiterates that were the documents actually forged, she would have never given them to the Finnish authorities in the first place.

At a later phase of the same interview, something unexpected happens, which interrupts the strict roles and institutional framework. The event paves the way for an understanding that the responses that are enacted shape the interaction between parties. The political dimension here lies in the fact that there is always more than one possible response and thus our reactions to the unexpected represent events of the political.

> ((The officer is typing the memo behind the computer))
> ((a bleeping sound is repeated))
> INT: £what that is that£ ((smiles))
> OFF: it's I'm getting email so it bleeps like that ha ha
> INT: aha [((translates and points at the computer))
> OFF:　　　[I'm so- em sorry hah
> (1.0)
> OFF: £it's because [of we are taping this it has to like with a certain (recorder)£
> INT:　　　　　　　　　[((talks to the applicant, but looks at the officer with a smile))
> APP: ((talks))
> INT: ((speaks))
> OFF: mhh wh so (3.0) yes so I'll ask one more question and then let's take a little break
> INT: ((translates))
> APP: ((nods))
> OFF: and after the break also the representative can [still ask if something comes to mind or
> REP:　　　　　　　　　　　　　　　　　　　　　　[((nods))
> OFF: ((looking at the applicant)) you can ask if something comes to your mind

After first trying to detect the source of the sound, the interpreter asks openly about it and thus disrupts the interview situation. At that point, also the officer seems bewildered, as she, despite her efforts, cannot block the arrival of emails. After excusing for the disruption, she presents her last question before the break and glances at the computer, which continues to bleep and interfere with the applicant's narration when she voices her thoughts about a possible return to Iraq in the case of a negative decision. The officer communicates annoyance and discontent through her body language: she frowns, and her lips and head twitch when the emails continue arriving. She has changed her body position and turned towards the applicant, as if to encourage her narration despite the repeated bleeping sound that echoes in the room. Only when the applicant finishes her answer does the officer reassume her position behind the computer and begin to type what the applicant has just has said. This pattern of behaviour differs considerably from the interaction that preceded in the interview. It is clear that what happened was not anticipated or intentional on anyone's behalf. At least momentarily the officer adopts a more informal tone and starts directing her talk and gestures towards the applicant. The officer, by so doing, discards the position of a distant listener and assumes a role as an active participant in the construction of the asylum narrative.

Besides unexpected events, open challenging of the institutional roles and positions also takes place in the interview. When, in the same interview, the officer inquires whether the applicant wishes to say something that has not yet been addressed, the applicant asks to talk off the record. The officer leans back in her chair and faces the applicant instead of the computer so that she can focus on what the applicant has to say. This disrupts the established setting of the interview, where the officer largely remains behind the computer and most of the time directs her focus towards the production of the written record instead of the reception of the story and creation of the interactional situation.

OFF: do you have now something to ask or a- add to this int- [interview
INT: [((translates))
APP: ((talks))
INT: so that the interview has ended right so I would like to say something
OFF: euh well this is still a part of this interview so that this has not yet ended (.)
      everything will absol- be written so that outside the record is said
INT: ((translates and gestures))
APP: ((talks))
INT: mm ((writes down))
APP: ((talks))
INT: mm ((writes down))
APP: ((talks))
INT: ((nods and talks to the applicant)) (.) well eum that off the record I just
      wanted to say that eum to ask that you are a woman and I am a woman these
      things that I have suffered you must feel and eum that you see and feel as a
      woman what [I have
OFF: [yeah
INT: happened
OFF: yeah em- this is why usually in this type of an asylum interview a woman
      interviewer is preferred over a man

During the asylum interview, the body becomes a political space, which does not belong to a political status or a collective entity but rather exposes political existence as an ontologically relational condition. This becomes manifested in the vignette, when the applicant pleads for the interviewing officer's understanding on the basis of her being a woman and thus presumably being able to relate to the applicant's experiences of domestic violence and the fear and distress that this has caused in the applicant's life. By so doing, the applicant asks the officer to come

84   *A struggle over the body*

out of her role as a professional and assume another kind of role through a double strategy: speaking off the record and making a plea as a female victim of domestic violence. It is impossible to say exactly what the effects of the changed dynamics of the interaction and the interruptions to their strict roles are. These events, however, disrupt the smooth operation of power in the interview and make visible the negotiations around authorship and knowledge. As they partially dissolve the institutional framework and result in more effort on behalf of the officer to maintain the communicative relation, the applicant may get a heightened sense that the officer is seeking to embrace what she says.

Events and what happens constitute a meaningful unit of analysis in an exploration of a politics that begins and ends with the body. A focus on evented nature, on how people enact themselves, dissolves the notion of a rational sovereign subject in control of their actions and presents existence as it happens and as it is shared. In Nancian terms, this represents thinking of existence as being-with-others, as exposure to others and the world. The presentation of the self and one's positionalities is a deeply relational practice and, as such, it cannot be determined beforehand or by focusing solely on either verbal accounts or intentional action. Yet, that which happens and how people respond to one another can play a role in how the actual interaction ultimately unfolds and whether the goal of addressing everything that is significant in the applicant's case is fulfilled:

APP: ((talks and gestures with her hands))
INT: mm-m ((writes down))
APP: ((talks and gestures))
INT: ((talks to the applicant))
APP: ((talks))
INT: well em I will speak [with a relative
OFF: [mm-m ((nods))
INT: I hope that they'll send them and then I hope that they can get some sort of certificate emm so that from the office of civilian matters one thing I forgot to tell (.) usually when you get the certificate of nationality
OFF: mm-m
INT: there are long queues
OFF: ye:eah ((looks at the interpreter))
INT: the officer has been sitting and he is filling in papers there is a queue everyone is so that there's a rush one is yelling another one crying ((gestures with his hands)) that that that even though there is no computer system
OFF: [ye:es ((looks at the computer and types))
INT: [and that is how it is possible that this thing happened
OFF: yes [I will write it here just a little moment ((types))
APP: [((talks))
INT: ((speaks and points at the officer))
APP: ((talks and gestures with her hands))
INT: ((talks to the applicant and nods))
APP: ((talks and gestures with her hands, touches her chest))

INT:	mm
OFF:	so was this an office for civilian matters what was it
INT:	((translates))
APP:	((talks and nods))
INT:	((nods, turns his gaze from the applicant to the officer)) yes
OFF:	((nods and types))=
INT:	=an office for civilian matters
	(41.5)
OFF:	((stops typing))
INT:	emm so for instance the officer who fills in eum so that this staff, so that these identity cards, it's the same as you are seated that 10 people they are in the room and outside there are thir[ty
OFF:	[mm
INT:	people in the queue (.) and then everyone is in a hurry (.) he understands that quickly (2.5) with my own feet I have gone there and that we have paid him the officer that he that he helped us quickly told [us
OFF:	[mm ((types))
INT:	that we're in a hurry

In the vignette, the applicant gives further contextual information that concerns the confusion about her identity documents. She discloses an important piece of information vis-à-vis the process of evaluating the credibility of her account, as giving out false information concerning one's identity is a crime in the face of Finnish law. If the applicant is suspected of such behaviour, this clearly does not enhance her position in the process. It is curious that the applicant does not voice this contextual information when the quality of her identity documenta-tion is under scrutiny. This may happen because, at that point, the applicant does not hold the same information as the officer concerning the problem with the documents and cannot understand why the officer claims them to be forged. Even when the applicant at the beginning of her interview admits that her year of birth is incorrect, she is not able to explain that, because she is more preoccupied with convincing the officer that the mistake in her documents does not annihilate her identity or that she would not be the person she all the time has claimed to be. The fact that the applicant has, by the end of the interview, been able to relax and find a narrating position for herself – perhaps due to the ruptures of the institutional framework that have changed the interactional dynamics – she manages also to provide important additional information on her case.

The evolution of the asylum narrative, and the negotiation that is involved in it, illustrate that constructing the identity of an asylum seeker is a deeply situational and relational activity. The positions between those present in the situation are not static, and applicants can call upon the officer to come out of his/her position and evoke a sense of connection and sharedness through both voiced pleas and the language of the body. In the actual asylum interviews, applicants take on dif-ferent positionings through which they advocate their cases. Applicants can bring their case forward through, for instance, familial, religious, ethnic or gendered

86 *A struggle over the body*

relations. These positionings are also enacted in the course of the asylum interview, when the account is presented to the officer through the interpreter. This interactional characteristic of the situation affects what is articulated and how it is done. As we will see in the following excerpt, verbality is merely one avenue:

APP: ((talks))
INT: and since that day I have considered him as my own son
OFF: mm
APP: ((talks and points straight ahead with his finger))
INT: and he considers me as a father
OFF: mm-m
[. . .]
APP: ((talks)) (.) ((holds a handkerchief in his hand)) (.) ((waves his hand above his head, talks and stands up))
OFF: yeah if you want you can take a little break so
INT: ((interprets and looks at the applicant))
APP: ((wipes his eyes, stands with his back turned to the officer and lawyer))
(.)
APP: ((cries and talks))
INT: not necessary to take
APP: ((returns to his seat))
OFF: yeah
APP: ((talks))
INT: no need
OFF: ((types at the computer))
APP: ((talks))
INT: mm
(.)
APP: ((talks))
INT: mm-m ((nods and writes down))
APP: ((talks, wipes his eyes)) (.) ((cries))
INT: ((looks at the applicant))
OFF: ((types at the computer))
(.)
APP: ((shakes his head)) (.) ((talks and taps the table with his finger))
INT: ((nods and writes down))
APP: ((keeps on talking))
INT: mm
APP: ((talks))
INT: ((nods))
APP: ((talks)) (.) ((cries))
INT: okay [( )
OFF: [would it be better to take a little [break
INT: [((translates))
APP: [((answers, shakes his head and finger))

A struggle over the body   87

In this vignette from another interview, exposure takes form as emotional upheaval, which causes the applicant to distance himself from his narrative by standing up and turning his back to the officer. Whether the officer considers his anguish genuine cannot be detected, but the applicant's emotional unrest disrupts the situation and evokes a response from the officer. The applicant, however, refuses to admit that he might not be able to go on, and both verbally and gesturally refuses firmly to interrupt his story. Both of these vignettes evoke an understanding that the body can neither claim certain knowledge nor be known unambiguously. Neither can the applicant know if the officer believes what s/he hears and sees, nor can the officer be certain that the applicant is telling the truth. As a result, both the applicant's and the officer's claims to knowledge are ultimately equally ambiguous. Such a stance situates the body between objectivity and subjectivity, identity and difference, inside and outside. Furthermore, it opens a space for a discussion of the political significance of exposure even in the face of restrictive policies and exclusionary practices. As a whole, these excerpts from the asylum interviews illustrate that in their accounts, asylum seekers enact a variety of "axes of demarcation" (Kynsilehto 2011: 1547) in order to communicate their cases. Asylum narratives frame persecution and multiple experiences of violence in terms of their embodied and sensuous effects, which are context-bound and situational instead of systematic, cumulative oppressions (see also Bürkner 2011; Kynsilehto 2011).

Conventionally, as Judith Butler (2004: 5) has pointed out, agency has been understood in terms of a singular subject, who is personally responsible for his or her actions. It is connected to valid interests from which authority, responsibility and capacity to act in history arise (Meyer & Jepperson 2000: 106). The coming together of these two aspects denotes what is conventionally meant by political action. There is political agency in/beyond the status and fixed roles, because people are not one with them. This implicates moving from politics to the question of agency in the political, which accounts for the plural and relational dimension of politics, thus destabilising the focus on the way sovereign logic constructs the visibility of the body (see Rajchman 1988; also Chapter 4). For me, politically significant are also acts and events, which *in their potential effect* can be understood to contest, interrupt or intercede operations of body politics, or exceed its limitations and expose one's being in a way that disrupts the smooth operation of categorical identities and political statuses. That does away with the prerequisite of intentionality for an act to be considered political. The opening that emerges enables us to consider also *events* of the political, where the political emerges through exposure, and not simply as a result of a singular subject taking action.

The approach departs from that where a person's situation in discourse is formed by them being addressed (see Butler 2004: 139). In such an approach, relations are established through categorising and naming the other in terms of the prevailing order, which is exactly what the asylum determination process aims to accomplish. For me, the political is exposed in the fact that the body under categorisation is not totally conditioned by its status, by the other's perception and way of address. Multiple "mobile and transitory points of resistance" (Foucault 1978: 96) and relationality thus begin to emerge. Foucault (1982: 781; cf. Butler

88 *A struggle over the body*

1997) has conceived all main forms of resistance as struggles that revolve around the question of identity – who we are. These struggles refuse a scientific or administrative "inquisition that determines who one is" (Foucault 1982: 781; cf. Zetter 1991: 40). When considered from a Nancian stance, the struggle involves the body's movement away from a substantial identity that would situate it in terms of a political ideology or ontology, in this case sovereignty.

The narrative or corporeal articulations that deviate from how the asylum interview was institutionally supposed to unfold may be problematic and questionable from the state's point of view. Yet, these articulations signal active directing of life, the person's search and quest to find a place for themselves, and the possibility of defining their own being and body (see also Puumala & Pehkonen 2010; Puumala, Väyrynen, Kynsilehto & Pehkonen 2011). In the frame provided by the ontology of the body as an ontology of being with, these acts are political, as they expose the applicant not only as a vulnerable victim, but also through the body's connections to political structures and various other bodies outside its political status. The events through which the body articulates itself and exposes itself in the course of the asylum interview creates movement between the conversing parties and affects the migration officer's body. The interaction illustrates the political potential that the body bears, together with the necessity of starting to think about the corporeality of (political) communication. (Puumala & Kynsilehto 2015). The perspectives that come physically together in the asylum interview, in the process of constructing an 'asylum narrative' (Shuman & Bohmer 2004), can have a rather ambiguous relation to one another (cf. Foucault 1980: 82).

Not only with their stories, but also through their bodies, applicants contest the functioning of sovereign practices and their endistic endeavours. Through corporeal acts that disrupt the flow of their account, applicants can expose the officer to their presence so as to influence the reception of their story or to point out the meaningful elements upon which the applicants build their stories and identities. In taking action that seeks to transform improbable into possible, the body moves to evade or change the nature of the grip of sovereignty. It signals reaching and stretching towards a transformation. This does not mean that the body's aspirations are fulfilled, or that the body is no more constrained by politics – it simply articulates a mutual exposure that takes shape through corporeal practice. The body is exposed to sovereign practices, but its response to those practices exposes sovereignty to itself by leaving the goal of governance and related knowledge practices unfulfilled.

When the migration officers' survey responses are combined with the actual practices of articulation that interlocutors adopt during the asylum interview, it is possible to see that the body constitutes a central hermeneutic element. Nevertheless, the institutional and political logic on which the whole asylum process relies fails to recognise this. Instead, it demands that, in the name of objectivity and transparency, the meaning of the body in knowledge production and as an arena of political expression is omitted. In practice, this reifies the exclusive communication relationship in which one party has, morally, the upper hand and the other is required to translate their views into a language that fits the prevalent political imaginary. Philosophically, however, the need to think about how the body, and a politics that begins and ends with the body, enters into the ambiguous relationship between asylum seeking, sovereignty and the international, is clear.

The body matters

The appreciation of the politics that begins and ends with the body stems from an understanding that being displaced fosters a particular take on the world, which makes asylum seekers highly attuned to and conscious of the frailty of those social and political structures upon which they stand (see Huynh 2010: 54; for a more thorough exploration see Chapter 1). The event of exposure, as it happens, reinvokes the bond that has been severed by sovereign imaginary. This imaginary neglects our ontologically plural condition, which is always political, yet never free from the sphere of politics. My collage, then, seeks to move beyond, but not negate, discourses of marginality and abjection. When considering acts and events that expose and articulate political existence, the said and done are not the most significant factors.

In the context of asylum seeking, it is important to understand what ultimately mobilises people. The act of seeking asylum is a relational one. It involves a reading of relations and connections and is driven by other relations and connections. It portrays movement both as a withdrawal and in terms of approaching; a move away from something/body and a move for/towards something/somebody. We would need to understand what matters in people's lives and to evade perceiving certain types of asylum-seeking bodies – such as young men travelling alone – as particularly threatening and inscribing hate and fear to them. The body does not exist and move alone. It conveys a message that is at least two-directional: it articulates hope and vulnerability. Seeking asylum is an act that communicates both to those left behind and to the state where the application is lodged. An engagement with an event where the ground for seeking asylum is formulated might help to concretise how the relational body is present in the plea and what kinds of connections it draws out.

OFF: and do you yourself still have something to add add to do you yourself have something that you want to add to these grounds for your asylum application or to why you left
INT: okay
OFF: to seek asylum
INT: ((translates))
   (.)
APP: ((talks and at the end of his turn he lifts up a finger))
INT: mm
APP: ((talks))
INT: mm
APP: ((talks and lifts up a cup of water and moves it in the air))
INT: mm

90 *A struggle over the body*

APP: ((talks))
INT: that I want to say that here is eh my yet eh I come here in Finland because of my wife and children but not particularly particularly exactly eh because of the child eh I come here
OFF: mm
INT: a:nd I eh would be ready that (.) that if eh he can no from there to Finland I myself do not want (-emm-) nowhere
OFF: mm
INT: I assure that I'm not advocating my own interests but (.) he
OFF: mm [yeah
INT: [his interests are the most important
OFF: yeah
APP: ((talks and lifts up a finger))
INT: and it is [ve- ((looks at the applicant))
APP: [((talks))
INT: a:nd yeah [so that it is extremely because
APP: [((talks and keeps his finger lifted))
INT: so I swear that I I will not step into Finland again if he could get
OFF: mm mm
INT: to stay in Finland
APP: ((talks))
INT: because both the child and the mother if they could stay [because
OFF: [mm
INT: a child needs a mother
OFF: mm
APP: ((talks))
INT: a:nd after this
APP: ((talks))
INT: if you can sometimes eh could help eh them then
OFF: mm
INT: it would be a good thing I for myself do not want anything
OFF: mm-m ((types at the computer))
      (.)
APP: ((talks))
INT: mm-m ((nods and looks at the applicant))
APP: ((talks))
INT: mm ((nods)) (.) because I look at this thing so that I do not want that that eh what I have gone through that I this that this would happen again eum with others
OFF: [yes
INT: [I don't want that [that these
OFF: [yeah
INT: bad things would happen to another [human being
OFF: [yeah ((types))

After describing the multiple forms of physical and political violence, exploitation and precarity that the applicant has experienced in his life, both since childhood in his home country and after leaving until the present day, the plea he makes seems at first banal. If he has been persecuted, why would he be willing to renounce his place in Finland? It would be easy to contend that the applicant does not suffer from a well-founded fear of persecution, if he is willing to go back to the conditions where he lived previously. However, at the end of the exchange the applicant contextualises his stance by contending that he would not want anybody else go through what he has had to suffer. For him, seeking asylum represents an act of love and responsibility as a the provider for the family. The applicant was willing to undergo travel, waiting and the bureaucratic process to save his foster son from the hardships he has had to face. It is also possible that the scope of the asylum interview has not been entirely clear for the applicant and, by making a plea for his family, he seeks to reverse the Finnish debate about male asylum seekers leaving their families to suffer while they selfishly try to secure their own lives and futures. Both the interpreter and the interviewing officer support the applicant's narration with their feedback, which communicates understanding of the situation but does not yet tell anything about how the applicant's story is actually received in terms of the process.

For me, the above vignette illustrates the need to try to understand the perspective of the other and appreciate that some things are more meaningful than others in people's lives. The fact that the asylum determination process evaluates the individual's case does not mean that a claim for asylum could be articulated in isolation from the relations and reasons for leaving that matter most in the applicant's life. In that sense, the act of seeking asylum is a question of affective value that cannot be isolated from the relations with, connections with and separations from others (cf. Despret 2013). The experiences of violence and persecution differ among the applicants. They are shaped by gender, sexual orientation, familial relations, age, class, religion and ethnicity, to mention but a few. Yet, none of these bodies exist alone; somehow their beings and fates intertwine with those of others. Seeking asylum evokes both deeply intimate and politico-historical relations; it is not an act of a singular subject.

The asylum seeking body is a 'growing' multiple that is formed through diverse practices and relationships. If this is not understood, there is a risk that the wider context behind the application is erased and expressions of relationality are easily interpreted in a deeply problematic manner, to the detriment of the applicant. The role of the body is much more ambiguous and central than what discussions about the asylum seeker's body as a target of evaluation would suggest. The asylum determination process does not concern abstract policies, faceless treaties or disembodied practises, but the human body measured against international and sovereign political norms, which underpin our conceptions of political life. The body is to be thought of as an essential dimension of interaction that plays an important role in the construction of reason and consciousness (see also Damasio 2000; LeDoux 1996; cf. Herlihy & Turner 2006). The co-constituted nature of

92   *A struggle over the body*

reality and our being is clearly expressed in the asylum interviews, where the applicant's story and being is constructed in the interaction between the migration officer, interpreter, legal representative and the applicant him/herself (cf. Edwards & Stokoe 2011). All of the bodies present in the interview play a role in how the applicant's presence is perceived, how his/her story becomes articulated and how a meaningful storyline is created within the account (cf. Stokoe 2014).

Writing about the ambiguity of the politico-corporeal struggle involved in asylum seeking, and claiming that it bears the potential to disrupt sovereign politics, requires placing emphasis on multiple modalities of being political and expressing the shared nature of our existence. Most often, these modalities of exposure are not associated with visible (sovereign) politics. Yet, as the empirical data discussed in this chapter lets me conclude, asylum seekers have multiple means of disrupting the smooth functioning of sovereign practices and making those practices engage with the "turbulence of migration" (Papastergiadis 2000; Squire 2009: 145–166). Even so, there seems to be an immense gap between both the interviewing officers' explicit acknowledgement and the evidence provided by the empirical data of how the body matters in the interview, and the officers' refusal to admit that anything else than the verbal account could count as a valid source of knowledge at the moment of decision-making. One respondent pointed out that emotional outbursts and body language "affect in the background, cannot be written down in the decision as such". And another respondent stated that the process of decision-making is only "seemingly neutral".

It would be crucial to understand why certain emotions appear in the course of the interviews. Thus, emotional reactions should also be clarified during the asylum interview, while now the focus is on the narrative structure and logic of argumentation. If this is not done, the meanings of bodily language are unlikely to enter into decision-making as legitimate sources of knowledge. Furthermore, it would be important for migration officers to reflect on their own responses and presence in the interview setting as well as their role as decision-makers who, on the one hand, have to distance themselves from the narration and, on the other hand, attune themselves to the multiple ways in which the applicant has voiced his/her case.

The shift that begins to appear in thinking about the state and the international in relation to moving and sensing bodies does not mean thinking outside of sovereignty. Rather, it means thinking both alongside (but not in line with) and beyond sovereign practices and the politics of asylum (see also Manning 2007). This tension opens a space for theorising possibilities of political life and the senses of the international. These senses are in a process of becoming when sovereign politics seeks to come to terms with the moving body and when the body constantly refuses to be known. There is a constant process of (re)presentation and withdrawal: the senses of the international are never finished, complete or final, but always unfolding in relations that evolve between people and sovereign practises, and among people, as they all move in relation to and with one another. The body represents a border or line of separation that allows beings to appear distinctively, and yet exist contiguously (Perpich 2005: 85). Understanding the body through

A struggle over the body 93

exposure exposes the body as a relation, being unfolding as being-in-common. Questions of existence, the political and community are inseparable from one another, as the body is always understood and intelligible only with others.

In-different positionalities

By adopting different perspectives towards the asylum determination process and the struggle that materialises through it, this chapter has highlighted how individual emotions and bodies are interwoven with social structures of knowledge and belief. Therewith, the chapter has facilitated a deeper understanding of how identities and collectives are constructed, negotiated and scripted. It has attended to the interactional and corporeal processes through which meanings and knowledge are conferred, negotiated and mediated situationally. As such, the chapter already paves the way towards the wide range of complex ways in which asylum seekers articulate their presence in-difference to the state, in the face of multiple structural and political constraints. The two following chapters will delve further into the dynamics through which the body of the asylum seeker disrupts state-centred conceptions of who we are and who we must as political beings.

In our thinking about how we live and are together, we need to move from the politics of in-common-being (where the common is the essence of being and political existence) to being-in-common (where being is what unites all people and constructs them as legitimate political bodies). The move articulates a whole new approach to the question of political participation and belonging – political community – and challenges philosophically the notion of "the modern international" (Walker 2006a, b). The challenge lies in understanding 'with-being' not only as 'in relation to', but also as a being-towards, which is ontological. Through a politics of its own, the body resists, interrupts and exceeds state politics. The body exists in-difference to the state, which does not mean that sovereign practices and politics do not give direction to and limit asylum seekers. But the relationship between a body and state practices is far from being static (see also Manning 2007; Walters 2015).

The relational, situational and contextual nature of communication undermines the notion of a pre-existing and shared understanding of the scope of the interaction, at least in the way assumed by the officers. Furthermore, it alters the scope of the asylum interview, from *whether* the applicant has a well-founded fear of persecution, to *how* such a fear is, or should be, acted out during the interview. The question focuses on sense-making both during and after the asylum interview, instead of neutral and objective description of the real world nature of the applicant's background and experiences. Davide Panagia's (2009) critique of using narratives as the standard for expressing ideas and determining valuable action, speech and thought also applies to the asylum determination process. Yet, the practices of information gathering and interaction in asylum interviews illustrate the obsolescence of rigid categories and statuses, as well as the evented nature of constructing political communities and articulating political conditions.

94　*A struggle over the body*

The political implications of the discussion suggest that we need to rethink the possibility of holding on to a foundational category of neutral, objectivist knowledge. Consequently, this might indeed require reassessing the assumption concerning the capacity to evaluate an experiential story according to pre-established criteria. It is crucial to understand the rich variety of experiences, points of identification and multiple relationalities that any account of seeking asylum entails and with which it resonates (cf. also Kynsilehto 2011). The act of fleeing and crossing a border does not annihilate these, but in many ways may strengthen them as asylum seekers articulate themselves and expose their presence to others. The whole experience of seeking asylum becomes meaningful and gains its meanings through the connections it breaks and the ones it forces or makes impossible. Most of these connections do not have an initial and explicit connection to the state, but displacement has resulted in a heightened sense of how statist accounts dominate our capacities for action and the connections we are able to foster and maintain. Even a partial bridging of the gaping discord between the perspectives that come together in asylum seeking would require that the incoherence that characterises the interaction at many points of the asylum interview be openly acknowledged. Furthermore, it would be vital to admit that the incoherence concerns both conversing parties, although the consequences of that condition are not equally distributed.

My own exposure to the demand to think about the foundations of my own identity in relation to the asylum seekers necessitated a further and more thorough exploration of state practices. Engagement with the ontological dynamics of the asylum determination process has meant exploring how things – and people – are kept together and apart at the same time (see Olsson 1991: 60). The question relates to the consistency of rules that define normality, and to the willingness to disrupt that logic of normality in order to arrive at an alternative theory of political existence and action. In the kind of framework that I have suggested, language and speech are not simply media of communication, but social and political gestures that uphold, reconstruct and deconstruct a particular expression of (political) belonging. The gaping discord between representatives of the state and asylum claimants illustrates that language, thought and action are rooted in ontology, if ontology is understood as telling us what belongs to the world and what bases are available to our thinking (Kynsilehto & Puumala 2013; Olsson 1991: 76).

The asylum-seeking body is adamant in not being reduced to bare life, a victim of political processes and circumstances. It does not simply acquiesce to the operations of sovereign politics or wait for the outcome of the asylum process. In rejecting and contradicting the position and role assigned to them, asylum seekers gain at least partial authority over the process that controls them and limits their bodies. An analysis of how multiple demarcated axes of power appear in asylum interviews encourages a move from subject-centred approaches towards exploring the complex ways in which seeking asylum evokes political, societal and historical developments in extremely intimate relations. The body articulates *the incompleteness of the international organised in terms of territorial, sovereign units, which function as the basis for political participation and expression.* The (inter)national body politics creates a need for asylum seekers to explore their means of taking political agency and expose themselves as legitimate beings. As the next two chapters continue to illustrate, their articulations not only comment on the process and its ontological background, but also at points exceed them.

Notes

1 Due to the highly sensitive and confidential nature of the data, I have agreed to guarantee the absolute anonymity of all participants. Thus, it is not possible to disclose any detailed information about the applicants, interviewing officers, interpreters or legal advisors. Besides six video recordings and related documentary data, I got access to the written records and decisions in the case of four additional applicants with whom video recording was not possible, but who still wanted to participate in my research.
2 The utilised transcription symbols are presented in Appendix 1. Original data has been translated from Finnish into English.

Event 4

Passages and dislocations

Ahmed is a tall young man. The gun-shaped pendant around his neck catches my attention when I take a first look at him. He is wearing a grey t-shirt and a cap and pants that both are camouflage-patterned. Ahmed has a tight way of speaking. The director of the detention centre told me that he was detained 11 days ago and tomorrow he is returned back to Norway. Ahmed himself does not know this yet.

When we begin to talk, Ahmed expresses his outrage at a policy according to which he could be returned even though he still has the right to appeal his decision in Finland. In detention, he has been thinking about his life, about "what's the next step". Ahmed recounts spending the last five years of his life in Norway, but that his home country is Somalia. He tells me that he has lost his brother, friends and some family members in fightings in Somalia. Ahmed informs me that he was a small child when his brother died, but still remembers the moment when men came to his home and took his brother away: "When I think about that, I can still remember the faces of the people who took him." Ahmed tells me that after his brother had been killed, he and his mother fled to Yemen. That was his first experience of displacement. Ahmed claims that growing up in a place where you see people being killed is quite unlike anything else. However, he feels that nowadays with the TV, news and the Internet, people all over the world know what is going on. "People can see, listen and understand what other people are going through. Then, of course, they can act as if they didn't," he ponders. "If you just close your eyes and imagine how it would feel to lose a brother, sister, mother or your family and then flee from your home, not knowing what will happen or has happened, then you would get answers."

Ahmed's mother decided to send him away so that he wouldn't grow up witnessing killing and violence and would avoid getting into trouble himself. Before Ahmed left, his mother used to sit with him for "five hours every day talking." "Five hours every day," repeats Ahmed. When I ask what she told him, Ahmed starts explaining and pauses for a while after each of her teachings to give me time to write it down. "She told me: trust yourself, be friendly with everybody, respect everybody, do right things, treat everybody in the best way, help others who have problems and whose problems are even bigger than your own and don't give up till you die." Ahmed says that his

98 *Passages and dislocations*

mother told him that life wouldn't be easy after leaving. He confesses that at the time he didn't believe what his mother told him, but now he realises that she was right. When Ahmed left, he was only 17 years old. He tells me that many people leave. "Some try to reach Australia, others Europe, some get killed on the way."

Ahmed applied for asylum and received several negative decisions during the time he spent in Norway. Having exhausted his possibilities there, he was ordered to leave the country. That is when he came to Finland. This is not, however, the first time that Ahmed has been in Finland. In the previous year, that is 2006, he spent three months near Vaasa, in Oravainen [Ahmed uses the Swedish name Oravais], in a reception centre. Ahmed protests against Norway and Finland for not accepting refugees and giving people protection: "I have travelled all over Norway, and I saw with my own eyes that the earth is empty. And Finland is empty, too. I saw that too. You see people killed and yet you tell them that they cannot stay. I came trough Ivalo, Tornio, all the way to Oravais, and there is nothing but trees here. Why are you sending people away?" Ahmed states that he would understand this policy if there was nothing but houses everywhere, that there would be no space in Finland. But there is space, he concludes.

(Interview with Ahmed, May 2007)

Ahmed's story could be broken down into many strands within international relations and migration theories. It would be possible to talk about the conflict in Somalia and the failure of the international community to rebuild this 'failed' state and establish peace. Or about exile, and the impact of refugee 'flows' into Somalia's neighbouring countries or the other countries in the region. Another perspective would open by taking on the European asylum system and its developments, either in terms of constructing the phenomenon of 'illegal' and 'undesirable' migration or the human consequences of this politics. Yet further aspects are transnational networks, human smugglers and the forms of business, precarity and injustice connected with the latter. Each of the approaches splits the mobile body into segments, loses sight of the intertwining of these aspects and how they are brought to the surface and come together in the body.

A discussion of the thoroughgoingness of exposure and understanding the exhaustiveness of seeking asylum together with the historical, social and political developments that have preceded the experience requires a different analytical category: *movement as an articulation of space*. As I have illustrated, the presence of asylum seekers was tangible as it unfolded before and in relation to me (Chapter 1, Events 1 and 2). The sensuous element necessitates that movement is approached not in the sense of massive flows, but as moves taken on and performed by the asylum seeker. Those moves are shaped by policies and sovereign practices, but neither of them manages to stop movement or control it completely. Thus, movement articulates space that cannot be conceived in terms of the territorial state or the system of such states. That emergent understanding invites me to think of sovereignty and the international as they take form through sensing and touching bodies in motion.

Movement shapes the body and by moving the body creates spaces. On the other hand, sovereign practices seek to construct various kinds of spaces of visibility to determine the movement that the body can undertake and the relations it can form through its moves. Everything moves in relation to everything else. Space and time appear through movement, through bodies and practices being exposed to the movements of others (see Nancy 2008: 27). In addition, movement changes the body itself and puts it into a constant process of becoming. The body, any body, as such becomes, appears, as a particular kind of body through movement. Thus, it is not surprising that the direction of, motivation behind, forms of and means of movement all play a central role in the evaluation of an asylum claim, and that the surveillance of movement reaches into the daily lives of asylum seekers. Yet, movement can be a means to disrupt sovereign practices, to position oneself in-difference to the state.

4   Moving (in) space

Seeing movement like a state

Sovereign borders continue to play a central role in politics, especially in the field of migration. Their importance has not by any means diminished, but merely shifted (see Andreas 2000: 3). Sovereign borders are thick. They thicken against and in relation to the moving body, as sovereignty is enacted both at the border and within the society. The administration of human mobility is extended and dispersed within the borders of the state through multiple practices. These practices are embedded within bureaucratic processes, put into operation technically or enacted through various networks that aim to govern and organise human life politically (see Bigo 2005; Huysmans 2006; Nail 2012; Squire 2009). They are designed to place the body within extant conceptualisations of politics, its space, forms and manifestations.

Within the logic of sovereignty, the possible modes of legitimate identities materialise most concretely in flesh-and-blood individuals, whose actions and movements are limited by the status created in governmental discourses (cf. Foucault 1979, 1982; see Chapter 3). The apparently simple lines separating states from one another produce specific forms of subjectivity, which on a daily basis and as sources of self-perception are extremely complex and contingent (cf. Walker 2009: 186). The idea of thick borders resonates closely with Peter Nyers' (2003) concept of mezzanine spaces of sovereignty, which are designed to give a specific materiality and visibility to the asylum seeking body. The notion of thick borders allows examination of the way in which knowledge about moving bodies is produced at various locations with their own epistemology and operations (see also Aaltola 2005). In his interview, Benjamin explicitly addressed the detention centre as a constructed space of visibility:

> You know, this place always makes me think about why I left, why I don't have the access to see the natural sun, to talk to people the way I used to do. I live like in a cage. I don't like it. [. . .] So, it worries me that I'm not outside. I am not a criminal, but I'm living in a place where they see you as something different.
>
> (Interview with Benjamin, June 2007)

102 *Moving (in) space*

The figure of the asylum seeker is constructed gradually, through a network of practices and operations. The construction of the figure begins when a person presents their claim for asylum to the receiving state. From then on, the identity of an asylum seeker is constructed within the bureaucratic process with regard to both the past and the future. That means examining the means of travel, the claimant's personal experiences before leaving and whether migration officers can affirm the applicant's claim for a refugee identity and, further, estimate what is likely to happen if the applicant is returned. The identity of the asylum seeker is a temporary one; it represents a passage. The temporal aspect is at various phases of the determination process used as a justification for additional practices of governance, like the need to live in a reception centre or as grounds for detention. If the person's asylum claim is ultimately acknowledged, s/he is no longer an asylum applicant or seeker.

The temporal dimension of the status makes it an unstable point of identification. Asylum seeking cannot function as a source of identity or self-perception, as it reflects in-betweenness and potential transformation from the state's point of view. The asylum seeker is, in the state's perspective, subject to suspicion, because the validity of the claim has not yet been proven, which results in the need to surveille the asylum-seeking body, the moves it enacts and the relations it engages in. However, the body's positioning in a mezzanine space of sovereignty and the problem-oriented approach to the body constructs a particular type of visibility and knowledge-system around the asylum seeker with regard to the wider society. The person subjected to the practices of surveillance and positioned in such spaces, like Soran in the following excerpt, is by no means ignorant of the effects:

> "I am not happy. Everybody here treats us badly. Everybody hates us." Omar has come to sit with Soran and me just in time to hear his lament. "You cannot say that, Soran," objects Omar. "Not everybody hates us. You cannot generalise like that. Not everybody here [in Finland] is bad. The fact that we live here [in the reception centre] affects us." Soran nods, but does not seem convinced.
>
> (Research diary, 11th September 2006)

Soran's claim that Finns hate asylum seekers describes his experience of his surroundings. Whether this claim is true, or to what extent it is accurate, is not under scrutiny here. Instead, it is worth noticing that asylum seekers are by no means unaware of the fact that at the level of public debate they are made to look culpable for taking advantage of the system and thus aggravating already existing prejudices. In particular, young Muslim men who seek asylum are the targets of extremely hostile language, and their bodies are made objects of hate and fear in the Finnish society. In the vignette, Omar counters Soran's interpretation by noting that hostility towards them stems from the fact that they live in the reception centre and thus have not yet had their asylum claim recognised. Omar seeks to point out that their positioning in Finnish society, and not their being/presence

Moving (in) space   103

as such, generates the feeling of being hated. For Soran this does not seem to make much difference when considered against the fact that he represents the 'unwanted' part of society, which puts him in a vulnerable position.

Soran's plight could be taken to represent an experience of a situation in which the body has been reduced to nothing more than a status and a set of gendered and racialised stereotypes which it cannot mediate (see Noland 2009: 199). As Squire (2009: 126–128) contends, the conditions in which asylum seekers live are some of the perhaps unintended and yet de facto punitive effects of migration policies. It would be relatively easy to conceptualise the asylum seeker in Agambenian terms as homo sacer, whose body is in most intimate relation with sovereign power. In Giorgio Agamben's thinking, the homo sacer is firmly situated in the sphere of sovereign decision, which limits human action and includes by exclusion (Agamben 1998: 83; see Dillon 2004). For Agamben (1998: 111, 140), sovereign power captures all life that falls within its sphere. Hence, bare life as such does not exist, but is both a product of the machine and its fundamental activity.

The touch of sovereign politics inarguably materialises on the human body through various practices of surveillance and governance. The asylum-seeking body senses their effects concretely. As the following vignette illustrates, in Benjamin's case, sovereign politics began to unfold as two people came together. The Finnish political community and its boundaries were imagined on his body, against his body. This transferred into a sense of hurt and incomprehension:

> One police lady came down here. She brought her camera. She was the person who's going to prepare my documents for travelling as I don't have travel documents. [. . .] You people didn't even consider my work or the people with whom I live. And now you are preparing my documents to send . . . So what can I say? I have nothing to say. If I leave, it's with almighty Allah. That's what I told her. And the policewoman [took the photos] "snap, snap" [snaps his fingers to demonstrate the sound of shooting a picture] and said that now I have to wait for three weeks. [. . .] I met her last week. I don't even remember the day. So, I'm here like a hungry lion, who's waiting for its meat. Yes.
>
> (Interview with Benjamin, June 2007)

Putting sovereignty beyond question as a foundation upon which political existence is to be fathomed signals a belief in national cohesion and the state's ability to provide a sense of belonging. Erin Manning (2000: 57–58) has criticised this "discourse of the ground" for its ability to think of the political only through identification with a bounded space. As Benjamin's account illustrates, sovereign imaginaries are enacted through intimate practices that reveal a "regulative ambition for a specifically modern political life" (see Walker 2006b: 57). From the state's perspective, movement represents a destabilising factor that gives rise to a large variety of mechanisms and technologies of surveillance and governance, which Benjamin's account presents in their intimate forms. Thus, simply by addressing the question of seeking asylum, this work must also address

104 *Moving (in) space*

sovereignty. The principle of sovereignty gives rise to citizenship as the prime design of political subjectivity and as a building block of political communities. It is this logic of belonging that asylum seekers counter with movements and gestures that expose the political. Logically, then, this work cannot be only a study of sovereignty and of sovereign practices, as the philosophical grounds for the kind of commonality on which the principle of sovereignty rests are being challenged by the phenomenon studied.

Sovereign communities are always imagined and enacted in a selective style. As Soran's and Benjamin's cases illustrate, the actual ways of enacting sovereignty involve multiple corporeal practices of categorisation in which statuses and visibilities are constructed (see also Chapter 3). These practices are designed to situate the human body with regard to the sovereign state, within its order. In this light, European efforts to harmonise migration policies, the asylum determination process and surveillance technologies put into operation in the field of asylum all represent international politics, which concerns the body and participates in the construction of a particular type of political body.

With their movements, asylum seekers complicate the limits between places and disrupt the notion of political life as something that takes place either between fixed insides and outsides or within unambiguously defined communities. Cross-border mobility reveals the inbuilt vulnerability and instability of the kind of political community built around a nation-state. Through a wide range of practices, the political community is undergoing a constant process of deconstruction and reconstruction (see also Isin & Nielsen 2008; Mountz 2010; Squire 2009; Weber 2008). International displacement and forced migration represent a potential failure of the sovereign logic, which is why the body of the asylum seeker in particular materialises the challenge of that thinking. Furthermore, asylum seekers bring to light the myriad ways in which a horde of institutions and actors regulate, practice, administer and (seek to) shape the human body. These practices and processes turn the body of the asylum seeker into a point of differentiation, in relation to which the community 'within' can build its sense of belonging and identity.

However, enactments of sovereignty do not result in subservience or acceptance, which transforms the moving body into a site of political struggle. Through the politico-corporeal struggle, multiple senses of the international appear and the political organisation of the world gains multiple interpretations and meanings. The singular-plural body brings to the surface the ambiguous relation between the individual, the communal and the international. It questions the boundaries within and between political communities and the limits between representations and experiences (see also Schildkrout 2004: 322). The movements of the asylum seeker undermine the spatial regime in which different expressions of what it means to lead a political life and be a human are flattened out and obscured by a vocabulary of security, organisation and efficiency. Movement can thus create new frameworks for a discussion on what belonging, displacement and being out of place mean and what their relation to political life is (cf. Manning 2009). Thus understood, movement is characteristic and constitutive of the relations between bodies and worlds. It rearticulates political community in a way that exceeds sovereignty both within the state and within the system of states.

Movement as corporeal articulation

EEVA: What about your dance, does it have a message?
BENJAMIN: Yes, it does have a message. Every movement has a message. [. . .]
Every step and move that you do, you have to give a message.

(Interview with Benjamin, June 2007)

Every move has a message. A move is a message. This understanding places the moving body in focus when thinking and talking about the political. Movement represents one analytical category through which it is possible to think about political expression and the political taking shape through events and acts. With this I am suggesting that more attention should be paid not to why, how and where people move, but to actual movement as a form of articulation that brings forward the body and its political potential. Does movement enable us to think of a "different kind of inhabitance" (see Ahmed 2004: 39) that exposes the body as a site of political and communal exhange? What is the in-difference towards the state that bodies moving alongside and beyond sovereign practices gesture? This gesturing is not intentional articulation, but rather works existentially through events of exposure. Asylum seekers' movement does not signal the losing of identity, but provides evidence of the body's capacity to transcend and stretch sovereign imaginaries. As sovereign politics can never fix the body in space and stop its movement, the value in thinking of movement as articulation is revealed.

There is a strong connection between the body and movement in Nancian thought. According to Nancy, the body is always on the verge of a movement or a dislocation, always about to leave. It also escapes knowledge and withdraws from the knowledge practices of the state, even when it presents itself and its claim to the state. This makes it immensely important to explore how people, through everyday practices and interactions, produce the space of being-with and unfold the (political relations of the) international through their movements, whether they are acts of withdrawing or approaching (cf. Tate 2007). The space between bodies and also between bodies and sovereign practices is not fixed, but oscillating. Bodies and sovereign practices resonate with one another. The adopted stance points towards conceptualising neither the (inter)national in terms of territorial communities nor the struggle of seeking asylum in terms of categorical administrative identities. Instead, it calls for an exploration of what alternatives there are to conceive of human life and how our understandings of relations between the body, politics and the statist/international change in the process.

If borders are, in line with William Walters (2006) view, conceived as multiplicities with complex dimensions and multiple changing functions, they imply lived relationalities both in migratory stories and horizons and in staying embedded (see Ahmed, Castañeda, Fortier & Sheller 2003; Howarth 2006; Soguk 2000). The space of politics delineated by borders is not exhaustive or constitutive, but contested and leaky. Thinking of movement as capable of evoking exposure directs the analytical prism towards the transformation and mutability of political space (see Walters 2006). There are studies that have explicitly raised the question of movement from the perspective of political agency. In most of these cases,

106 *Moving (in) space*

however, movement has been approached in the form of mobility, not in the actual movements of an asylum seeker and the gestural politics taken on by the moving person (e.g. Aradau, Huysmans & Squire 2010; Squire 2010). A focus on movement as an other of language or as a means of articulating an ontological demand that concerns existence persuades us to look at movement, not from 'above', but by focusing on the moving body. Such a focus makes it meaningful to explore even minute moves and gestures and think about their significance with regard to sovereign practices and "border's capture" (Soguk 2007). Movement as a force that can transform notions of political space and the space of politics altogether necessitates that we adopt a notion of politics that both begins and ends with the body, and also that we relinquish the idea of a sovereign subject who acts intentionally and is in control of his/her actions.

The body's movements articulate political space in terms of events and thus unfold space as a relation within which the political takes place. The change of perspective offers unanticipated avenues for resistance, contestation and interruption as well for the forming of connections and acts of reaching. Political agency, resistance and engagement are all matters of co-existence between two or more bodies. In this light, movement represents one possible means of questioning being political in the world and consider how we have come to think of ourselves as separate, sovereign subjects in the first place (see Edkins 2005b; also Nancy 2000). At least philosophically, the political mode of belonging created through the state is as precarious as the daily lives of asylum seekers. The ways in which marginalised people, through various strategies, evoke compearance – the ontological vulnerability that characterises existence – needs to be explored if we wish to understand the struggle they are involved in and the political relationalities that they evoke (see Chapter 2; also Coward 2009; Edkins 2005b; Odysseos 2007; Vaughan-Williams 2007; Puumala 2013; Puumala & Pehkonen 2010; Puumala, Väyrynen, Kynsilehto & Pehkonen 2011).

Nasren's story begins to unfold the politico-corporeal struggle that movement represents from the asylum seeker's perspective. Her situation reveals the tension between the sensory experiences of being subjected to sovereign practices and the efforts to transcend the effects of those practices through movement. In Nasren's case, experience of the regulative ambitions through which sovereignty seeks to institute itself gives rise to a strong sense of dislocation and rupture. No matter what one thinks of people like Nasren, who travel from country to country seeking asylum and try to find a place for themselves, one can claim with reasonable assurance that this politics is not functional from anyone's perspective.

> Nasren sits on the sofa with her head buried in her hands.
> Her whole body shakes as she cries for her unborn child.
> I'm witnessing the other side of forced migration,
>   the one initiated by the state.
>
> Doesn't anybody care?

Moving (in) space 107

After the negative decision in France, we went to Italy.
From there; back to France.
We were told to leave the country, so
we returned to Iraq. We tried to stay.
It was not possible.

We have a document that proves that we left Europe.
                    see, here.
                            But,
our names were – not – clearly *written*.
The translator marked this down with a *?*
The police do not consider the document valid;
The migration officials refuse to investigate –
Poor handwriting undermines our claim.

See, we have the plane tickets.
                            But,
no proof that we boarded: Check the passenger lists!
But we were told that there are no resources for that.
Nobody cares about what is true.
Or about what will happen to us.
Professional duty.
        That's what matters.
The end.

They are sending us to France.
With no accommodation.

A late night phonecall from Paris,
                the city of love and light.
A sense of desperation communicated.
Two weeks later another phonecall.
From Helsinki.
We want the officials to examine our case.
We are entitled to that.
So we returned.

To emphasise the various levels and forms of movement, motion and mobility, I chose to formulate my notes from my encounters with Nasren from August 2013 till March 2014 in a poetic shape. The form of writing and layout reflects the movement between an asylum seeker and the state and the international, as well as the ambiguity which characterises the practices that control people's movement. It is noteworthy that while investigation is a central part of the asylum determination process, there it serves the interests of the state. Documentation can be scrutinised to find out whether identity documents are genuine or forged, accents and bone structure can be tested to prove origin and age; a whole set of practices is harnessed to determine and potentially undermine the validity of the applicant's asylum claim.

108 *Moving (in) space*

However, as Nasren's account illustrates, when resources should be used to find proof to support the claim, a sudden austerity appears. The set of possibilities and responsibilities is highly unbalanced between the parties, which makes it practically impossible to challenge sovereign practices from within their logic of operation.

In her account, Nasren points out that legally they would be entitled to have their case investigated in Finland, as they resided in Iraq for more than three months after leaving France. But as the form that would prove their being in Iraq was filled in with poor handwriting, and as Finnish officials refused to check whether Nasren and her family had actually boarded the plane, their case was not considered and the family was returned to France. By returning to Finland, they contradicted this interpretation and illustrated the dysfunctionality of the Finnish return policy.

The senses of the international materialise on and shape all kinds of bodies; those residing comfortably, those tortured and dismembered, those fleeing the torturing, those fighting and those escaping and perhaps seeking asylum – bodies, some of which are far more privileged than others (cf. Agathangelou & Ling 2004). Thus, sovereign practices can tear bodies apart, but people also come together and expose the international at unexpected places and in unwarranted manners. Nasren's case illustrates that despite the multiple vulnerabilities and risks that movement bears for the asylum seeker, it is a central element in the politico-corporeal struggle. Her story makes evident both that the risks and vulnerabilities that movement materialises are context-dependent and that sovereign politics is bound to fail in its aspirations to control movement. By moving, the body articulates its own politics, which is foreign to and disruptive of sovereign logic.

Movement as articulation demands reciprocity in action and thought. This, just like being always in motion, can be exhausting. Unlike citizens and permanent residents, asylum seekers are not able to stop, pause, root or speak from/of a place. What is available for them is movement as engagement, as an ability to 'speak' out of place (see also Moulin & Nyers 2007). Movement exposes a politics of the body, with which asylum seekers establish points of contact and articulate the political as a relation that unfolds through events.

Sovereignty in transition

Nancy (2000: 36) challenges us to think of sovereignty as "the 'nothing' of the 'with' that is laid bare"; sovereignty in the end is nothing but a singularly plural spacing. How are we to think of sovereignty against domination? The challenge represents the transformation of political space as *a transition*, a distancing and plurality that opposes the concentration of interiority that political sovereignty demands. Nancy's way of re-treating the concept of sovereignty means that it can no longer work as an entity that imposes a common order on itself, a concept that understands order to be its own project and that constantly (re)invents itself through this project (see Wagner 2006: 96). Re-treating sovereignty signals also re-treating the political.

Nancy's take on sovereignty could easily be dismissed as a utopian ideal far removed from the actual realities of the world. Yet, those realities show the necessity of thinking otherwise. The migration crisis that Europe faced in 2015 illustrates the shortcomings and failures of sovereign states in responding to and dealing with people's movement. The task is not easy, but the situation demands a response, one that could think of movement along different lines. If nothing else, the moving people have forcefully illustrated that the political project of sovereignty always is and will remain incomplete in the face of the body. In Nancy's (2000: 36) words, it illustrates that sovereignty is "nothing but the *com-*", "always and indefinitely to be completed". The moving body can, therefore, deconstruct the spatiotemporal horizons of the sovereign state as the necessary prerequisites of political life (see Walker 2009: 180; cf. Schwarzmantel 2007). It urges us to dismantle the territorialisation of space and to think of postnational space.

Movement and the moving body articulate sovereignty as a presentation of being-with. It is a space for our compearance, for the presentation of the fact that we as human beings appear to one another only in coming together. People appear only with others – they compear. Thus, there is a strong connection between space and compearance: if there is something or someone, there are several who always already concern and touch one another, and withdraw from any attempts to substantialise their being (see Nancy 1992; Wagner 2006: 97). Space, in this framework, takes form as an interval or a transition that does not have a specific shape, focus or content. In the context of asylum seeking, the approach necessitates going further than merely analysing the lack, direction or scope of asylum seekers' movement and gestures. Instead, I will engage with movement in terms of acts and events of exposure that articulate space in terms of a transition, as a move towards or a withdrawal from.

Movement and sense are intimately connected. The kind of Nancian thought on which I build my argument is interested in worldly engagements that seek to address the world in terms of a "multiplicity of sense" (see James 2006: 94). Within that frame, both sense and meaning – Nancy uses the French word *sens* – are constitutive of the existence of space. *Sens* exists as a passage. It represents a movement-to, which "*is* the space of the world as meaningful, intelligible and experienceable" (James 2006: 102, italics orig.; also Nancy 2003b: 8). Being, the world and the spatiality of being-in-the-world take form as an infinitely open-ended relational spacing of both sense and meaning, where being needs to be conceptualised always as *being-to* or *being-towards* (Nancy 1998: 8; also James 2006: 93, 103).

In presenting their views and sensuous experiences of living in a mezzanine space of sovereignty, asylum seekers like Benjamin, Nasren and Soran postulate that not everyone has similar space or possibilities to move. The senses of the international are dependent on the experiencing body. But their movement also unfolds sovereign practices in terms of an opening of sense, which makes it possible for them to gain bodily know-how through which, prior to cognition, bodies orient themselves within an intelligible space (see James 2006: 106; also Manning 2007: 10; Wall 2008: 58). Rather than a point of separation, the border as an event of enacting sovereign practices takes form as a bodily point of contact:

FADI: [. . .] on Wednesday the police, they came. I was in the class room, learning *suomenkieli* [the Finnish language]. I'm taking a *kurssi* [course].

110 *Moving (in) space*

EEVA: Ye-es – and they brought you here [to the detention unit].

FADI: Yes. I said "what's happening?" The police said: "We are here to deport you." I got my final decision in October 2006, so about seven months ago. Why did you not deport me in that seven months? When I wanted to apply for a residence permit on the basis of work, after I first found work, you say: "Now we are here to deport you." Seven months, it's a long time. The police said [that the reason for detention was]: "Because we are scared that you might run away." If I knew where I could run, I would have run away eight months ago. That [the reason stated by the police] is not evidence for putting me here. I don't accept what they do to people.

(Interview with Fadi, May 2007)

Fadi's account evokes a sense of limits, where limits and limitations unfold through events as bodies come together. Fadi talks of touch, of a double rapport of attraction and repulsion between bodies. By no means is his story ignorant of the highly unequal consequences of the event of coming together; yet it also addresses the capacity of touch to expose dimensions and the edges of singular beings. The body is, ultimately, the limit itself – as "face, manner, gait and aspect of the delimited being" (Nancy 2004b: 47). Understanding sovereignty as a transition implies a constantly unfolding relation that exposes the limits of all political subjectivities in terms of singular beings. In fact, as Georges Van Den Abbeele (1997: 15, italics orig.) points out, the community that Nancy envisions is "founded upon the compearance of singular beings in the commonality of their *difference*". Nancy's thought, hence, opens a radically different way of thinking of otherness, namely because his philosophy disconnects communal identities from demarcated geographical spaces. Fadi struggles with this same logic, and refuses to accept its operation and its being brought into play through his body. Fadi's example also clearly points out the unease that movement causes from the perspective of the state.

Moreover, it is possible to contend from Fadi's account that movement neither has to be directed towards a particular goal or nameable place, nor follow conventional routes in order to become a subject of unease in the eyes of the state. Movement as such bears political prominence. In order to think about postnational – and not merely post-topological – space, we would need to engage with the space of the political in terms of a transition that becomes manifested through events. For me, the kind of transition that Nancy addresses unfolds as and like poetics, as it denotes an experience of spatial and communal differences which speaks of the "unheard-of verticality of sense" (Van Den Abbeele 1997: 16–17; see Chapter 1). The political potential of movement, then, lies in the body's ability to contest and exceed those processes of historical change that a particular political order has fixed in space. Movement exposes the world in terms of the separation and distancing of sense, which is an event simultaneously of touching, spacing, sharing, positioning and disposition (James 2006: 138). The body moves in relation to and against other bodies, and through this, it exposes itself as a limit.

The body as a limit

EEVA: How long did the journey take? Since it is not, it must not be all . . .

TAHIR: Yeah, it is no . . . from 25 to 30 days.

EEVA: Mmm, several weeks.

TAHIR: Yes.

EEVA: What then, when you reached Finland, how did that feel? Did you think that you had reached safety?

TAHIR: No, no. The smuggler told me to go to the police station to meet the police, so that they would help me. Then, when I went there, I thought that maybe I am in a neighbouring country of Afghanistan. There the policeman asked me where I was from, and I told him I am from Afghanistan. And then when he showed me Finland on the map; how could I be so far? I felt that I might never meet my mum again and that was a huge thing. Now it has been two years since I last saw her.

(Interview with Tahir, April 2007)

Tahir articulates a world of bodies in motion. In his account bodies weigh on one another, against one another, with various degrees of force as their movements intertwine with the movements of others. In Nancy's thought, weight represents the materiality of the body and the carnation of philosophy and politics. The body's weight exposes a finite experience of the international as it takes form through sovereign practices and wider patterns of human mobility. It manifests the local and material (be)coming and construction of political community (cf. Nancy 2008: 93–97). Bodily sense discloses the international in and as a movement of dispersal or passage, which articulates an experience of the body as a limit. Sense exposes the events of being, which occur as transitions, infinitely open-ended relational spacings (see James 2006: 132–133).

When Tahir described the shock of realising where his movement had taken him and an impending sense of what it might mean in terms of familial relations, he actually articulated his finite experience as a movement of dispersal and passage. Not only his body, but also his sensuous experience of being, is in transition. Tahir is not in control of the possible meanings that transition might hold for his life, and thus he cannot articulate a sense of closure (see Chapter 5 on sense).

Meaning, like sense, travels through the body. Through the body-as-limit, both identity and difference are constituted. For something to appear *as* a determinate something entails spacing and separation, which signals that meaning is relational. It is created through a network – circulation – of contacts and touches. Things and people become meaningful in relation to others, as they appear to one another. Like in Tahir's case, the act of embarking on a journey with a human smuggler attained its ultimate meaning only retrospectively, but in a way that cannot be closed. Much like with Tahir, we can see through Farzad's story that the meaning of movement is open-ended. There is no closure, just a *dis*closure of existence:

My family is in Afghanistan, or at the moment I don't know where they are. I just hope that they left the village in time. It is a bad village, where the

112 *Moving (in) space*

Taliban still try to rule, so there's constant violence. I hope that my mother and two little brothers left that village, and Afghanistan. When I arrived here, I wrote a letter to them, gave it to the social worker, who sent it to the Finnish Red Cross in Helsinki who sent it to Kabul, where somebody went and tried to find my family, but they were not there. They couldn't be found anywhere. And now I don't know where they are. After my father . . . (pause) Who's going to take care of them now? I always think of them. I'm a human. She's my mother. I will never forget her. It is not easy to worry about my family and not know what will happen to me here.

(Interview with Farzad, September 2006)

Farzad's and Tahir's stories do not, actually, present the meanings of movement as such, although both of them refer to family relations and the way in which movement has disrupted their understanding of those relations and roles within the family. Rather, both young men's stories articulate a sense or feeling of what happens, which escapes understanding if it is taken to denote a closure of sense. Their accounts posit movement as much in terms of a dislocation as an act of approaching. Their stories tell of the intensification of the body's presence in relation to others as a result of movement and also in the course of movement (see Perpich 2005: 84–85).

A moving body also puts into motion those bodies that are exposed to its movement (see also Foster 1995: 16). Movement, therefore, exposes every body's potential to participate in, resist or exceed the forms of political production that are underway (see Foster 1995: 15, 1996; Noland 2009). Moving is a gestural act which brings in a type of experience that subverts and interrupts the sovereign logic and inserts a corporeal language of transition. Thus conceived, movement represents an event of the political and a form of political practice.

The movement of asylum seekers exposes the practices of sovereignty in terms of spatiotemporal events that are bodily and finite. Concurrently, the international is not a space within which we move but rather a political project, which takes form as bodies move (cf. Massey 2004). Asylum seekers move against the logic of sovereignty not by asking us to necessarily believe their accounts, as Nasir points out in the following excerpt, but by requiring us to engage with their moving bodies and to respond to the demand that their bodies articulate.

These authorities here, in *Ulkomaalaisvirasto* [the Immigration Service], they don't believe refugees and the stories refugees tell in the asylum interviews. If they don't believe, they don't need to believe, those stories. Ok, we can be content. Just, if they just went and saw for themselves how people come and reach Europe. If they observed them on the way, they would understand, why they have left their country. It is not for some silly, stupid reasons. They take risks, great risks and endure many hardships and difficulties. Those would be reason enough for the officials to understand that refugees do have some problems for which they leave their countries and try to reach safer places. [. . .] Many people have died after they have survived in their own country but they could not survive on the way to a safe place. They died on their way. To a safe place. People have drowned in rivers, drowned in seas. People have come with balloon-boats (inflatable boats). People have crossed the sea with those boats. From Turkey to Italy or Greece. Just imagine. And they would pump (inflate) it with their own mouth. Very few reach safely. Many drown.

(Interview with Nasir, March 2007)

Nasir describes the moves that asylum seekers have to perform before they can even present their claim for asylum. Surpassing the physical dangers of the travel does not equal overcoming one's troubles. The body-as-limit does not conform to the flattening representations that the political order based on sovereignty seeks to impose. The story that Nasir voices is about movement as exposure to the distant and the uncertain, to the perils and possibilities of drifting and an arrival. The moving body measures and senses space, monitors pressure and friction and accommodates its moves on the basis of its finite and sensuous experiences.

Irregular migratory movement subverts fixed notions of space (see also Mezzadra & Neilson 2003; Walters 2006). Asylum seekers cross borders and inhabit places without authorisation, resist deportation and, from the state's perspective, move in unexpected ways in unanticipated directions. An exploration of sovereignty as transition and the body as a limit can start with an analysis of how people are embodied within and impress themselves upon (the political organisation of) the world. Because an experience of movement shapes the moving body, it might in the end transform the political culture itself. Such a take on movement launches a cartography of beings side by side, beings "dispersed in an ocean that is each time and at once an other and the same, configured around a different shore" (Nancy 2004b: 51).

The event of exposure (or perhaps rather ex*peau*sure) that the moving body brings about, with its full (ontological and material) weight, signals arriving and departing with no given coordinates. It articulates a temporal spatiality of coming and closing, a transition, that raises the question of political life. Bodies crossing seas with "balloon-boats" articulate a presence, which signals simultaneous nearness and withdrawal. The movement of these bodies repeats the idea of a sense in action, which denotes the sharing of sense and meaning between people in the interval. Movement enables the asylum-seeking body to explore its conditions of possibility, within which its political existence and potential can appear (see Puumala & Pehkonen 2010).

The politico-corporeal struggle is strongly present in people's movement and their oscillation between here and there, past and present. Exchange and the element of sharing make bodies in motion resonate with one another. Movement can throw bodies off guard and bring them into contact. In any case, it is a central element in asylum seekers' lives, as they usually are very conscious of the slippery social structures on which they stand, where a firm foothold is nothing but an illusion that might one day be there and the next day be gone. In fact, the vulnerability of asylum seekers makes us confront our own vulnerability and the vulnerability of the world as we have come to know it.

114 *Moving (in) space*

Seeing states through movement

> When I came, I spent four days at the Serbian border. There were so many people on the move. We were standing in lines, waiting. I did not know what to do. Everybody else seemed to be travelling in groups and I was alone. Then, on the fourth day, a police officer came to me, gave me food and helped me. I am so grateful to him. Now I am grateful to be in Finland. It seemed that everyone to whom I talked during my travel was heading for Finland. When I asked where are you going, everybody answered "Finland." I asked why, but nobody seemed to know exactly. They just said "we want to go to Finland."
>
> (Interview with Hamada, September 2015)

As Hamada's account illustrates, the grounds for choosing destinations are ambiguous among asylum seekers. Their movement takes direction based on a perception of the place that they would like to reach, and that perception is shaped by the rumour and stories that spread on social media and through informal networks, and that people on the move tell one another. The lives of asylum seekers are ripe with rumour, as Moorehead (2006) has put it, and hear-say plays a great role both on the way and with regard to the asylum determination process. The variations in the number of arriving asylum claimants are largely beyond the control of the states. The routes change in response to the practices with which states seek to curb applicants from reaching their sovereign territories. As people, and smugglers who facilitate their movement, are not limited by the principle of sovereignty, they are able to undermine the working of sovereign practices.

However, Alison Mountz (2010: 20) has suggested that refraining from establishing set policies regarding the reception and processing of "spontaneous" arrivals is also in the interest of the state. It permits the development of creative solutions such as the negotiation of bilateral agreements between states to return asylum claimants to the country of origin, or adopting stricter return policies and revising guidelines on countries of origin designated safe. The politico-corporeal struggle unfolds constantly and exposes the vulnerability of the moving body to sovereign practices and the vulnerability of sovereign logic to the moving body. Shiva's story, which I will take up next, helps us to understand that the relationship between the two is extremely unstable. It opens up a different conception of space, one that is stratified, fragmented and yet well-navigated when necessary. It already begins to resonate with how asylum seekers perceive states, instead of the other way around, and what kinds of responses sovereign practices evoke.

"I am a journalist of mass communication, so I used to write news for the local newspaper." This is how Shiva began his story when I met him in the detention unit in Finland in June 2007. Through his movement, I will illustrate the way states are constructed of, on and against bodies, but also the way bodily movement forms and transforms the body that moves and that also moves notions of space. The form of my writing highlights that states are, ultimately, formed through practices whose materiality takes shape against moving bodies. First, Shiva's moves take us from Nepal to India, where he was able to rejoin his wife, whom he had left in Nepal at the time of his own flight.

I worked
for four years in
that newspaper. There was a
riot in the parliament before our
country went under the, you can say, ter-
rorism of the Maoist. I used to write in this
newspaper during that time. I wrote both good and bad.
They evacuated the children from the schools, and they
took them to terror camps where they were given training.
Now the supreme commander is going to be the president
of Nepal. They will all receive a proper salary, a very
good job. In this way they were motivated. Some 1000-
2000 children. And, similarly, they had taken, with the help of the
Indian Maoists and Naxalites, weapons and made bombs and guns. I took
photos of children with weapons in the camp. These pictures, they were
pub- lish- ed. Our newspaper was accused of being an enemy
of the Maoist and of the republic of Nepal. Most
of this news were written by me. They declared the
death punishment. They declared the
death punishment. Didn't hang
me, I was out at the
time.

So, in
order to save
my life, I went to
India. And, we met in
India and we came here.
But we didn't come here
directly.
From Nepal we im-
mediately, after that night, my wife was
not …, because they traced her, my neigh-
bours also, if anybody gave her shelter. It   was
not safe at home, so they told me to go to India. So I came to   India. Later,
my wife could run away from the Maoist camp, went to our place and a neighbour told her
that I was in India. So she came to India. In India, we arrived at   Delhi   first.
In Delhi, there are many people who have left their homes in Nepal because   of the Maoist insurgency. We meet among us and they were our cover… and we   were
introduced to a man who took us to his home. Our contact had lived about
three years in India. He had migrated with his family. We lived
in their rented house and we helped in the hotel. They have
a hotel, a small hotel in Delhi, India. It was near the
railway station. We helped them. We stayed about
20-30 days there arranging things so that we'd
come here. We sold all our property; told our
parents to sell it. We collected some money.
India is not our home land and we can
meet some Maoist even in
India, because they have
good connections.
So, staying was
not safe. That's
why we made
the decision
to come to
Europe
…

116 *Moving (in) space*

The first part of Shiva's interview described how the necessity to seek international protection was aroused and the logic upon which the decision of to choose Europe as a destination was taken. Furthermore, Shiva's account addresses the various networks that are activated and relations that are formed in moving between states. These networks and relations exist within states, but are not limited by the statist imagination and have strong transnational dimensions. Asylum seekers, as Vicki Squire (2009: 162) has also noted, are active in constituting political communities, which undermine border regimes and exceed the territorial frame of the nation-state.

Shiva's account illustrates that senses of the international are produced both at and through borders, and that those senses are also contested and alternative senses exposed through bodily movement. In other words, the border defines both a particular political reality and multiple political possibilities. The limit of meaning (*sens*) lies at the border, which is revealed to be as much a site of inscription as a site of exscription. In accordance with this line of thought, Shiva and his wife's moves between countries articulate a choreography, which counters topographical mappings and politics (cf. Puumala & Pehkonen 2010; also Olsson 2007; Parviainen 2010). The moving body articulates various "relationscapes" (Manning 2009), which arise from the organisation of the modern international with sovereignty as its founding element. This body opens the door to a different set of actions, which have the potential of restructuring (inter)national imaginaries (cf. Tyler 2006: 192). In keeping pace with Shiva's moves as he recounts how he and his wife arrived in Lithuania, their first country in Europe, we will soon find out that the border is an extremely active site.

We came using our relatives' passports. We came
as students. We had arranged everything with them already,
for we contacted a Lithuanian colleague in Nepal. There nobody
knows that well where a country called Lithuania is in the world. In India
they had a connection to the school, and they paid a very huge amount, the
college fee. This way I came to Lithuania as a student. In Nepal, the level of education
is very different, so I came to complete my Bachelor's degree. We came only to
stay for the time being. We paid 6.500 euros for our trip. But the person hadn't in
the end paid the college fee. So, after two or maybe after three months the college told
me that we have to pay the balance. I told them that I had already paid, but he said
that there was nothing paid and what I was telling him was not true. And he
said that I should pay the amount in two months. If we could not
manage the balance money, which was around four
thousand euros, they would send me back
to the migration office and we would be taken
back to Nepal. And for this reason, we took
a month's time and tried to convince our
parents to sell their property, but we
couldn't get four thousand
euros.

Moving (in) space   117

Shiva's experiences and movement in Europe enable an examination of political life at various sites where the modern political imagination has come to think that hardly anything – apart from routine-like border formalities and bureaucratic proceedings – happens (see Walker 2006b: 57; also Haddad 2007). Ultimately, Shiva's moves actualise a narrative of the modern international: where its boundaries are located, how its relations function and are put into operation (see Walker 2006a, 2006b). The body of the asylum seeker articulates a different ontology, which questions the basis on which people can make claims in relation to societies and political communities. It actually questions the whole rationale of a bounded and sovereign political community. Shiva's account and his wandering body, placed between states, makes it obvious that borders are not simply a set of policies or governmental practices. They are material practices through which certain political and socio-economic relations are enforced and in which desire, fear, hope and desperation intertwine (see Walters 2006: 150). In fact, the moving body undermines the whole rationale of a bounded and sovereign political community. The difference between a desirable and undesirable body becomes inscribed in the flesh.

> So we
> went to Austria to seek
> asy-   lum. And in Austria they said
> to us, whatever that document is ..., and they
> said that Lithuania is your first country to seek
> asylum. You must seek asylum in Lithuania. In Austria,
> when I was in Austria, I came to know that there is a new law.
> That where you come first, you should seek asylum there.
> So they didn't grant me asylum. They did not listen
> to my   problem at all. Because they said, it's not our
> res-   ponsi-   bility to give you asylum. We don't want to investigate your case over
> here.   We went to Austria with the same passports and we bought the air tickets and went
> we travelled by airplane, arrived by plane, we bought the ticket, the transport, and arrived
> at the airport and   the policemen and the immigration were there to
> lis-   ten to our problems.

Shiva's moves materialise the fact that a border crossing, or sometimes even arriving at a mezzanine space of sovereignty (e.g. an airport or a transfer zone), can annihilate one's identity and make one a susceptible body without identity in the eyes of the receiving state. The country's 'truth' and the person's 'truth' are two different things in Shiva's account (see also Chapter 3). In his story, the political is reflected in the body creating and being involved in a mobile network of relations. Despite being placed in a highly disadvantaged position, Shiva and his wife's movement illustrates that power and resistance go hand in hand (see also Abu-Lughod 1989; Foucault 1978).

There are many people who want to come to Europe without any reason. Or, you can say, who are not eligible for asylum. And this is hampering the people who really need help. Or protection. The Finnish officials told me that

118   *Moving (in) space*

it takes about 45 days for them to find out my identity. Though I have given them the real identity, but they didn't believe me. [. . .] Now they are saying it's [his situation] because of the Dublin Convention. Now, maybe this is true for the country. Because there is the background that in Europe you have people who don't have problems. [. . .] I think that is the main reason why it is now said that you need to seek asylum in the first country where you entered. This may be the reason. But sometimes that creates problems, like in my case.

(Interview with Shiva, June 2007)

Shiva proves capable of relating his position with regard to the European policies concerning the harmonisation of the asylum system. He reflects on the connection between his situation and the Dublin protocol, which determines the state responsible for investigating the person's asylum claim. Already, at an airport in Austria, Shiva encountered the effects of European asylum politics, which took on even more corporeal meaning and intimate senses in Finland, where he was detained. In the mezzanine spaces of sovereignty, people are processed and their mobility is regulated (see also Isin & Rygiel 2006: 190; Squire 2009: 152–156). Practices undertaken in these spaces are enacted so that the relation between the moving body and the state can be determined and solved. They represent the claim of the sovereign state to monopolise the political (see also Chapter 3). Following from that, people's possibilities of constituting themselves as political agents and claiming access to socio-economic services and goods in a particular community are reduced.

The asylum determination process, and the preceding determination of where a person can, should and must seek asylum, transforms the moving body into a site where political relations are (re)produced. The body comes to represent either a victimised or demonised other against whom the national community can be built and strengthened, and on whom the state's more powerful position vis-à-vis the person can be affirmed (cf. Nast & Pile 1998). However, the body is not made immobile after being subjected to sovereign practices. Sovereign politics cannot annihilate the politics of the body or the capacity of the body to articulate its politics and presence through exposure.

The political is reflected in the body that is creating and being involved in a mobile network of relations. Rather than being solely perfomed, subjectivities are constituted in interactions in relation to and against one another (see also Chapter 3). Hence, the body is capable of actively seeking alternatives and reversing the understanding of sovereign subjects or sovereignty as a ground for a community. In fact, migratory movement, according to Sandro Mezzadra and Brett Neilson (2003: 22; also Walters 2006: 153), is a spatial form of political agency capable of initiating transformation and political change.

Through Shiva's account, I began to understand that movement across borders and within state territories both causes the rise of reactive political practices and reveals bodily movement as a form of resistance, protest and relationality. After being rejected by Austria, Shiva and his wife return to Lithuania.

Moving (in) space 119

...and there we sought asylum. But   they
said, at the Immigration office, they said that since you have already applied in Austria, you cannot seek asylum here. You have lost the
right to seek asylum here. So they made a decision to send us back to Nepal
once our visa had expired . And we requested them to give us one month,
so that we could pay the fee. Otherwise they could send us back. They said, no,
you don't have this right either. When they made the decision, they gave the decision
paper to us and we stated all the reasons why we cannot go back to Nepal. They called
the police director. Then, they said that we must pay within one month, and in this way
they left us. So then we tried to collect the money from our parents, but they were not able
to send money. So, with the help of, you can say, friends we raised three-four
hundred euros and came here to seek asylum here [in Finland]. And in
Lit-   huania, me and my wife, they asked us to sign a paper
in the name of the Migration department, in the
Migration office in Lithuania about our asylum case.
Saying that I am a citizen of Nepal and declare that
I will not seek asylum in Lithuania, apply for asylum
in Lithuania. And they made us sign that.
And if they now send us back, we have
already declared as they asked us
to write that we don't seek
asylum.

No European state that Shiva and his wife entered was willing to examine whether they were actually in need of protection. Instead, the prime concern of the representatives of these states was locating the state to which their case administratively 'belonged' and shifting the burden of the asylum process there (see also Uçarer 2006). The tactics of governmentality in the field of migration control function both to dispose of and order populations, and to produce and reproduce subjects, practices and beliefs in relation to specific policy aims.

In her analysis of the relationship between politics and loss, Judith Butler (2003b: 467) has claimed that a fractured horizon allows space for that which is irrecoverable to become the condition of a new political agency. When viewed through a sensuous perspective, Shiva's movement gives shape to a body that understands itself as international and possesses agency within its spheres. Shiva and his wife are in fact negotiating with more than one sovereign state on the potential of their bodies. Their movement raises an awareness of an international more physical and sensuous than what political programs and documents – such as the international and European treaties that concern and regulate asylum seeking – suggest. Shiva's movement is a response to sovereign politics, which regards community as its own project. It is a form of resistance in the sense that the body refuses to accept a particular collective form of life and instead articulates political life that transcends statist boundaries. Shiva's movement, however, also articulates a sense of disorientation and dislocation: a being-here at a time when one would rather be elsewhere (cf. Curtis & Pajaczkowska 1994).

Continuous movement represents a refusal to conform to the practice and function of the sovereign power. Movement is a form of corporeal struggle that the body takes on so as to represent itself – to intensify its presence with regard to

120   *Moving (in) space*

sovereign practices. Movement, thus, can evoke or be fathomed as one potential avenue for exposure to take shape and happen. It is a corporeal and sensuous way of enacting the political. Yet, there is scant romance in movement as resistance (cf. Abu-Lughod 1989). It is constant struggle and awareness of always being on the verge of movement – either voluntary or forced. Movement can, therefore, be both resistance and the only viable option for the body. It exposes the possibility that the body ontologically is. The moving body is capable of transforming and appropriating political discourses and presenting nuanced interpretations of them (see also Chapters 3 and 5). Borders are not only separating elements, but also points of connection and spaces for transformation. The turbulence of human mobility disrupts territorial borders, but the reaction it evokes is most often a defensive one (see also Papastergiadis 2000; Squire 2009).

Now, I
am here…
with   a humble
mind   First, they
said I don't have an identity. Now, they say
they got my identity,
but they want to send
me back to Lithuania.
But they are giving a
decision that my wife
can stay. They are sep-
arating us. Why do you
try to separate us? There
is disparity in my op-
inion. The lawyer
gave us the advice
that later I can come
back from Nepal. It is impossible. I already spent 6500
euros, and I don't have anything
now. If I could come later, why can't
I stay now? I don't know, they don't tell me
clearly. Even when you ask for the reason.
I came to know from my wife, she's under-
aged, that some people, I don't want to
give any names, have advised her also
to get a divorce. Now my main worry
is that we'll be sent to Lithuania,
because yesterday I talked to my
wife and she does not want to
stay here alone.

…

Moving (in) space 121

Shiva's movement, together with the reactions it spurs, makes it evident that the international and the world are not synonymous (see also Walker 2009). If the two are coincided, the international is put beyond political consideration, and the spatiotemporal spectre according to which states seek to orchestrate bodily movement is naturalised. It is clear that Shiva's body falls victim to the exclusionary logic of sovereignty, but it yet manages to articulate a different ontology of the international. An engagement with Shiva's moves turns the question of otherness from a problem of containment into an ontological and ethical exploration into the possibilities of political life within and between bodies variously positioned within the international. Such a claim is possible because, at heart, Shiva's story emphasises the exchange that in movement comes to take place between bodies, and the multiple ways in which bodies resonate to/with one another as they move across borders and within political communities. This resonance gives birth to multiple senses of the international that as they are shared and transferred into meanings begin to direct and shape movement.

As a whole, Shiva's account of his search for safety signals a crossing, which is the fundamental sense of experience "as the chance of an *arrival* upon some other shore, close to another proximity" (Nancy 2004b: 50, italics orig.). Seeking asylum represents a struggle that also takes form through movement and oscillation between here and there, past and present, possible and probable. In dislocating fixed notions of the 'communal', asylum seekers expose the slippery social structures on which political life has been constructed and on which we all stand. Ultimately, in the very end, we are all equally vulnerable. Movement questions "the immanence of nationhood and those discourses that are evoked and maintained to legitimise it" (Van Den Abbeele 1997: 15). Hence, the moving body actually exposes the existence of a nation as a-real, without foundation. In Nancy's thinking, the concept of a-reality (*aréalité*) signifies both the nature of an 'area' and a lack of reality, or perhaps more accurately a suspended reality (Nancy 2008: 43). The moving body communicates dislocation.

According to Van Den Abbeele (1997: 16), the arealisation of the nation places it at the limit and exposes it between a variety of differences. Thus, contrary to Agamben's thought, where sovereign power turns the human body into bare life, Nancy's philosophy makes sovereignty vulnerable to the body, which in its movement is always beyond practices of control. So, while it is true that the effects of international borders place people between or within state territories (e.g. Haddad 2008: 113; Nevins 2008: 27, 78), which makes asylum seekers inevitable consequences of those borders (e.g. Doty 1999: 597), people's bodily movement nevertheless lays bare the impossibility of separating out the real, areal and a-real senses of the international (cf. also Puumala & Pehkonen 2010: 62). Reality, necessity and possibility intertwine in the political vision of the world that is built on the system of states but, as became clear from Shiva's story, the relation between the three is far from stable.

Sensing space

Movement, in the context of seeking asylum, varies from the 'spectacle' of the border – from enacting return policies, deportations and cross-border policing – to

122   *Moving (in) space*

the minute practices designed to direct and intercept movement within the sovereign territory. Practices with which the moves and possibilities of asylum seekers are limited, directed and surveilled are manifested in extremely mundane areas that would be easy to ignore or omit as politically irrelevant. However, if we take the reception and detention centres to represent spaces where sovereignty is enacted and where sovereign rule seeks to take control of the human life that falls within its sphere, it becomes meaningful to explore how the body senses space and meaning in these spaces (see also Mountz 2010).

The body, for Nancy, is the site or place where sense and meaning take place. The world of bodies is a world in which bodies "initially articulate space" (Nancy 2008: 27). The body discloses existence in an interrelation between discourse and matter (see James 2006: 131). Exploring existence through such an interrelation signals a move beyond the biological given and the positionalities constructed through discourse. It signals a move beyond identity as something substantial or something that could be substantialised in the first place. There is no essence to our being, which directs attention to the multiple means and avenues through which a person can articulate their body and presence to others. It can take place through claiming or deviating from, for instance, politico-legal statuses or gendered, religious and familial positions and others' perceptions of the body on the basis of such positions. The tactics of performing the self are various, and the body makes creative use of them. In putting the other's perception of itself in flux, the body makes space for an event of exposure that evokes political relationalities between people.

With such a perspective on the body, I will now take up asylum seekers' bodies as sites of contestation that seek to withdraw from the logic of sovereignty and articulate their in-difference to it. Asylum seekers adopt multiple ways of working through the wait and the everyday experiences that characterise their lives in the reception centre. Mostly, these ways are directed towards changing the tedious rhythm of life and daily routines, but the strategies adopted are variant. In my exploration, I am keen to find out whether the moving and gesturing body can be understood as seeking to understand something about the gesture that the movement is, the political environment this movement creates and affects, and the capacities and limits of the body concerned (see also Noland 2009: 106). In case speech or language cannot adequately communicate one's feelings or thoughts, the body can through movement or gestures seek to resist and contest, but also understand, the political dynamics at work. Movement does not necessarily signal a conscious effort towards a goal, but is a political and relational gesture in itself. It spaces the body, which then moves to fill the space with alternative meanings and senses. A political engagement with movement requires us to change the rhythm of our own thought.

In order to fully appreciate the moves and political engagements that asylum seekers evoke, and to recognise their moves and gestures as events of the political, it is imperative to understand that in a reception centre for asylum seekers there are concrete limitations and practices of control and surveillance in operation on

Moving (in) space 123

a daily basis. As the views that Benjamin and Soran presented in the first part of this chapter illustrated, the physical surroundings, and the practices embedded in those surroundings, play a role in people's perception of their own position within society and in how they feel that others perceive their presence. As the idea of the centre as a mezzanine space of sovereignty suggests, it is not only the asylum seeker's body that gains a certain visibility by being located in this space. Rather, any body who enters this space is subjected to sovereign practice and its politics of constructed visibility, where people are thought to have clear identities that are separated from one another and that relate to one another according to professional roles or positions constructed through bureaucratic processes (see also Event 2).

Resulting from this, in the space of the centre, the researcher's body also becomes explicitly entangled in the webs of sovereign power and practice. Thus, while the centre was a convenient and apt place for me to locate potential partici-pants, it was also a site of control with certain expectations towards my presence. As mentioned, my fieldwork practices involved more than formal interviews: they consisted of informal chats, mundane encounters and futile debates with my participants – and also with those who in the end did not wish to participate in my research, but who yet wanted to talk and needed me to listen to them. Such research practices are hard to explicate beforehand as they cannot truly be antici-pated, which from the methodological point of view is not surprising as the nature of ethnographic work involves improvisation (see Chapter 1; also Cerwonka & Malkki 2007). Yet, this makes it difficult to communicate them to the staff in the centres in a consistent manner.

In the early days of my fieldwork, I very soon noticed that hushed conver-sations in the lobbies and corridors, undertaken in order to guarantee at least some privacy for my participants, did not match the staff's idea of the kind of fieldwork I was supposed and permitted to do. Therefore, my body and the rela-tions I developed also turned into subjects of surveillance. In the end I found out that the staff's concern was not only about me and my position, but also about the potential results of my presence. They felt that my interest in some of the resident's actions and views encouraged them to behave in unwanted manners:

> When I get back to the staff office after finishing an interview, Heidi, the leading counsellor, asks if we could have a talk. We go into a room that is used for the meetings between residents and their lawyers. There Heidi voices her concern. She explains that because I don't have experience of this kind of work [work in the reception centre], "they" are now a bit worried that my sample or group of interviewees doesn't represent the whole very well. In other words, they are worried that the material I collect will be biased because certain people (Soran and Benaz mentioned by name) seek contact with me. In addition, Heidi reproaches me for confusing the "clientele" with my research practices. I ask where the concern stems from and whether any

124　*Moving (in) space*

residents have said so themselves, but she merely contends that this is how the staff feels.

(Research diary, 26th September 2006)

To a great extent, Heidi's latter concern, about my research practices creating confusion, sprang from a methodological choice I had made: the use of photographs as tools with which people could explicate what matters in their daily lives. The experiment was short-lived, because of the concern that it might compromise the anonymity of both the staff and the asylum seekers living there. In order not to make my stay in the centre impossible, I had no choice but to conform to this view. However, in a different light, Heidi's concern was about me disrupting the order of the centre. The other major source of concern was to do with my connections with the 'wrong' people. While Heidi mentioned Soran and Benaz by name, they were not the problem as such. She felt that my profession and gender, combined with the fact that I did not refuse to talk with Benaz and Soran, encouraged them to cause problems in the centre. Thus, what worried her were the relations that evolved and began to unfold between me and them during our talks, and the encouragement that the staff felt that Soran and Benaz got for their actions through my attention.

What I encountered, or what my field strategy and contact with Benaz and Soran made me encounter, was the reactive nature of practices through which sovereign imaginaries are upheld. This politics will never arrive at its scope, because the body's movements and the political relations that take shape through those movements expose sovereignty as a form of authority which is without a firm foundation; it is a-real (see Nancy 2000: 36). When a relation starts evolving between a citizen-body, as an ideal design of political belonging, and an asylum body, as deviant from this norm, the surveillance and disciplining efforts of sovereign power extend to control this relation and the possible forms that it might take. The daily practices of sovereign control extend their reach beyond the asylum body, which illustrates that the principle of sovereignty concerns all potential forms of subjectivity within its sphere. Even though I did spend time talking with Soran and Benaz, and tried to understand what motivated them, what Heidi and the rest of the staff did not know was that I also had debates with them. Sometimes I objected to their views profoundly and questioned them about their interpretations so that it would be possible for me to understand what was going on under the surface (cf. Taylor 2005). Why was it that they provoked the staff and caused trouble? What were they protesting against? What did they want to express through their behaviour?

I will engage with Benaz's moves to articulate a shift from politics as something that takes place in a delineated space, to the body as a space that exposes the political as an event. The point of departure for the following discussion is Squire's (2009: 72) notion that even if securitising moves and exclusionary politics lack continuity, they can have political effects and limit the scope of contestation. I will make a spin-off argument to that notion and claim that the body's

Moving (in) space   125

gestures and moves do not have to be continuous or even intentional to have political significance. Indeed, Benaz exposes multiple forms of political engagement as his body's creativity in enacting itself politically looks for alternative expressions. Another lengthy journey based on my fieldwork will thus follow, but it is a journey that plays with relationalities and points of contact between bodies.

> Benaz is a journalist by training. In Finland he has written a book on "how having black hair affects you negatively: I look outside and see the other building where similar people to myself are living in their own flats where they have their own showers and bathrooms. And then I think about myself and us living here in this centre. Why do we have to share the shower with 15–16 other people? Why can't we have the same life as Finns? Couldn't more foreigners fit into Finland?" He explains that when he meets with the staff, who tell him [to do] something, he smiles, but inside he is extremely angry. He would like to shout.
>
> Benaz describes the thing that he finds especially upsetting: "I shower, and I clean my room. And then they [the staff] come to my room [there are regular room checks in the centre], put on rubber gloves to protect themselves and start sorting through my rubbish. I am clean, why do they put those gloves on?" Benaz tells me that he cannot get into bars, because they ask for his ID. He has only the resident's card from the centre. It is not an official document, and hence most places do not accept it. "Then they ask me to leave. People here do not want to touch you because of your hair or skin colour," he adds.
>
> (Research diary, 24th August 2006)

During our discussion, Benaz often elevated his voice and gestured wildly making his frustration and anger obvious. Yet, instead of suggesting that the story is indicative of a newly developed awareness of the restrictions on movement and possibilities of action, I would like to claim that Benaz's gestures and movement indicate him having gained a sense of those forms of power that become operative when the body is categorised politically (cf. Abu-Lughod 1989: 49). Benaz, hence, does not become suddenly aware of the actual restrictions set for his body, but perceives the political power at work in relation to and on the surface of his body. Yet his body is capable of changing its direction, (s)pace, rhythm and choreography. The body unfolds constantly, and in this sense it always outdoes sovereign practices that seek to fix it firmly on a grid.

Benaz made use of various intersecting positions in his protest. He framed his presence as an ethnic and gendered body, and illustrated how these elements materialised in his daily life and what kind of reactions they caused in him. He protested against the fact that when people look at him, they already see a particular kind of a person, one who is often connected to certain trouble-oriented discourse within the society. That unprivileged position was further aggravated when his status in Finland was revealed because he did not have any official documentation of his identity. Benaz's ways of evoking exposure, even though they at

126   *Moving (in) space*

times took on gruesome verbal and corporeal forms (see below in italics), exposed the materiality of every body and also the fleshiness of politics.

> A week after my first meeting with Benaz, I was informed that during a recent talk with a staff member he had acted in a threatening manner. I am also told that soon after his transfer to this centre he was involved in *a knife fight* and caused another disturbance by *lowering his trousers in public*. He is also suspected on two occasions of falsely *setting off fire alarms* in the centre. When the staff took these things up with him, Benaz simply stated that he was a bohemian character. He then told that if the staff tried to restrict him, he would get the knife from his room and might *kill himself*, but wanted *his eyes to be sent back to his home country*. Or, then he might get his knife and *slit somebody's throat and take the head with him back to his room*. Heidi, the leading counsellor, tells me that Benaz can be stable and friendly, but in a couple of hours he might come to the office and start *miaowing* like a cat. The staff considers him to be unpredictable, and they are not quite certain about the state of his mental health.
>
> Immediately after my talk with Heidi, I come across Benaz in the lobby. He is talking on his mobile, but finishes the call in order to greet me. I tell him that I now have the information that he requested concerning his publishing prospects in Finland. He promises to wait for me in the lobby while I go and get my papers from the office. When I return, Benaz is sitting on one of the sofas. We shake hands. I take a seat on the other sofa facing him, but soon move next to him as I try to explain his publishing possibilities in Finland from my papers. He seems to be interested and grateful. I have a hard time relating those things that I have just heard with this person. Undoubtedly some characteristics are there, but I am not sure whether there is something 'wrong' with his mental health or whether he is just lashing out his frustrations with the help of his imagination and wild visions/ideas.
>
> (Research diary, 1st September 2006)

In my interpretation, Benaz's hostility to the practices of surveillance, control of movement and requirements to behave in a particular manner exhibits resistance. Instead of speech or a verbal account, Benaz articulated his discontent and frustration through his gendered body, a voice that made no sense to the staff, who saw his actions only as the type of violence and threats that are connected with masculine subjectivities. I do not intend to suggest that the kind of actions to which Benaz resorts, threatening or assaulting others, are in any way laudable or justified. I am not seeking to justify them. My key claim, in fact, does not concern Benaz's acts in themselves at all. Rather, I take his behaviour, which happens in wanton disregard of the regulative ambitions and the disrupting effects of that behaviour, to illustrate a protest against the rationale that debased him and viewed his presence and body strictly in terms of a political order which he himself was not ready to accept (see also Puumala 2013). Benaz's agency and gestures thus may have risen prior to cognition, from the sense of dislocation that the loss of control caused.

By interrelating certain political discourses about asylum seekers and his material body, Benaz contested, resisted and interrupted the working of disciplinary mechanisms through his body's irregular movements. Such gestures and moves keep the asylum seeker's potential for politics open. Moreover, movement reveals the centre as one place where the struggle between politics and the agentive body culminates on a daily basis. In terms of the dialectics between movement, the political and the international, such a view suggests that movement is characteristic and constitutive of the relations between bodies, communities and worlds (see Manning 2007: 132, 2009).

A protest does not have to be explicit in its expression to be understood as resistance to a particular spatial organisation of political community. When put alongside mass protests or social movements, the body's resistance and its acts of exscription are perhaps less romantic or heroic. Because of their ambiguity and multiplicity, however, the singular body's ways of political expression are all the more disturbing for those who receive them. Through a minor defiance, a reach towards or a move beyond, the body discloses existence in ways that displace or rupture the spatial frame within which our political existence is supposed to occur. Consider, for instance, Benaz's miaowing: the act caused consternation and made the reception centre staff powerless in the face of his protest. They did not know how to interpret and respond to this behaviour. Through his body, Benaz momentarily dissolved the separation between people, exposing the limit of the sovereign subject and the relationality between various political subjectivities.

Bodies are extensive, in the sense that they extend. In the politics of the body, the body, although subjected to governmental power, opens the possibility for controversial politics. As in Benaz's case, contradictory forms of resistance, contestation and transformation address the notions and corporeality of politics. They mark the international, sensing body and political community coming into existence and gaining meaning only with and in relation to one another (cf. Van Wolputte 2004: 258). Thus, it is not adequate to conceptualise political agency in terms of self-empowerment, self-worth, self-emancipation or resistance (cf. Muldoon 2001: 38). To be sure, all of these dimensions can be present in bodies expressing themselves politically, but concentrating on one body alone or even a collective body formed through the idea of 'common-being' is never enough.

As above with Benaz, the body's experiences are always outcomes of involvement in diverse, potentially changing positionalities, activities and institutions (cf. Solis 2004: 197). Perhaps an apt way of addressing asylum seekers' moves and gestures would be to conceive them as passages, that is, as movements-to, which open space and construct it as meaningful, intelligible and experiencable. Thus, their gestures and moves are capable of evoking exposure and articulating an understanding of the relationality of our existence (see Nancy 2003b: 8; also Soguk 2005: 433). In other words, gestures and movement are ethical and political stances, which contest and exceed the ideas and practices "associated with the singular, the original, the uniform, the central authority, the hierarchy" (Benterrak, Muecke & Roe 1984: 15, cited in Muldoon 2001: 46). Benaz's unpredictability represents a subversion of the body allegedly known and placed within the Finnish political order. His acts are not

128 *Moving (in) space*

only gestures and moves that try to do the impossible, but also interventions into a social reality that he has encountered in Finland. These interventions change the coordinates of what is perceived to be possible in the first place (see Žižek 2000: 671–672). Indeed, the body can redefine what counts as political and what is the space of politics. This is possible just because it can opt out of moving in synchrony with practices of surveillance and sovereign politics.

Gestures and moves force a response. At any given moment, asylum seekers are capable of disrupting the smooth and frictionless functioning of the sovereign logic and disclosing the vulnerability of those structures and practices that found notions of politics, communities and identities. Seemingly minute acts are extremely powerful in indicating some of the foundational problems of the modern conceptions of politics. Sovereign politics never totally defeats the body or its movement; the body constantly pushes through, evades, resonates with and withdraws from the principle of sovereignty and renders it incomplete. A politics that begins and ends with the body is a politics of touch and potential, senses and meanings. It is relational, unfolding and open. It is unstable in a sense that it cannot be written into agendas or formulated into dogmas, like the projects of sovereign politics, which give certain stable bodies a voice (see Manning 2007: 31). The presence of the asylum seeker's body demands that we expose our citizen selves to the touch of a body that moves according to a different tune. The event of exposure is not comfortable or pleasant, but can cause disquiet and worry – in a way it makes our perceptions of our existence anxious.

The bodily event of the political

Living as an asylum seeker is constant struggle. It is warding off, challenging and negotiating stereotypical images. The label or status 'asylum seeker' is intelligible only in relation to a certain political order, its operations, reconstructions and reinstitutions on a daily basis (cf. Tate 2001). Asylum seekers' movements and gestures seem to be directed towards a place which they cannot yet name, but which gains some form in their movement. Asylum seekers struggle for the possibility of becoming, which the accumulation of knowledge and experience condition (cf. Biddle 2001: 188). The senses of the international reflect interaction between the body, the surrounding world and others. Nancy (2008: 15) calls this "local being", where local does not refer to a particular place, but to the coming of the world on the surface of the body in the sense of local colour (see also Chapter 5). This can happen either through the body's response to politics or through sovereign practices leaving restrictive marks on the body. Although there is no firm place for belonging available for asylum seekers, there is movement between places, change in rhythm and being as it happens. This movement opens up the possibility of reconceptualising the fluidity of political space and political community (see Puumala & Pehkonen 2010). The possibility for a transformative politics is embedded in sovereign efforts to capture and limit, which cause the body to expose itself, to place itself outside itself and in front of other bodies.

Moving (in) space 129

Movement as a form of political articulation may point towards or mobilise the shortcomings of the international as we have come to know and organise it, and gesture towards a need to mobilise our thought concerning political communities. The negotiation of space and of the potentialities of becoming through movement expose an event of the political. The moving body withdraws from the linear and bounded conception of space-time proposed by state sovereignty (cf. Manning 2007: 59). It relies on acts and events of relating and touching, rather than on touch and relation as such. The refusal to embody a substantial identity enables asylum seekers to recombine various positions in a subversive way in relation to sovereign politics. No single identificatory marker defines the asylum-seeking body totally, as it moves between a number of potential positions and makes creative use of them. This marks an important twist in understanding the body not as a standpoint of a rational and intentional subject-mind, but as something created through movement, non-teleologically and even unintentionally. Political agency turns into a question of a political and politicised body moving in relation to and together with others, rather than the capacity of a disembodied sovereign subject.

Movement, as a modality of exposure, is capable of re-treating the space of politics. In its own way, this Chapter has critically reflected upon the way identities are spatialised and positioned within a spatial – or rather territorial – spectrum. Furthermore, through asylum seekers' moves and gestures, it has sought to provide an answer to what 'being many' might mean in terms of sovereignty and the international. Movement bears the potential to articulate the consequences of those bodily spaces that sovereign practices in the field of migration policies create. At the same time, however, it exposes the body as always being-towards others. The senses of the international take form in corporeal conjunctures, in which bodies come together and a shared space for communication begins to unfold.

EEVA: Do you think that people in Finland, I don't know how much you talk about this with your friends or others, that they understand what it means to be an asylum seeker?

TAHIR: Yeah, it's difficult. I don't know whether you've seen Jenni Linko's documentary Asylum? I was in it. I explained there what kind of problems we have here. [. . .] Even though I thought we might have problems, if the movie went to Afghanistan, perhaps I was afraid . . . But people here don't know that there are problems here also. And they don't know why we are here. Then it is better if somebody dares to do it [the documentary]. I'm happy that we got to do that video, and I know it has been broadcast in many places.

[. . .] I was in town last Friday or Saturday. I went to a disco. After that in the morning, when I headed home I met a woman who was a bit tipsy. She asked me "have you been on telly?" and I said "yeah, I have." Then she started talking with me and she said "before we were racists, the whole family. Then we saw the documentary, and we cried for you and

130　*Moving (in) space*

after that we decided that we are for your case." Then the woman wanted to give me 100 euros, but I didn't accept. She said "I thought wrongly about you and I wish to repair that." And I told her "no, because now you know how things are, that is what . . ." Then she got us a taxi, and she paid it. It was 30 euros.

(Interview with Tahir, April 2007)

The meeting between Tahir and a Finnish woman in a taxi stand after a night out shows how stories, once communicated, have the potential of moving people and fixed mind-sets. Thus, the political potential of the body does not lie only in openly political acts (Puumala & Pehkonen 2010; also Puumala, Väyrynen, Kynsilehto & Pehkonen 2011). I will not speculate about the role that alcohol might have played in the event, nor raise the problematique of buying a clear conscience with money. Rather, for me, Tahir's story crystallises the inherent capacity of the body to engage with others both through and beyond the label, articulate exposure, and thus it also articulates a potential transition in thinking about the space of politics and relations that can be meaningful within it. The space that appears is not a static constellation. It does not have a specific shape, but takes form in the event of exposure that articulates compearance.

Compearance does not necessarily imply long-lasting contact or even physical immediacy. It is a philosophical concept that concerns bodies' movement towards one another, but in such a way that the body is always on the verge of withdrawal from the other's grip. Withness is intrinsic for the political and a question of its essence (Lacoue-Labarthe & Nancy 1997: 133). The political is our state or situation (Lacoue-Labarthe & Nancy 1997: 110). It is, in fact, *an ethical commitment* without moral superiority. Such an understanding presents responsibility as "response-ability" (Sullivan 2001: 103) to others, which can take multiple forms and add a plethora of different shapes to politics. Nancian thought invites us to rethink space and spatiality, not as objective and measurable, but rather as exteriority and in terms of extension, in which dualisms cannot operate. In this idea of the interval, space transforms into a temporal unfolding in which singular-plural bodies mutually expose themselves (see James 2002: 136–137; also Manning 2007: 128). A sense of this kind of a space is tractable in asylum seekers' movement and the ways in which they and the people and practices with whom they interact expose one another. These events of exposure shape the senses of the body's presence with regard to and in-difference of sovereign power.

Asylum seekers enact movement as a form of engagement and as an ability to speak out of place, in-difference to the state. Informal and expressive forms of resistance, articulation and engagement are important channels through which exposure can be evoked. By exposing itself, the asylum-seeking body presents a demand for reciprocity in action and thought. It demands that we think of postnational and yet political space. Bodies' movement engenders a complex spatial spectre. It points to the incapacity of western political thought to think about community beyond the state. Indeed, according to Nancy (1992: 374; Nancy 2000: 101–143, 145–158), this tradition of thought has annihilated the arsenal of

Moving (in) space 131

meaning(s) of community by making the community an end in itself, in the form of a sovereign state. The politico-corporeal struggle that unfolds on and through the asylum-seeking body involves exploring those multiple ways of how international relations and sovereign practices mark us and our bodies and how we are their marks (see also Nancy 1992: 389).

A critical engagement with the struggle does not permit absorbing the body into the collective body of the nation. It argues against founding our thought of political community ambiguously or exclusively on either the state or the system of states. This may seem like a utopian ideal, but if we look at the asylum crisis with which Europe started struggling in 2015, the immediacy of and necessity to engage with the challenge that movement presents to our political imaginaries becomes evident. The discussion in this chapter allows two important contentions to be made. First, the border is not where it is supposed to be. Borders are much more than geographical and governmental lines, which makes sovereignty not only a territorial construct, but also a topological one. Second, the body is not where and what the sovereign practices suppose it to be. When sovereignty and the networked practices and institutions through which it is enacted are engaged with the challenge that bodily movement presents, complex choreographies and corporeal cartographies begin to unfold.

Event 5

The feltness of sovereignty

Abdi left Somalia to escape the conflict that has ravaged the country since the early 90s. In Finland he found himself placed in limbo. Abdi is a well-educated man, who had led a comfortable life back in Somalia. But life had not been easy for him. The scars on his legs and stomach remind him of the beatings that he suffered from early 1991 until the late 90s. Furthermore, the scars remind him constantly of the situation he left his family in. Abdi suffers from insomnia, depression and other stress-related illnesses. His liminal placement has begun to aggravate his mental troubles. To cope with his pain, Abdi was prescribed anti-depressants and sleeping pills. He, however, felt that the medicine did not provide him with enough help, so Abdi started drinking. Then he received news from his family about his eldest son being killed in a shooting. In addition, his family had to leave their home and flee Mogadishu. They contacted Abdi, and told him that they needed money and were counting on him sending it to them. He had already sent on a monthly basis all he could afford from his living allowance, but the sum that the family required was too big for him to cover. Abdi had to ask for help from the Finnish Somali community. His pride and sense of self-respect were deeply hurt when he had to rely on his countrymen to help his family, a duty that he considers his own. As a result, Abdi started to feel that returning home under any circumstances was impossible and that his separation from his family was permanent. Abdi could not cope with the situation and constant uncertainty of his own faith, which caused him to attempt suicide. Tears run down his cheeks, when he now tells me about failing his duties as a husband and father. He points at his chest and gestures that it feels like something is always moving up and down in his throat.

(Interview with Abdi, August 2006)

Abdi's story made me realise that in many cases the price of survival was shame (see also Bohmer & Shuman 2007: 625). Along with other distressing factors and negative emotions, the shame Abdi experienced for not being able to fulfil his responsibility towards his family made him resort to self-harm and attempt suicide. The gap between what Abdi thought his role in the family was and the powerless and vulnerable position where he found himself was too great to bear. The condition of asylum seeking was intertwined in Abdi's case with cultural and religious perceptions of his roles and responsibilities, which cannot be left

134   *The feltness of sovereignty*

unaccounted for if we wish to understand the reactions and acts to which he ultimately resorted.

First, listening to stories of extreme vulnerability and distress made me want to move beyond the research participants' administrative positions or the label 'asylum seeker' in the ways in which I was to analyse those stories. It seemed too harsh and unbearable to think and write about stories like Abdi's, as doing this so easily places asylum seekers as mere victims of sovereign politics or depicts them as mentally unstable. In many ways, asylum seekers unarguably live in spaces which not only physically separate them from others but also simultaneously reduce them to silent victims. Then the element of sense emerged, or actually I became aware of the various sensuous responses to the status, the living conditions and the past and future in my empirical data. Concurrently, I started to struggle with how to think about the scars and of the immense amount of emotional distress I had come to witness in terms of their political significance. Most often trauma is explained and analysed from a psychological perspective and interpreted from an individualist standpoint. Why was I still feeling the necessity of thinking about the political in the utterly vulnerable condition in which many asylum seekers lived? Could scars, wounds, distress and self-harm be interpreted without adopting foundationalist politics and without reducing them in the sovereign subject (cf. White 2007)?

EEVA: What is it like to live in the centre?

AYAN: In what?

EEVA: In here.

AYAN: Really, I have lived for a long time in the centre. In this camp and in another camp. You know, when you live in a place like this, you encounter problems sometimes, because you don't live alone. You live like this. People with whom you share a room, come and put the lights on in the middle of the night. Because they have problems, and do not sleep. Then, you can't sleep because you feel the problem they feel. Sometimes people can say, for instance "you can't sleep now, I want to talk to you."

EEVA: Mmm

AYAN: [pause] I am just so tired. Toilets and kitchens are so dirty here. Sometimes I don't feel like cooking there, because I'm afraid of bacteria, because it's so dirty. Because so many people live here. And, if you clean now, they make it the same, leave all things and don't care really. Your life is like this. These people, they have problems. It is so hard in the *vastaanottokeskus* (reception) centre. [laughs] This is how life is. Having your own house, and what you see here, it's different really.

EEVA: Yeah.

AYAN: Most of the time I don't stay here but go somewhere else because I can't stay in this place. I think a lot in the nights and then I tell myself that if I stay in the camp maybe I become crazy. I want peace of mind. If I think a lot, then in the night I can't sleep . . . I go to sleep at 2 o'clock, and I get up at 7 o'clock in the morning. So I don't sleep really. And I feel much headache.

You know, we don't get help in this country really. I don't need all this. They give us money for food, but I don't really need this. I want to know

The feltness of sovereignty   135

what I can do and how I can get on with my life, but I don't want to stay like an animal to eat and sleep and get up. [pause] But the nurse, I don't know . . . She always sends me to the doctor who gives me medicine. How much medicine do I have! I say that "I have *pää kipee* [an aching head]," she says "you have to take this, this, this, and this." I think that this headache never passes if I continue thinking. Maybe sometimes the doctor gives you medicine [laughs] to sleep. This is not good, really! It is not that you need medicine. We need to have peace of mind. If you stay two days or three days in the bed without getting up, what will you think? When you think a lot, you get tired here [points to her head]. Your body is not tired, but your mind is tired. Really, in the mind.

I think that this is such a hard life. [pause] My life has not actually changed. It's the same as before. Now I have peace, that is different, to know that I don't die, that if I go outside, I know I won't see a person who says "I want to kill you." That I have. But, otherwise, it's the same in my life. I lost my future in my own country, when I was a child, I didn't go school, because of the war that began in 1991. Now, I am 22, so it has been 16 years without a future. Then I came here, and I have to stay in the camp . . . like an animal, really.

(Interview with Ayan, October 2006)

When I asked Ayan to describe her life in the reception centre, she emphasised how different everyday life is compared with life in a reception centre. In the centre, the living arrangements are often very austere and crowded. The 'camp', as those living in centres term them, is not a proper home. It lacks the kind of intimacy and privacy that is necessary for a proper sense of home to develop (cf. Fox O'Mahony & Sweeney 2010). More interestingly, however, Ayan connected the experience of her immediate surroundings to the wider condition of being an asylum seeker. She recurrently took up the theme of thinking too much, of not being able to get rid of harmful thoughts, worries and traumatising memories. The thoughts that bothered Ayan were related to both the past and future, but had a sensuous effect on the present as well. Ayan was worried for her father who had had to stay in Somalia, and who was experiencing severe problems with his health. She was also preoccupied with the lack of direction in her own life. These, and the incomprehension and perceived lack of sense concerning the rationale of the Finnish asylum politics and policies, had all begun to cause her bodily symptoms. Stress begins to travel; it circulates in her body, first in the mind and then by causing physical symptoms like headaches.

Ayan was prescribed both sleeping pills and a medicine called Cipralex, which is used to treat depression and panic attacks related to agoraphobia. She laments the medicalisation of her condition and feels that many of her problems stem from her inability to pursue a normal life, which makes it difficult to incorporate the traumatic experiences from Somalia as parts of who she is now. Ayan claims that in Finland she is safe from open and random violence, but nothing else has actually changed in her life since the temporary nature of her status prohibits her from

136 *The feltness of sovereignty*

being directed towards the future. Ayan is left in a liminal position. What makes Ayan's account particularly interesting from the perspective of political studies and international relations is the connection that she makes between the status and her thinking, resulting to a great extent from the gap between the past and future that living with the status opened. The present takes shape as a senseless gaping that leaves Ayan ambiguously located, and where sovereign practices cause her concrete headaches.

Stories and experiences like Abdi's and Ayan's point towards an understanding that asylum seeking evokes a sense of history and politics that cannot be located within a sovereign, individual subject. This understanding paves the way to discuss not only the praxical challenge with which asylum seeking presents the sovereign state, but also the philosophical challenge with which it presents the international. A focus on sense represents a call for a different political project of the international. Could senses and sensuous responses in their various forms be indicative of the politics of the body? Instead of resorting to existing analytical frameworks, which would render asylum seekers mere victims of sovereign practices, I decided to engage with the meanings of hurting and healing bodies in politics and sketch sensuous and corporeal means through which the international turns into local colour.

5 Sensuous politics, political sentiments

On sense and sensing

The importance of the role that sense and sentiments play in the struggle of seeking asylum was not clear to me from the beginning. In terms of my research, they only emerged as a relevant channel to negotiate the touch and effects of sovereign practices on the body through my own exposure to asylum seekers. It is not possible to dismiss the emotional, felt and sensuous when thinking about the question of asylum seekers' lives and their forms of resistance (see Ahmed 2004; Hall 2010; Ross 2010; Svašek 2010). In engaging with *sens* – with a reference to both sense and meaning – I am interested in understanding how people react and respond to their exclusion, what kind of sensuous experiences are involved in it and what kind of negotiations are related to it.

> When I ask Abdi about things that he is looking forward to or that make him anxious he begins to speak about Somalia. "In Somalia they think that in Europe everything is better. They think that Europe is a paradise. Here, you have peace, but nothing else." He is about to cry. "I have no morale left, no morale to work. My mind is in Somalia, but I am here. I still feel I am Somali. [. . .] Everything is hard for me. I cannot imagine life, the future right now, when everything is complicated. [. . .] I am a human, you know, I feel. When I eat, I wonder if my children are eating or if they are hungry. I think about what they are doing during the days while I am here. My children were expecting a better life when I left." I ask if he would like to go back to meet his family, if it were possible. Abdi negates and laments "it's shameful. I am ashamed that I haven't been able to help my family. I cannot go back, it would be shameful."
>
> (Interview with Abdi, August 2006)

Abdi's case brings out the way in which various stress factors intertwine during the experience of seeking asylum (see Event 5). The pressure and stress he experiences result partly from the asylum determination process, but also from the worry he bears concerning the well-being of his family. Furthermore, his identity as a provider for the family has been severely impaired and thus Abdi perceived

138 *Sensuous politics, political sentiments*

himself as a failure as a father and husband, especially as his decision to leave was taken in order to enhance their standard of living and perhaps pave the way for a potential new life in Europe for the whole family. Abdi's perception of his own state had made it impossible for him to think about the future and left him without the morale to even try. He himself conceived his situation as "shameful". To expel such failure or badness from oneself, Sara Ahmed (2004: 104–105) opines, one feels the urge to expel oneself from oneself. This has led her to claim that prolonged experiences of shame bring people perilously close to suicide, which Abdi had attempted. In Abdi's account, experienced stress turns into a part of who he perceives himself to be and that perception, in turn, feeds into the ways Abdi behaves and acts (see also Zarowsky 2004). For me, that circulation functions as a point of departure to explore the senses in terms of politics and as a form of political expression.

It is generally acknowledged that asylum seekers suffer from mental disorders, distress and trauma, and that the asylum determination process can be traumatising (see Bohmer & Shuman 2007; Gerritsen et al. 2006; Herlihy & Turner 2007; Keller et al. 2003; Salis Gross 2004; Steel et al. 2004; also Chapter 3). Detention, in particular, has been noted to be harmful for asylum seekers' mental health (e.g. Keller et al. 2003), which has initiated demands that the state's responses to asylum seekers should not be based on practices that further aggravate already existing mental health problems (e.g. Steel et al. 2004).

In the Finnish context, Riitta Lukkaroinen (2005: 17–18) has coined the term "asylum syndrome", which refers to the uncertainty, unsatisfactory living conditions, lack of privacy and differences of opinion between nationalities as key factors which lead to re-traumatisation, especially of torture victims (cf. Chapters 3 and 4). Depressive reactions, as well as difficulties in sleeping and in concentration, are common among asylum seekers (Halla 2007; Lukkaroinen 2005; Pirinen 2008). This is what Abdi's story starkly communicated, but with much less euphemism. Lukkaroinen (2005: 21) further contends that the lack of control over one's own life leads over time to a social state of deprivation, which causes depression, hopelessness, aggression and self-destructive behaviour. She points out that when the asylum determination process takes more than a year, the need for psychological support and mental health services among asylum seekers increases dramatically. This causes Lukkaroinen, at the time a director of a reception centre herself, to suggest that mental health problems represent the biggest and most problematic question in the daily work of reception centres.

Traumatic loss, pain and suffering, as Kate Schick (2011) has claimed, are not irrelevant to world politics (see also Caruth 1996, 2001; Edkins 2003; Howell 2011; Philipose 2007; Scarry 1985; Wall 2008). In relating the sensuous and the political, self-inflicted violence, emotional outbursts and responses and refusals to act in line with sovereignty represent relational acts, acts from body to body. In fact, in his examination of self-harm among refugees, Joseph Pugliese (2002) suggested that these seemingly singular acts are already double, as they "conjoin the anguished body of the individual refugee to the larger corpus of the nation in a complex relation of power and violence". This is how political community

Sensuous politics, political sentiments 139

intertwines intimately with the body. In my interviews, asylum seekers have mentioned the head, heart and stomach as places which have been damaged by the experience of displacement and their marginal position in the receiving society (Puumala 2012, 2013). This makes it meaningful to think about the political significance of both sensuous and embodied emotional stress, together with their capacity to rearticulate the space and time of politics and political relations between hierarchically positioned subjectivities.

In experiences of refuge, medical biography intersects with political and historical forces over which the singular person has no control. Several studies have concluded that adapting to a situation of forced migration entails severe social, mental and physical challenges (e.g. Coker 2004: 16; Schick 2011: 1840). It is no surprise, then, that often attention is drawn to the psychological suffering of traumatised asylum seekers and the emotional and physical scars, sense of loss, despair and helplessness that characterises their lives. In fact, as Vanessa Pupavac (2001: 358) claims, viewing experiences through a therapeutic lens, trauma counselling and psycho-social intervention have become an integral part of the humanitarian response to the refugee condition. However, viewing trauma and social suffering through a health paradigm, which regards trauma as an attribute of dysfunction, raises questions over asylum seekers' capacity for self-determination (also Ahmed 2004: 39; Pupavac 2008: 279–280). The experience of displacement disrupts the sense of time and space. The conditions under which people leave, travel and arrive at their destination are not orderly, but somewhat chaotic, so that their sense of self-control and direction can be severely affected. Turning suffering, trauma and hopelessness into pathological states can carry significant political and social consequences for the person and their ability to articulate or perhaps even conceive themselves as political agents instead of simple victims.

Besides the sensuous consequences of political practices and previous experiences related to persecution, it is important to explore whether and how people's experiences represent events of the political through the sensuous. In such an approach, the body is the existential ground of culture and political life on which liminality is worked through and through which new attachments are created (e.g. Csordas 1994). In the condition of asylum seeking, political, cultural and personal narratives must be recreated from a chaos that has been experienced and that has left its marks on the body. This process of reordering and recreating can be fathomed to represent local colour, the meanings that are attached to the experience of displacement and the ways in which the experience comes to matter in the person's life. The reordering of the self and the relations of the self to others need to begin with the reordering of the body (Coker 2004: 17). This reordering marks a sensuous event of exposure, where the body looks into its possibilities of becoming and negotiates its possibilities with and connections to others.

As a whole, the present chapter delves into the sensuous bodywork that asylum seekers perform and through which it is possible to examine how suffering, displacement and sovereign practices are expressed on and negotiated through the body. Concurrently, it explores how the political takes shape through the body in the sensuous experiences of displacement, the suffering that is related to those

140   *Sensuous politics, political sentiments*

experiences and the process of (sensuous and emotional) healing that asylum seekers undergo. Even in the absence of language or in the case when nobody listens, people inherently reach out into the world with their bodies (see Tatman 1998: 27; also Marcus, Neuman & Mackuen 2000). My field experiences have taught me that asylum seekers have an urgent need to talk with someone who will surrender their imagination to their stories without adopting a professional or institutional role. By professional and institutional roles, I mean in this context the interactions that asylum seekers most often have with health care workers, psychologists, psychiatrists, migration officers or the police. Someone coming from the university is different in their interpretations: a (quasi)neutral party, whose interest in hearing their stories is not conditioned by a strict position. People make immense efforts as they struggle to become understood, communicate and find words for their experiences and gain a human(e) response.

Despite statuses and categorical and hierarchical identifications, reaching out to others is always possible because the senses cannot be regulated or surrendered to restrictive politics or sovereign practices (see Manning 2007: 86). A sensuous approach thus emphasises the body's capacity to transcend limitations, find ways of communication and articulate its presence in and through the limited body. It also allows for a focus on the undeniable sensation of suffering/pain that is involved in seeking asylum, where the pain experienced is sometimes medically inexplicable. There may not always be a medical condition that would explain the experienced physical and psychological symptoms. That we are tempted to look for them reflects the western tendency to intellectualise and individualise suffering (see Coker 2004: 19; Grimwood 2004: 67, 69).

Perhaps senses articulate, with the most force, the demand that asylum seekers present. Even when language fails, the body does not stay silent. The body can expose itself in multiple ways, even when it seems that nobody listens or cares. My interviews with mental health professionals who work with asylum seekers confirm that experienced hardships, distress and insecurity transfer (into) the body with multiple consequences. Suicide attempts, scalding, burning or cutting oneself, self-destructive thoughts, overdosing on medicine, excessive use of alcohol, pulling out wisps of hair, pounding one's head against a wall or table, anxiety, psychosis, desperation; all of these represent practices to which asylum seekers resort in order to communicate with others and expel felt desperation from within and bring it to the public sphere. What combines these practices is that they are all inflicted on one's own body and articulate a sense of desperation and a lack of direction in one's life. Sensuous responses reflect the figural voice of the other that is felt on one's body and that the body seeks, although perhaps not intentionally, to reverse.

In writing about sensuous connections between bodies and politics, there is a heightened sense of ethics present on my part. In engaging with 'deviant' acts and forms of behaviour, it is crucial not to represent asylum seekers as somehow fundamentally different, not to sentimetalise or pathologisise them. It is equally important to avoid feasting with people's pain and thus evoke mere pity, a sense of voyerism or a false sense of altruisim (see also Dauphinee 2010; Doty 2010).

Sensuous politics, political sentiments   141

With the latter, I intend a condition where a person such as myself, whose own position and background is fundamentally different, claims a position of being able to enter the other's place and feelings. I have adopted a philosophical stance to the practices and acts of distress and desperation. Had I in the first place sought to focus explicitly on senses in my research, I most likely would have felt much more compelled to make sense of them as a phenomenon. As it is, I do not seek to close the meaning of the sensuous body. Rather, my focus results from the vulnerability, openness and incompleteness that such acts have arisen in me. As a result, I started to think about asylum seekers' finite experiences in terms of a bodily disclosure that articulates the political as a (figural) wound on the body. The body exposes the flesh affected by sovereign practices and through the flesh communicates itself to others, perhaps evoking a sense of exposure in the other.

Local colour

Paul Sullivan and John McCarthy (2004: 291) have contended that studying lived experience means adopting a perspective that makes the feltness of experience local. It involves understanding that experience is always connected to the body and, before becoming a question of reason and meaning, experience is a question of the senses. An engagement with the sensuous responses that an experience provokes allows us to make sense of how that experience matters. Such a focus suggests that, instead of a rational agent, the body should be understood as a sense in action, which in exposing itself presents politics as ethics and ethics in terms of the political. Once again, in my attempt to connect experience with the body and, furthermore, to articulate the linkage between the sensuous body and the political, I put Nancy's thought into operation. Nancy (2008: 15) uses the expression "local colour", which tells about an event's reverberations and marks on the body. The exact ways in which an event reverberates and the marks it leaves on the body are context-bound and situational, mediated by, for example, gender, religion and culture. The same event can have different senses and it can thus matter differently depending on the person and the basis upon which s/he constructs his/her identity. Having said that, I need to emphasise that such an approach does not suggest the return and reification of the sovereign subject. Rather, as there is no single form of exposure, there is no 'model' body that could exhaustively account for the meaning(s) of politics and the senses that events can gain.

The meanings of an experience are negotiated in the event of compearance, and the body can articulate and evoke exposure with multiple means. Local colour, as it takes shape in the struggle of seeking asylum, refers to a carnalising of politics and the international. In this chapter, it equals the way states, borders and sovereign power feature on the body, and the way asylum seekers feel their intimate effects, respond to them and in their responses evoke a sense of the political as a shared condition. It refers to the ways in which people take note of their previous experiences and "immediate present" (Junka 2006: 358) and how sensuous responses are rationalised, various agentic positions negotiated and mutual vulnerabilities exposed. The political logic of sovereignty and its multiple

142 *Sensuous politics, political sentiments*

biopolitical practices and networked ways of governance can never totally close the meanings and senses of the body. In this section, I will engage with Asad's case, which illustrates the concrete hold of sovereign politics over his body. But at the same time, his body is a testimony to complex corporeal and political horizons of relationality, separation and connectedness.

The experience of the marks that sovereign politics and asylum seeking leave on the body are multiple. On the one hand, asylum seekers are keenly aware of the way in which their bodies and presence are perceived (see Chapter 4). On the other, they carry with themselves traces of their home countries, their travel routes, their stops and the asylum determination process. The dynamics that enter into self-perception are complex and further reflected upon by how people regard their being, positions and possibilities in the political community. In order to understand the extent to which sovereignty can inscribe itself on the person's own experience of him/herself and what matters in asylum seekers' lives, I started a collaborative photographic project titled "How would I like to be seen?" with asylum seekers.[1] That is also how I met Asad. The photographic project spanned from August 2013 to February 2014.

The aim of the collaborative photographic effort was to create portraits of the participants that would communicate those senses, emotions and feelings that they themselves wanted to express. They could choose the places where they wanted to have the pictures taken and pose in any way they wanted and felt comfortable with. It was my task to listen to their thoughts and ideas and try to capture their presence with my camera as they would like to be encountered. After each photo session I developed the shots, and then looked at and talked about the photos together with each participant. In the end, they could choose the ones that in their view communicated their presence and bodies the best. They also received printed copies of all the photos for themselves.

My interest in such a research method was not primarily in the photos. Rather, I wanted to understand the process and practices of identity formation and negotiation that take place within the condition of asylum seeking. That process lies at the core of the politico-corporeal struggle. The photographic project was an attempt to find a form of interaction that would demand mutual exposure and thus could help to conceptualise the possible ways in which exposure actually happens and the forms it takes. Instead of simply asking people what they thought and how they felt, the portraits privileged the body, as only by looking at the pictures were meanings given to presence and the person's relations to others reflected upon. Methodologically, the project was also an attempt to place myself outside of myself and to let participants see what I saw when I looked at them. All in all, the collaboration sought to understand what mattered in the daily lives of asylum seekers and, hence, enter into the affective sphere instead of remaining in the rational or verbal realm.

"*This is a sad picture,*" contended Asad when he first saw the portrait where he was sitting under a tall pine tree that reached for the skies in the vicinity of the reception centre where he lived. He looks away from the camera; his eyes are fixed on the horizon that opens on the left side of the portrait. Looking at the photo from

Sensuous politics, political sentiments   143

a western perspective suggests that Asad is looking into the past, and the height of the tree makes him seem very small; his back is against the trunk. The picture was taken on the day of his first 'anniversary' in Finland, and the main feeling in his mind at that time was endless waiting. The asylum determination process had taken longer than he had expected. According to Asad, the photo brought to the fore the multiplicity and shifting of emotions that characterised his life at that moment. In a sense, our collaboration provided him with a means to explore his experience of seeking asylum and to make sense of all that was related to that experience. In his portraits, Asad himself could see the scars on his back from the beatings he had experienced in Greece, the tattoos on his arms and neck to commemorate a dead friend and to urge him to keep on fighting. The "NoMercy" tattoo on his left wrist reminded him that people in Europe have shown no mercy towards him or others like him. All those past, present and distant struggles and relationships condensed within the portrait as Asad's body, which – through its position, place and gait – brings forward interconnected geographies and histories (cf. Squire & Darling 2013: 61).

Asad's movements and activity in looking for a meaningful place where he wanted the photo to be taken enable us to fathom the political as an event that happens in encounters with others and that articulates a presence. An engagement with the daily lives of asylum seekers can result in a more nuanced view into the evented nature of the political, which allows us to pose important questions about the practices of sovereignty and the categorisation of human bodies that results from the principle of sovereignty. In such a fashion, the body can represent an index of the international and its dimension. Asad's body, and his finite sense of his own body, materialise a language that both defies and demands our understanding. Seeking asylum and the multiple forms of control, processing and surveillance that follow from that are experiences that reverberate on the body, that enter the body. They articulate sovereign politics as something that concerns the lived body in its entirety – entering into people's self-conception, perception of others and material bodies.

For me, Asad's interpretation of his portrait represents an instance where he becomes aware of the effects of seeking asylum on his body and, importantly, the way he looks at himself. This brings me back to the concept of local colour as something that refers to an event of existence (see Nancy 2008: 16–17). A relational political statement takes form as local colour, which in highlighting the sensuous element of sovereign practices carries with it the potential for unexpected ways of political expression. As mentioned, senses are not an unfamiliar topic in social sciences with regard to subject formation, although the focus has mostly been on self-harm or body modification (see e.g. Brandt 2004; Caruth 1996; Hewitt 1997; McAllister 2003; McLane 1996; Pitts 2003; Sullivan 2001). The political significance of self-harm has been addressed through various perspectives, some with a focus on agency, others on biopolitics or abjective subjectivities (see Edkins 2000; Edkins & Pin-Fat 2005; Nyers 2008; Pugliese 2002, 2004). However, although self-harm is the main way in which the study of senses has entered the condition of asylum seeking, I do not want to focus on it. It features in my writing, but does

144 *Sensuous politics, political sentiments*

not form the core of it. Rather, inspired by Asad's reflection on the multiple ways in which asylum seekers' finite experience of themselves and their positioning is informed by the senses, together with how and with what consequences sense enters into the body (e.g. Oliver 2010), I wanted to explore how senses matter in people's lives. What can senses tell us about the workings and effects of sovereign practices? How does the emerging understanding, in turn, enable us to make sense of the responses those practices evoke in the people subjected to them?

Senses produce those surfaces and boundaries that allow the delineation of the individual and the social as if they were objects (Ahmed 2004: 10). They emerge between bodies, which turns political existence into a matter of tact (Nancy 1993a: 198). In the condition of asylum seeking, senses are not 'in' the individual, as they point towards historical and political developments that cannot be totally claimed by or reduced to the individual subject (see also Dossa 2003: 53; MacLure, Holmes, Jones & MacRae 2010: 492–493; Pugliese 2004: 33). The whole question of asylum, actually, surpasses the notion of a sovereign subject. Fathoming senses as something that connects the person to others and articulates being in the world, they can – like Parin Dossa (2003: 53) has suggested in relation to silence – represent a way of knowing, giving meaning and articulating it to the other.

Sensuous experiences such as pain and suffering are temporal because they resist exhaustive definition and at times also language (see Wall 2008). They cannot be adequately addressed through verbal accounts, as Asad's case illustrates. In the temporality (openness) of the senses lies politics – the politics of the body. Sense opens the body to the world, exposes it to others. The idea of exposure offers a radically different conceptualisation of the sense as something that cannot be contained within dichotomous thinking. Sense and sensuous experiences bear the potential of multiplying the spaces of politics and the forms of political exchange. They contradict the notion that political beings should be constituted through clear and distinct ideas, which are publicly and verbally articulated (see Palladino & Moreira 2006). This, in my view, carries the potential of the senses being a political strategy, a way of evoking exposure, which results in non-disclosure in the face of the demand to speak (see Muldoon 2001: 43; cf. Dossa 2003: 60). Sensuous experiences and responses incorporate language, voice and meaning in the body in a way that does not succumb to sovereign practices and politics. This turns the body into a wound within the state, which struggles to identify, locate and categorise the body according to its own practices. The senses and sensuous articulations can provide a means for asylum seekers to disrupt and resist the sovereign politics at work, if there is no way to speak in-difference to the state or resist being framed by its logic.

Asad's reflection on how the past, present and unforeseeable future intertwine in his body represents an empirical example of how the body can be seen as a sense in action. For Nancy, the body gains its meaning and appears *as* a determinate body only in relation to something else. Through the limit, both identity and difference are constituted. In the Nancian sense, meaning, claims Diane Perpich (2005), is not intentional, as in based on the intention of a subject, but rather created through a network, a circulation, of contacts and touches. This was brought to the fore in Asad's case. The asylum-seeking body proliferates the meanings of politics as it resonates to and circulates those meanings that have been attached to it through sovereign practices. A multiplicity of potential political spaces open through Asad's body. Hence, senses can refer us to others, make us share "our naked existence" (Nancy 1990: 48). A focus on the expressive and sensuous body brings forward a register of various affects, gestures and silent languages of pain and compassion. In a way, the asylum-seeking body, no matter its administrative status, is not only wounded by politics or sovereign practices, but also a wound within the international itself. These bodies mark the failure of the principle of sovereignty to unambiguously organise relations between states and to build a code of conduct between various actors. Could sensuous articulations of experienced vulnerability, marginalisation and discrimination be thought of as politically interpretable action that challenges our knowledge of the ways identities and belongings are articulated and formed?

Making sense of the senses and sentiment

Trauma experienced in the past can also remain a part of and be carried with the body (see Das 1998; Väyrynen 2013; Väyrynen & Puumala 2015). It can affect perception of the present, and sometimes asylum seekers exhibit similar habits and fears to those that were present in their lives before leaving:

> I remember one day, when I said to myself "today's the last day that you are in the war." There was this man who kept talking to me. I told him that I only wanted to take the bus. He said that "you can't take the bus, if you take the bus, I will kill you." I asked "why? I don't have any money, why do you . . . what do you need from me?" When I get up in the morning, I remember all these things. Once I went to buy something, not far from where I lived, and I saw a militia man with a gun. I started to run and he came after me. I asked him, if he wanted to kill me. I remember such things from my past. Here I imagine crawling under a piece of furniture to cover, to hide from him so that he couldn't see me. But then I get up and tell myself that "you're now in Finland, not Somalia, you don't need to hide." But you don't just forget these things. You still think about them, they are with you for you to remember.
>
> (Interview with Ayan, October 2006)

Because of her memories from Somalia, Ayan described fearing that somebody might break into her room and threaten her. She also told of having a feeling that somebody was following her in the street in Finland, which made her rush to her room and hide under the table or bed. She also talked of imagining where to hide if such a situation ever came about and then having to remind herself that in Finland she was safe. Edward Said (2000) has theorised this similarity of habits being an unavoidable by-product of being out of place (see also Huynh 2010).

In the politico-corporeal struggle of seeking asylum, suffering, loss and pain are understood to result from and be shaped by contact with others (cf. Honkasalo

146 *Sensuous politics, political sentiments*

1998: 38–40). For asylum seekers, formal channels of political representation are not available, so informal and expressive forms of resistance and engagement are important ways of making oneself heard and making one's presence felt (see Ross 2010: 124). The sensuous and emotive body, in other words, seeks to reassume and reorganise its relations to others by turning into an "active agent of meaning-giving" (see Honkasalo 1998: 41). Sensuous responses and contacts communicate in various ways the possible meanings of leading a political life and the contours of political life within the international (see Herlihy & Turner 2006; Panagia 2009). In my interviews, asylum seekers have mentioned how various senses could either mediate or aggravate their sense of being out of place. For Adan, the smell after it had rained evoked memories from her home country: "After the rain, especially in the mornings when it has rained during the night, it smells the same as in Somalia". Adan told me that she quite liked the smell, as it made her feel that she was in Somalia again. For Soran, on the other hand, the odours of the reception centre caused repulsion. In saying "there are no voices here. Life does not have a good taste", Abubakar pointed out the lack of normal voices of life in the reception centre, which caused him to feel isolated, whereas Benjamin felt that music played an important role in bridging his former life with his present condition in the detention unit. Physical touch can be made sterile, which can be interpreted as a sign of impurity or signalling contamination, as in Benaz's case (see Chapter 4). Senses, thus, mediate our being in the world and our perception thereof.

Sensuous perceptions are only one manifestation of how the experience of seeking asylum is made sense of. Emotional outbursts can also evoke a sense of exposure. Thus, my interviewee laughing or crying during our talk, or telling of having done so in a certain context, is a radical manifestation of the connection between senses, body and politics. Both, although in different manners, are gestures that put whomever witnesses them, to quote Carrie Noland (2009: 205, my emphasis), "in contact with a *prepersonal* motor system that is invisible to the colonizer's gaze". Sensations and their manifestations suggest awareness of the limitations of the body as well as of the possibility which the body in itself is. The self is not a stable and sovereign entity, but an inherently – ontologically – relational process that escapes substantial identifications. Through the senses, asylum seekers insist on witnessing what sovereign practices and politics feel like, what those practices mean to them and what the sovereign imaginary requires from them. In projecting the senses and using them in articulating themselves, asylum seekers also try to make sense of what happens. Sometimes this means an attempt to make sense of what seems senseless. This process of sensing and making sense of the senses represents the body as a space of the political within which meanings of politics and policies are conferred within the international.

Sense-making does not necessarily have anything to do with rationalisation. It refers to an understanding of how things matter in people's lives, not simply what they mean. It stems from language never being an exhaustive or even an adequate substitute for the vitality of the body and its forms of articulation. In his analysis of self-harm, Pugliese (2004: 27) has argued that even when the voices of asylum

Sensuous politics, political sentiments 147

seekers are inserted within networks of communication, their subalternity is not superseded. He argues that tears in the flesh are asylum seekers' way of speaking otherwise in the face of the other's refusal to listen and bear witness. Self-harm, in Pugliese's interpretation, becomes a corporeal form of poetics in which the liminal body and the frame of interpretation of the contours of political life are transformed. In a similar vein, the senses, when understood as ways of articulation and meaning-making, connect the person to the community and political structures. Sensuous experiences and responses communicate the person being situated in community, or perhaps even coming into being in community (see also Reischer & Koo 2004; Tabar 2007: 19).

Asylum seekers are usually very well aware of political realities and discourses, or quite quickly become so. They are far from being ignorant of what goes on in the world. Rather, their bodies as such resonate closely with politics. The ways in which people seek to cope with and make sense of what happens take shape through the body either corporeally or by projecting experienced injustices and frustrations to others. The politics of the body takes form as a corporeal expression of one's vulnerability, exposure. It does not openly seek to advocate a change in sovereign politics or practices, but articulates a human response to extreme senses of loss, hopelessness and frustration that are aggravated by waiting and constant uncertainty about one's own well-being and that of those left in one's home country. Expressively, these acts are sometimes quite clear, but yet extremely difficult to engage with institutionally or personally.

> Two days ago one young Afghan man had made a suicide attempt in the reception centre. He had laid down in the middle of the street in front of the centre with a note taped on his chest saying that "it's better to die quickly than to die little by little." The February weather was bad and it was already getting dark outside, which meant that visibility was extremely poor. It would have been very difficult for the drivers to notice him in time. An accident was avoided, because a passer-by had come to inform the staff about what was going on. They had taken the man back inside the centre, from where he was sent to hospital. There, however he had taken an overdose of Marevan, a warfarin-based anticoagulant. (Warfarin was originally introduced as a pesticide to control rats and mice and causes death by internal bleeding due to decreased coagulation.) In the end, the person was committed to psychiatric treatment in a mental hospital.
>
> (Research diary, 1st March 2007)

Pugliese (2004: 28) has claimed that self-harm is a means for asylum seekers to reclaim and resignify their exilic bodies. In my interpretation, self-harm is not only about expelling an identity and position that one is not willing to accept, but also a way of articulating togetherness controversially through evoking the potentiality and prospect of death. In the politics of the body, gestures and the articulation of sense replace language (see Hewitt 1997). The body represents a sensuous site of political and communal exchange. Sensuous articulations have

148 *Sensuous politics, political sentiments*

the potential to question the boundaries of what it means "to live together, to live apart, to belong, to communicate, to exclude" (Manning 2007: 9). Thus, the various ways in which the person seeks to make sense of what is happening and of resulting sensuous reactions can be interpreted as efforts to relate one's being and body politically to the world or to reorganise and reassume one's relations with others (see Schildkrout 2004). The waiting that characterises the lives of asylum seekers feels endless and meaningless – it can be given no other attributes besides those senses and as such it escapes reason and the verbal realm.

Sensuous articulations of the experienced effects of waiting and uncertainty make use of the body as something that is always in the making: constructed, deconstructed and reconstructed incessantly in relation to others and through relations with others. The asylum-seeking body can make its presence sensed, although it cannot change the situation it is in. In the following three sections, I will further elaborate on that thought through thematic examples that focus on common sensations and sensuous reactions to sovereign practices.

Sensuous protests

> The [Finnish] government is just ignoring everything. And I received this rejection. They said that the district where I came from is safe and that I can return. And, I wondered. I said, where the hell did I talk about the place being safe or unsafe? I never talked about it being unsafe. I don't care, if it's safe or unsafe. It is not safe *for me. I* have problems there. I never mentioned this, this, this issue. *I have talked to you about my problems! And you are telling me it is safe! Who the hell cares!?* I will talk to you for hours, for *days*, if you understand reason and if you understand logic. They (the officials) don't even think for a second that they could be wrong. They have this prejudice against us that we are lying and they're always right. If they could think as educated persons, that he or she could also be incorrect in her judgements, in his judgements, or that *we* could also be right. That we could also be telling the truth. It is not that always we are wrong, and that always they are right.
>
> (Interview with Nasir, March 2007)

The interview with me became a means for Nasir to question the asylum determination process and the interpretations that the officials had made about his asylum interview. Nasir transforms the line of argumentation in the process and makes it his own. The discrepancy between the two viewpoints becomes clear from the beginning of Nasir's account. He is ready to admit that the district where he came from may be safe from a general perspective, stating that he has never claimed that the region in itself was unsafe. Yet, he counters the interpretation that he could return and points out that it is not safe *for him*. Nasir's voice manifests a shift from the realm of truth to the realm of meaning and sensuous experience: from what it is generally like in a particular region to what it means for a person to live there. Nasir's account of the everyday in Afghanistan is based on local colour, which does not equate with the view that the Finnish asylum officials have adopted based

Sensuous politics, political sentiments   149

on the information available to them. Nasir's feelings are especially negative if he is made to think about his return to and future in Afghanistan. To understand what happens in the interview it is necessary to move from Nasir's account (what he says) to his voice (the relations he evokes and addresses).

Nasir is angry, and anger gives rise to his agency. The anger and frustration that asylum seekers go through tends to be directed at everything that makes their story or their identity as asylum seekers politically possible (cf. Ahmed 2004: 38). This notion counters the often-presented view that anger is an irrational force that obstructs, annihilates or negates political agency (Dugan & Reger 2006: 470; cf. however Marcus, Neuman & Mackuen 2000; Ross 2010). According to Andrew Ross (2010: 116), there is a variety of affective processes involved in the politics of protest. Anger and discontent may be the most common emotions that have been expressed in my interviews. Anger is a commentary on the relations and identities that have been constructed during and through the asylum determination process and other daily sovereign practices. As such, anger manifests hopes, fears and grievances. If we, however, take anger to be focused on a unified object, we miss its force (Ross 2010: 117). It is crucial that we learn to hear the anger of others without turning it into defensiveness of our own positions (Ahmed 2004: 178). This is not easy, as asylum seekers' anger exposes the limits of our being and the vulnerability of the foundations of what we regard as knowledge.

Anger is an extremely political sentiment that is, however, neglected in its philosophical mode. It is also the prime sentiment of resistance (see Abu-Lughod 1985: 251–252). Besides the interpretation that the Finnish officials have made, Nasir's anger is directed towards the instrumentalisation of the human body in sovereign politics. Nasir's anger carries traces of earlier experiences of injustice, which then intertwine with vulnerability, a sense of alienation and powerlessness (see also Chapter 1). It is easier to understand anger as a communicative position if the profound experience of distrust towards the officers and the asylum determination process, together with people's concern for their lives, are kept in mind (cf. Ross 2010: 120). Nasir's anger spells out emotional connections and relationalities that for him are inadmissible and intolerable. He refuses and resists the interpretation made and the logic upon which the process has been built and thus also a particular way of constructing political communities. This refusal and resistance is a step that, for Nancy (1992: 375), goes "beyond all that can be accomplished reasonably – in order to open possible paths for a new negotiation of the reasonable but also paths of an uncompromising vigilance". Nancy posits that without anger, politics and communities created through sovereign practices would be nothing but accommodation and trade in influence. Nasir was not willing to accommodate the view of and decision made by the Finnish authorities.

Emotional and sensuous ways of evoking exposure and articulation are normatively complex, which brings me back to Soran (see Chapter 1 and Event 2). In looking for a target for his anger, Soran actively engaged with and responded to various others all at once (cf. McCarthy, Sullivan & Wright 2006: 433). In terms of sovereign practices, his story represents how the policing act of taking the

150   *Sensuous politics, political sentiments*

asylum seeker's fingerprints turns into a corporeality, which again initiates certain emotional, fluid and open-ended relations between bodies, places and practices:

> I meet Soran when I enter the staff office. He has come to ask Lumi, a counsellor, to write a note stating that he would like to cancel his asylum application in Finland and leave the country.
>
> He looks tired, fed up, and frustrated.
>
> Soran wants to know if his fingerprints will be deleted from the Eurodac-system when he leaves. Lumi tells him that this is not the case, the prints will stay.
>
> "Why?" he wants to know. He repeats time and again to me that he is going to leave Finland and "go to Europe." For him "Finland is not Europe. The Finns do not think. I don't want to be here, I will leave."
>
> [He has burnt the back of his hand with a cigarette, and while we are talking, he keeps picking the spot:
>
> pink flesh in the middle and burned skin around the edges.]
>
> I ask if he has a particular place in mind.
>
> "Sweden."
>
> I ask whether he is aware of the fact that Finland, Sweden and a good number of other European countries have agreed to share the prints. This means that people are returned to the country where they first arrived. I contend that he must know about those people in the centre who live there for some weeks after which they leave – or disappear. I explain that some of them have been returned to other countries, but that many of them are people like him; people who have wanted to go and live in another country, but that is just not possible as an asylum seeker in the EU.
>
> He gets increasingly frustrated.
>
> (Research diary, 19th October 2006)

Soran had received his first temporary residence permit some months before our discussion because his return could not be enforced. The constant waiting and uncertainty that pertained to his status had started to weigh on him. Soran wanted to find a way out of the liminal state he was in and, as that could not be done in Finland, he had decided to leave. For Manning (2007: 49: also Wall 2008), making a decision marks a moment of reaching-out, while the political represents an instance of decision that engages one towards the world and an other. Soran's decision represents an event of the political, where he reaches out to others and seeks to force a response. At the same time, his decision engages him towards others and other possible futures elsewhere. During our discussion about the Dublin Convention, the Eurodac system, the Common European Asylum system and the restrictions pertaining to his temporary status, he got frustrated with me as well as the situation he found himself in. Feelings of frustration, anger and disillusionment affect Soran's reading of the present and his relation to his surroundings. They had made him resort to the 'culture' of self-harm prevalent among asylum seekers, and his pain was open for all to see. He had moved it from within to the

Sensuous politics, political sentiments   151

public sphere. His body exposed the hurt and pain that sovereign politics cause, and his wish to feel something caused Soran to keep the wound open.

Soran opposed the reading of his presence in the Finnish society and acted accordingly. Ahmed (2004: 174–175) claims that "being against something is dependent on how one reads what one is against". This reading affects not only the perceived space within which one can act and articulate oneself, but also the forms of action and expression. To an extent, like with Nasir, anger was also Soran's action: he felt that he was against the Finnish and European system, society, people and at least momentarily me, but he had not yet discovered what he was for. This inarticulateness could not be turned into 'positive' action – that is, campaigning for something – and it had not made him withdraw into himself. In expressing his anger, Soran tried to translate his frustration to me. He attempted to participate in the discourse that had immobilised his body, but on his own sensuous and emotive terms. Soran's presence intensified in our coming together, and the resentment he felt towards his situation and surroundings evoked a demand for relationality, potentiality and "response-ability" (Sullivan 2001: 103).

During our conversation, Soran accused me of not knowing anything, since life had always been easy for me – "When ever has it been difficult?" He addressed me as a white, middle-class woman who could stay comfortably rooted within society and the kind of familial institutions that are accepted within it, and not be truly bothered with the troubles of the world. Although Soran presented an understanding of our beings (political identities) being related, he pointed out that they were not mutually exposed. The interpretation is possible because the conception of voice on which my writing relies suggests that it is not enough to study what is actually said; the wider context in which something becomes said ought to be entertained. Soran's protest thus discloses the effects of the multiple demarcated axes of power that are at work in the struggle of seeking asylum.

In order to allow space for the voice and articulations of the marginalised body to appear, it is necessary to take the senses – both as actual feelings and sensations and as attempts to understand what happens – into account. Soran manifested political existence as being always situated in a body that has lived and moved through borders and categories, as well as it happening between bodies. What Soran actually said, and whether it was true, is not under estimation. What makes the discussion interesting is the way in which our voices intertwine and form responses to one another, which makes it possible to think of them as an event of exposure where both parties look for a ground on which a meeting would be possible.

"I have been to Greece, where I lived with two other people, and before that I was in Italy. In Italy they took my prints, but nobody found them here."

Soran's ideas about living in Italy and Greece are ultra-positive.
There everything was good, whereas here everything is bad.
He says that any place would be better than Finland.

152 *Sensuous politics, political sentiments*

He would maybe like to go to Iceland,
his friend told him that there they don't take the prints. Or then to Canada. [. . .]
I ask Soran if he then has thought about going back to Kurdistan to live with
his family. He starts thinking about that. I ask if he misses his family, and
he looks at me bewilderedly, as if he didn't understand my question. "No, I
don't, I haven't lived with my parents in Kurdistan for a long time. I lived
with my aunt, who didn't have a husband or children. Why would I miss my
parents?"
He tells me that he has decided to leave, and I still say that he should think.
Go some place outside the centre, calm down and think.

He says that he is still going to leave, but what if he buys an expensive ticket
and then is returned to Finland?

(Research diary, 19th October 2006)

Soran's voice built connections and relations between different bodies when
responding to my voice and European asylum politics. His original intention to
leave Finland after cancelling his asylum claim signaled an attempt to take charge
of his future and move on in his search for a better life and more promising pros-
pects. Any desirable path of action proves to be beyond his reach, because his
fingerprints have been filed in the Eurodac system. As a result, Soran could not
direct his actions towards a goal, but was left hovering between different choices,
which all seemed equally undesirable. He began to grasp the grip of politics on his
body through my presence (see Sullivan & McCarthy 2004: 295). Soran voiced a
frustrated, undetermined form of agency, which sought to create a sonorous meeting point or a speaking position rather than advocate for a single cause. As Sullivan and McCarthy (2004: 306–307) have put it, activity can be expressed through
weighing up alternative possibilities and committing to one over the other. Soran
articulated himself as a political being through actively pondering his potential for
action through movement. Simultaneously, as our voices intersected, they created
politico-corporeal conjunctures of responsibility and relationality within the international. (Also Puumala 2013.)

A Nancian stance on voice actually designates nothing but the interval. Central
to Nancy's idea of togetherness – with-being – is that existence, which is always
plural, takes place in an interval (Derrida 2005: 111–130; Heikkilä 2007: 15).
The interval is the space between us which makes the notion of 'us' possible in
the first place. It signifies access to 'together' or 'in-common' as the reality of
our being, even though this reality is inaccessible as such (Nancy 1993a: 318).
All being is being towards something, which means that sense emerges out of
relations between us (Heikkilä 2007: 76; cf. Nancy 2004a: 9–10, 27–28, 1998).
In questioning the logic and rationale of their position in Finland, both Soran
and Nasir sought a way out of the relational framework that sovereign practices
had bestowed on their bodies through the asylum determination process. Yet, the
frustated voices and articulations spurred by anger are no more Soran's or Nasir's

Sensuous politics, political sentiments   153

than mine. They were built together through sharing, which emphasises the connectedness between those who can have a part in the territorial political community and those who cannot. Treating either one of these bodies as singular or in separation from others can never result in a compelling and comprehensive picture of political existence, its preconditions and its shadow practices. The senses of the international emerge out of relations between bodies.

A shared sense of vulnerability

In a strange way, hope and hopelessness intertwine tightly in asylum seekers' lives at many points of the experience, from the reasons for leaving and travel to waiting. Because distress, anguish and hopelessness penetrate the experience of seeking asylum so thoroughly, they cannot be ignored when studying the lives of asylum seekers. For me, they presented both the demand and a means to try to understand intimately and concretely what the politics that begins and ends with the body entails.

Even if I bring hopelessness within a framework where the body in pain and under distress is a site of radical political relationality and proliferation, it needs to be stressed that the human suffering is very real. We cannot lose sight of this, but yet the asylum seeking body should not be reduced to medicalised, individualised or marginal positions, simplistically victimising the whole condition. Rather, it is necessary to think about the complex relation between acting and being acted upon, so as to make stories of hope and hopelessness understandable in terms of corporeal, sensuous politics. An understanding of politics that is responsive to sense and touch involves centring relationalities as they take place in and through the sensuous body.

> Nasren goes through her papers and tries to explain to me how the decision on their case is flawed. She does not understand – is not ready to accept – the reasons stated by the officials. As her English is limited, she goes to ask a friend of hers to interpret. Nasren wants to know how she can reverse the decision they got, because she is not willing to return to France. She asks me to contact the police or the Immigration Service for her, but I have to explain that she needs to proceed through her lawyer. Nasren expresses her discontent with the lawyer and phones him. When he replies, Nasren passes the phone to me and asks me to talk.
>
> I introduce myself and explain that Nasren is feeling quite anxious at the moment and wishes to find out what her options are. The lawyer listens and explains the situation: that the family will be returned, most likely, in a couple of weeks. Then he contends: "I have spent hours discussing with them, nothing seems to go through. I have tried to clarify to them what is going on, why things are like this and what their options are. To no avail. I wonder if that is caused by stress. That they are experiencing so much stress that they cannot take anything in."

154 *Sensuous politics, political sentiments*

After I hang up, I explain in English what the lawyer said. Nasren's friend translates this into Arabic. "No. I'm sure he could do more, but he does not want to," Nasren replies. Again she makes a plea to me, but I tell her that there is not much I could do. In case they really want to change the lawyer, I could ask if there is a person who would be willing to take their case and if s/he feels that there is indeed something that could be done. I could also help them explain the need to change the lawyer to the staff from the centre, but I point out that they themselves need to go and ask for this. (For doing just this, I was reproached later on by the director of the centre, who felt that I was interfering in the process.)

"Perhaps," Nasren ponders, "they will not return us now as I'm pregnant. Perhaps, the baby will change things. Or, perhaps the lawyer will have found a way to help us by the time the baby has come and we could have our case investigated here."

(Research diary, 30th October 2013)

In Nasren's case (see also Event 1 and Chapter 4), it is possible to gain a sense of how the experienced ambiguity that concerns the logic of the asylum determination process is a source of hope. The uncertainty related to the process pertains to the arrival of the decision, the result of a complaint or the exact time when returning will happen. All this makes the process emotionally harder for the asylum seeker, because any uncertainty evokes a sense of hope. However, that hope can turn abruptly and easily into despair. For me, Nasren's situation and the discussions I had with different parties – her interpreting friend, lawyers, staff from the reception centre, solidarity networks – around situations such as hers opened up a sense of space where familiar became unfamiliar, hope turned into despair and vice versa.

In Nasren's story, places, travels and movements lost their 'objective' referents and turned into bodily senses and experiences; Nasren's response to her situation was affective. When that what has happened and what the person expects or fears will happen is felt concretely on and through the body, it becomes impossible to articulate oneself clearly. As Nasren sought to articulate the senses of sovereign practices from her perspective, and the sentiments that they engendered in her, she used her gendered body as a hermeneutical place (see also Kearney 2015). She sought to expose a sense of vulnerability in whomever listened to and witnessed her story. I, for instance, could rather easily understand her worry for her children, being myself a mother to a child the same age as Sahar, Nasren's daughter (see Event 1). Exposure, in communicating the situation through the senses, can evoke a shared sense of how that what happens or could happen matters for the person and how a similar situation might matter for ourselves.

Expressions of one's own vulnerability, fear and despair gesture reaching because they invite the other to ponder one's own complicity in the setting. Sensuous articulations communicate ontological, and not only epistemological, exposure and sharing, which seek to make it difficult to hold on to our learned positions and foundations of our identities (see also Dossa 2003; Morris 2009).

Sensuous politics, political sentiments 155

Most often, vulnerability, helplessness and passivity are considered human qualities, but ones that are not a part of a proper agent, who must be rational, responsible for his or her self and actions and in charge of his or her life (see Meyer & Jepperson 2000: 107). Inarguably, the asylum-seeking body is produced and governed through multiple sovereign practices. Yet, the liminal or marginal body of an asylum seeker is ontologically equipped with a variety of dispositions, capacities and potentialities that allow for agency and proliferate the space of politics (see also Vaittinen 2015). The vulnerable body is also productive of relations and engagements that challenge or exceed the sovereign imaginary and illustrate the necessity of thinking about how that proliferation matters with respect to political life and its contours.

The pressure that the applicants feel during the asylum determination process as a whole, not simply in the actual interview, has come up time and again in my fieldwork over the years. It results in a feeling and fear of becoming crazy and losing one's mind. And, in time, the stress can cause psychosomatic symptoms, which are reflected in the body in multiple ways. The symptoms are treated and the person medicated so as to alleviate the experienced pressure, which feels overwhelming. This, in turn, can lead to the abuse of prescribed medicine, which has been the most pre-eminent form of self-harm among my research participants. Vulnerability, and the way it is expressed through the body and how it enters into bodies, represents a part of the politics of the body. These sentiments and discomfort are caused by the body's exposure to others. Because we need to acknowledge our own complicity, it is not possible to focus exclusively on the condition of seeking asylum or the experiences of asylum seekers in research on the topic. The question of seeking asylum is inseparable from the question of citizenship. And, furthermore, both of these questions are inseparable from the wider politico-philosophical question of community. Asylum seekers relate their position to others and articulate their being in relation to others:

> In jail . . . No, it's never good. To be in jail. And I haven't done anything wrong, I am an asylum seeker. [. . .] But to put me in jail, after you told me that you don't give it to me. You cheat me. [pause] It's a cheat. [. . .] You know, I pity myself. [. . .] This place reminds me all the time of my story: why I left, why I can't see the natural sun and talk to people as I used to do. I really live like in a cage. I don't like it. [. . .] So, it worries me that although I am not a criminal, I'm living, you know, in a place whereby they regard you as somehow different.
>
> (Interview with Benjamin, June 2007)

The difficulties in rendering the determination process and daily experiences intelligible give shape to Benjamin's melancholic contemplations. It is not a new idea to connect migratory movements with melancholy. The idea is rooted in an understanding according to which migrants both challenge and are challenged by what 'we' think a good and happy community is (see Ahmed 2010). The idea of the subject that is based on the principle of sovereignty suggests that identifying

156 *Sensuous politics, political sentiments*

with a nation makes people individuals and gives them a place of reference from which to act (see Ahmed 2010: 137; Walker 2009). Taking after Ahmed (2010: 138), migrants become melancholic figures, who either refuse or are not allowed to play a part in "the national game" (Ahmed 2010: 142). In Benjamin's case, that experience is articulated as a feeling of being cheated. As a sensuous experience, melancholy is often connected to radical ambivalence or ambiguity of the political experience (see also Agamben 1993: 20; Žižek 2000: 658–660). Sensuous responses to and experiences of those practices through which sovereignty is enacted in the field of seeking asylum turn the body into a "melancholic translational space" (Tate 2007: 10) within which meanings of politics, the body and political existence are negotiated.

Benjamin's melancholic contemplations were directed towards a future that was unattainable, a past that was irrecoverably gone and his surroundings in the detention centre. For Benjamin, being detained was to some extent an inarticulate, although profoundly sensuous, experience (see Butler 2003b: 467; Lash 1998: 157–159; Tabar 2007: 23). The ambivalence and ambiguity that characterise melancholy escape verbal expression and require bodily translation if they are to be communicated. In Benjamin's story, melancholy is articulated as a type of longing and sadness that is related to the body's capacities and condition. Melancholy, then, becomes understandable as a form of incorporation, while melancholic articulations indicate the creative and inherently political ways in which the body seeks to communicate and convey loss (see Nancy 2003b: 82–86; Tabar 2007: 6; Tate 2007: 11). The way in which Benjamin utilises melancholy to translate difference, rupture and exclusion gives rise to his agency and positions his existence politically.

Benjamin's account could be also understood to evoke an event of the political. When he described the experienced effects of detention, he actually offered the potential to understand how the boundaries of the social and communal are instituted and maintained (see also Butler 1997: 167). That what cannot be taken or accepted as a part of one's being and body, the inassimilable, becomes a site of melancholic critical agency (Tate 2007: 4). Benjamin does not protest against a particular practice or demand a change, but points out that he does not accept the way in which the Finnish state responds to his body. Melancholic articulations are not manifest in asylum seekers as merely conveying a sense of loss and sadness to others or as a critique of sovereign practices. Moments when engagement beyond the status seems impossible are also instances for melancholic expressions, which then take form as withdrawals from others.

Forms of agency and expression that arise from the condition of seeking asylum bear a trace of loss: loss of family, self-image, future or control. Benjamin's metaphor of living in a cage illustrates the experience of being cut off from the political community, from others. Detention in particular violates one's possibilities of engaging with others. Perhaps melancholy represents a refusal to incorporate the image of oneself conveyed through sovereign practices. It originates from hopelessness and the perceived lack of meaning in the asylum determination process, which frames melancholy in terms of limits. Scott Lash (1998: 159) has

Sensuous politics, political sentiments 157

termed melancholy a politics of the "outcasts" and "wild zones" and, furthermore, one of innovation. Melancholic articulations politicise the space of the present, expose the asylum seeker's body through introvertion and inarticulation. Melancholy became the relation that Benjamin adopted towards the Finnish society. As such, it formed a corporeal way of making sense of the world and the political organisation thereof.

Melancholy can open up potentialities for solidarity and relationality, as it exposes a sense of multiple forms of belongings that are based on more inclusive identities and community (see also Tabar 2007: 12). The attempts to communicate melancholy and vulnerability, and the ways in which these sensuous experiences enter into the body, represent an invitation to think about the contours of political life. Engaging with them can help us understand the political dynamics that are enacted whenever we address others as representatives of categorical identities.

Corporeal refusals and aversion

> "You know we Muslims believe that our faith is in Allah's hands. . . . But I would like me and my family to live in happiness and safety. I do not expect anything great, just normal life and small things. But my brain and heart will be fixed only, if something changes for the better in my life." Abdi feels frustrated that his hardship has not ended, but just differs in kind. "I am not thinking about death, but looking for a life. Everybody dies. . . . But when alive, you need a life."
>
> (Interview with Abdi, August 2006)

Abdi's story brings together two aspects of seeking asylum. His story resonates first with the production of refugee populations, and second with the produced statuses becoming lived. Abdi tried to negotiate with the sensuous effects of his condition, but still felt that it had severed his brain and heart. He protested against the positioning of his body by pointing out that "when alive, you need a life". The waiting and uncertainty that characterised his present day had put his life on hold, which limited the scope of his actions and resulted in a loss of morale. Abdi's represents a case where the body's weight becomes too great to be supported. The political imaginaries inscribed on the body – the reasons for leaving one's country, the hardships experienced during travel and after arrival – cannot be accommodated in or taken as a part of the body, but yet their effects seem too overwhelming to be actively countered. This understanding paves the way towards seeing the political in passivity and numbness.

Not all forms of sensuous articulation that asylum seekers enact are resistance or protest against asylum politics and sovereign practices. Partly, they represent a wish to numb oneself to the effects of politics as they are sensed on the body, and through numbness escape the grip of this politics (cf. Pugliese 2004: 29; Tatman 1998: 29–30; Turp 2007: 240). Omar, who sought to convince Soran that not everyone in Finland hated them (Chapter 4), was treated in a hospital for stress-related chest pain shortly after our discussion. His optimism, perhaps an attempt

158 *Sensuous politics, political sentiments*

to convince himself as much as Soran that their situation was not hopeless, gradually transformed into passivity and apathy:

> Omar's situation is discussed at the staff's coffee meeting. He has skipped school for two weeks, and his teacher has contacted the reception centre expressing her worry. Omar has seen a psychiatrist and discussed with him about a traumatising memory that now will not leave his mind. He was prescribed medicine for this. Omar, however, constantly overdoses the pills, which makes him passive and apathetic. He has told the staff and the nurse that he is aware of the problem, but the medicine makes him feel good, or not feel anything at all.
>
> (Research diary, 31st October 2006)

It is often claimed that asylum seekers wish to be included in or integrate with the receiving society. However, I am not quite certain that this wish for inclusion is all there is to it. Perhaps sensuous articulations, especially when these articulations do not openly and explicitly strive towards or protest for any kind of change, present a more profound philosophical demand. This demand concerns the foundations of political belonging and necessitates that the condition of seeking asylum is fathomed under different lines than hospitality. Nobody wishes to be(come) an asylum seeker, and integration may not be easy either.

As Omar's case demonstrates, the asylum seeker's body is not a clean slate; politics enters into, transforms and is sensed on the body in multiple ways and with complex consequences. These consequences are reflected in how the body directs itself and the responses it forms to others. If the pressure caused by the asylum determination process, combined with traumatic and painful memories from the past, is felt so intensely that it is best to feel nothing at all, it is meaningful to discuss political existence in terms of the senses. Passivity, as noted above with Omar's example, can result from self-harm in the form of drug abuse. It can result from melancholy and loss of hope, when there is no will to try, nothing more to say or no accurate words to express oneself. Acts of self-harm threaten the binary opposition between inside and outside, public and politics, and thus expose the body as a site upon which trauma, politics and their meanings are negotiated (see Oliver 2010: 119, 126). Even when passive, the body gestures through withdrawal.

Omar's case, together with the total loss of morale that Abdi described feeling, enable the examination of passivity and numbness as corporeal refusals that are politically significant (see also Pugliese 2004: 32). Acts of closure represent psychic reactions to trauma and traumatising conditions. They are strategies of survival in the face of past violence and the institutional violence of exclusion and marginalisation experienced on a daily basis. It has been noted that asylum seekers' structural exclusion gives rise to experiences of suffering, which concern isolation from others and the lack of possibilities for work, education and other forms of social engagement (see Dossa 2003: 55; Hewitt 1997: 120). Missing normalcy is felt thoroughly and complicated even further by the intertwining of multiple elements of violence and abuse.

Sensuous politics, political sentiments 159

As the person's status as an asylum seeker is thought to be temporary, the waiting that characterises it has not been systematically problematised, at least in a way that alternatives would have been actively sought. During the asylum determination process, asylum seekers are in a way cut off from both the past and future, which leaves them unambiguously residing in a lacking present, with no promise of a (better) tomorrow. The relations of the body to both directions of time have been broken, and the status quite effectively breaks the person's means to establish relations in the present through direct participation and engagement with others. In practice, the effects of the wait are concretely sensed and the body invokes multiple forms of agency, which develop an aversive relation to the reality which it inhabits (see also Chapter 4). Gestures transform the body that performs them (see Noland 2009: 212).

Asylum seekers' passive bodies articulate withdrawal and refusal. They express passivity in relation to something and as a commentary on political connections and daily realities (see Nancy 1993a: 27). Passivity is not in Nancian thought an opposite of activity, because neither is "of the individual". They are dimensions of our corporeal exposure to the world. Passivity does not necessarily represent a relapse or isolation, which would imply simple victimity (see also Grimwood 2004: 62–64). It comments on the politics that regulates speech and acts. Furthermore, it goes against conceptualising the state as a closed and consistent space where political existence and agency are mostly written in terms of the citizen. I am tempted to fathom passivity as an affective and sensuous bond which reaches beyond the imaginary provided by the sovereign state and the political community within. The passive body refuses to think in line with sovereignty and instead acts in-difference to it. Passivity does not need to represent incapacity to act, but is perhaps a stance that emphasises that the body escapes knowledge; it can neither be known, nor can it know, and yet it is not ignorant of its surroundings and the power that operates on it. Politics and practices that refuse to engage with this thought will leave both asylum seekers and citizens equally unhappy about the responses that are created in the field of asylum. The passive and apathetic asylum seeker remains unintelligible from the perspective of the state, and from the point of view of the asylum seeker, the enacted policies are sensed only as further violations that limit the body's possibilities for self-control.

Like other forms of sensuous articulations, passivity involves a reading of contact (see Ahmed 2004: 8). It is important to consider the conditions of appearance that affect the ways of articulation and the forming of a position from which one's presence and views can be articulated. In the face of being closed into a mezzanine space of sovereignty (Nyers 2003: 1080), asylum seekers' passivity signals the proliferation of the space of politics just because it resists a similar closure to the one with which the body struggles. It cannot be denied that passivity can be fathomed as depoliticising, medicalising and imposing further victimity on the body. Importantly, however, it cannot be completely verbalised and brought within the sphere of sovereign rule. Although it is utterly sensuous, passivity remains senseless because it escapes thinking and reason. In this sense, it exposes

160 *Sensuous politics, political sentiments*

those who witness it to the finiteness of their own being. Passivity centralises the body: the fragile, vulnerable and exposed body and the interval between bodies.

Expressions of corporeal refusals and aversion to the present can be taken to express asylum seekers' hope for another kind of world, one that is unimaginable at the moment. This unimaginability, and the uncertainty of a change in one's life, is not easy to bear. There is nothing towards which to strive, only a profound sense of injustice and distress. This, together with spatial liminality, can lead to forms of articulation that are thought to move asylum seekers beyond politics, leaving them without political agency. Sensuous articulations direct the body towards others in that they raise a different relationality. They sum up the "ambiguity between resistance and complicity" (Farber 2006: 249), expressing political action even in the face of exhaustion and despair. As far as these acts and conditions are understood to express grief, distress and the pain caused by politics, they suggest a critical engagement with and relation to sovereign practices (cf. Schick 2010). Sensuous articulations are events of "flesh becoming mirror" (Nancy 2010; also Farber 2006: 247–249). Through such articulations, asylum seekers can be interpreted as reflecting the representation of themselves in the eyes of another. Everything in the body exposes itself, and thus, instead of isolation, senses articulate the relatedness and ontological similarity between bodies.

Senses form a prominent aspect in the study of exposure, as they are largely beyond control. The inability to regulate the senses offers potential for reaching beyond words (see Manning 2007: 86). This inability also points towards an understanding that senses and the events through which the meanings of local color are negotiated are not intentional. The experiencing person, like Omar, does not have control over that what happens, as sometimes events escape rationalisation. A focus on senses and sentiments move us away from the verbal realm, as they cannot be captured linguistically (see also Manning 2007: 20). This focus offers a way to approach the body as intelligible and articulate, although not necessarily verbal. Conceptually, this means that it is no longer possible to differentiate between a biological, political or individual body (cf. Ahmed & Stacey 2001; Van Wolputte 2004: 254). These are conflated in a Nancian understanding, which, however, does not suggest that a stable body would exist. Existence is the bearing-under the exposure of our existence, in Nancian thought. That means that we all suffer the world, that our being and sense of self is always vulnerable to the other, although the intensity of that suffering and vulnerability varies greatly as a result of unequal power relations (Wall 2008: 59; also Devisch 2011: 2–3).

Sensuous articulations of the political

BENJAMIN: Me, I do dance anytime. Yeah, if they see a dancer looking like this [Benjamin choreographs some moves as he walks around the room] while he walks on the street, people might say that he's sick, because there is no rhythm there. But I know what I'm doing. Yeah. So, that is how it is.

EEVA: Do you feel it helps you? To express your feelings and . . .

Sensuous politics, political sentiments 161

BENJAMIN: Yes, it helps me a lot. Because if I can't express my feelings, it's like having something *bad* inside me. . . . I don't like it.

(Interview with Benjamin, June 2007)

Dance was Benjamin's way of expressing his thoughts and feelings. The holding of feelings inside affected him negatively, and being detained had not changed the need to express himself and his experiences. Veena Das (1998: 85) has claimed that pain should never be kept inside; it should be communicated. Yet, as Benjamin's case suggests, together with the other stories that have been discussed in this chapter, language is not necessarily the best or even a possible medium to communicate pain. That does not mean that pain in itself is inarticulate and that all the suffering person's connections with others have been broken. There are multiple ways of expressing the political life of sensation or political life through sensation. These sensuous, utterly corporeal articulations resonate with the idea of the body sliding, being spread out, grafted and exchanged (see Nancy 2008: 107). Sensuous articulations, when analysed in-difference to sovereignty, although not in-ignorance of it, provide an alternative way to think about political life and community within which political relations occur. Yet, they cannot as such found an alternative account of asylum, because they are not teleological and clear in their aspiration. An engagement with these acts and expressive events cannot establish a common locus for agency or identity among asylum seekers. Rather, the acts pluralise and proliferate the spaces of politics.

The exploration of the political potential of the senses, the sensuous and the sentiments is closely related to the problem of representation. The approach seeks to overcome and mediate the problem of colonising the experiences of marginalised subjectivities, which would result in and affirm their political erasure (see Chapters 1 and 3; Spivak 1988). Emancipation does not follow from forcing a language and signification to describe events and experiences that escape them. Through either victimisation or medicalisation of the person's experiences and condition, language can also raise a "mentality of erasure" that further denies agency to those under scrutiny (Grimwood 2004: 65). Yet, the body is not hermetically sealed and isolated from others (cf. Pugliese 2004). The body communicates and articulates its position forcefully, in a way that forces a response, but refuses knowledge and full understanding.

Individual acts of protest and self-harm have been addressed as both powerful and insignificant in studies of migrant resistances and agencies (e.g. Edkins & Pin-Fat 2005; Huysmans 2008; Squire 2009). Critical voices have suggested that a focus on the body and the bodily acts of an individual asylum seeker fails to engage with the wider mobilisations that politicise such resistances. The critique is accurate in pointing out that asylum seekers should not be regarded as a separate issue, detached from wider social networks and mobilisations. The asylum body should not be turned into a primary site of resistance, the one on whom the struggle over the limits of the political unfolds or the one who struggles for inclusion. However, the critique fails to acknowledge that the asylum body is not separate, but ontologically plural. It exists as that particularly categorised body

162 *Sensuous politics, political sentiments*

only in relation to others and the wider social and political networks (see also Dossa 2003; French 1994). When a body comes into contact with and is perceived by others, it never is truly individual or sovereign. It never is separated from networks, mobilisations and various others who compose the political community (see Hewitt 1997: 122; Reischer & Koo 2004: 303). There are no primary or secondary sites of resistance. Rather, there are various ways of engaging with the wider social and political frameworks, be it singularly or plurally.

Because the body is always towards others, it makes the boundaries of notions, such as subjective and objective, discursive and material, personal and social, obsolete. In the body, the politico-corporeal struggle that unfolds between sovereign practices and the person is firmly connected with the production of selves, belonging and identities. The body, within this frame of interpretation, becomes intelligible as the material infrastructure of the production of those politico-spatial relations that fall under under the term international. Yet, although sovereign practices are designed to tame, control, discipline and categorise bodies and human life in multiple ways, sometimes even a seemingly single and isolated body can undermine the various control mechanisms and gesture towards a sensuous politics of its own.

For asylum seekers, a simultaneous functioning of securitising, criminalising and humanitarian discourses effectively closes down the space of political agency and acceptable ways of addressing their presence and possibilities in Finnish society. In my data, people counter the perception of themselves as either perpetrators or victims with determination. Their voices emphasise the relationality of being human and living a political life. Like Ayan, they claim a right to have a life, with a future and a past:

> I don't know, how the people [here in Finland] help me. They help only by giving money and medicine. And we don't need these things, really. It is not that we need medicine. We need to make peace for the mind. . . . Because I have not come here to take medicine to forget everything. It's my life, I have to know it. I only came to get my future.
>
> (Interview with Ayan, October 2006)

The meaning of a body's presence and existence, as Ayan implicitly points out, is negotiated and travels between bodies. In her account, the response that the Finnish professionals have adopted views her being in a way that she herself is not willing to accept. She firmly refuses the victimising interpretation, while still acknowledging the effects of traumatic experiences in her daily life. Ayan claims her body and its position as a valid locus of agency. Sensuous articulations direct attention at webs of affect, interactive processes and relationality that are generated, communicated and negotiated in the pulse of everyday life (cf. Ross 2010: 120–124). However, they do not and cannot be taken to form a basis for a collective form of identity. Their value lies in their capacity to point out that the marginalised body assumes and continues political life, not in a direct and open relation to the state, but via the creation of alternative channels of articulation

Sensuous politics, political sentiments   163

beyond the grip of sovereign power. This does not mean that asylum seekers are indifferent to or ignorant of the perceived injustices and actual limitations that the categorisation creates on their bodies. These modify and shape, but do not annihilate, people's ways of making sense and articulating themselves.

Political statements can well be communicated through the senses as sentiments and affective states. Sensuous expressions (re)tell or (re)inscribe bodily-being as a possibility of being otherwise. Sensuous responses are not intended to give signification to the body, to make it intelligible (see Nancy 1993a: 198). The sensuous body communicates the politico-corporeal struggle that unfolds as it faces constraints and pressure while all the time seeking to overcome its separation from others. The sensuous politics of the body comprises a plurality of acts of presentation and withdrawal, of multiple ambiguous events that resonate with but do not succumb to the principle of sovereignty and sovereign practices. Yet, these acts and events do not necessarily aim to change the status quo, or at least they do not have a particular result in mind. They take place in the struggle between the body and sovereign rule that concerns the political organisation of human life in the world.

The body represents the tension between being as it happens and as it is politically designed to happen. It gestures being-in-the-world through the senses and bodily activity rather than cognitive reflection. The political takes form as affective responses and scattered sensations, rather than organised narratives. Sensuous articulations of the political do not resonate with reason and rationalisation, that is, through the cognitive parts and abilities of the brain, but enact the limbic system, which deals with emotions (see Damasio 2000; LeDoux 1996; Marcus, Neuman & Mackuen 2000). Exposure works beyond consciousness, as a political event of existence.

The sensuous body is an index of the international yet to be fully engaged with in its philosophical mode. It articulates what it means to live in this world. A focus on the sensuous and the multiple vulnerabilities that such a focus creates does not imply acceptance and subservience to oppressive circumstances or conditions. It invites us to think about ways of leading a political life and participating wholly and corporeally in this world (see also Tatman 1998: 38). The body resists the closure of meaning and sense. It resists the closing of itself into an essential political identity and its exclusion from yet another political community. When those spaces, practices and networked processes that are designed to complete the erasure of the political existence of the asylum-seeking body are read to the contrary, the mind-set of an apolitical, isolated asylum body is disrupted and multiple connections are revealed. An engagement with the political potential of sense allows us to conceive of it as bodily know-how, which can build intelligible spaces within which to orient ourselves and construct significations out of a perceived chaos (see James 2006: 107, note 10; also Wall 2008: 58). The approach enables the fathoming of alternative ways of knowing, thinking and being human, and picturing agencies and solidarities in-difference to the constraints of sovereign power.

As the body withdraws from the grasp of sovereign power, it articulates the ambiguous and shifting nature of the kind of body politics which divides people into different nationalities, migrant groups and peoples. Even small, seemingly insignificant acts, intimate gestures and sensuous reflections can articulate being as it happens, beyond ideologies, political projects and statuses. Events of exposure might not be anything but evanescent moments, in which two people positioned and categorised differently in the spheres of the international cross paths and touch momentarily. But bodies leave traces on one another. These traces are remainders of gestures, acts, words and movement. In mixing with other traces, they remind us of a shared existence.

NASIR: And all of us have one thing in common. We all strive to live a normal life.
EEVA: Hmm, I think all people have that in common. But many people have their normal lives and don't have to look for it.
NASIR: Yeah, they take it for granted.
EEVA: Yes.
NASIR: And we strive for it. And I guess we have a right to have a normal life. Just like any other person.

(Interview with Nasir, March 2007)

Note

1 The method utilised in the project was that of empowering photography. It is a form of photography developed by Miina Savolainen, a Finnish community pedagogue and photographer. The aim of the method is to communicate appreciation and worthiness at times and in situations where words have lost their meaning.

Collage of a politico-corporeal struggle

You see clearly, says Asad and looks at me with a serious face. We are seated over a table in a small café in an even smaller rural village where he lives. We have been looking at portraits that I took of him during our collaborative project, titled "How would I like to be seen?" During our collaboration, we have met several times in places that he has chosen. Some of which were located in the vicinity of the reception centre where he lives, but we have also visited other places. After each photo session, we met to look at the portraits and to discuss them. We talked about what we saw when we looked at his pictures and about the feelings and thoughts that the portraits evoked. Asad has also used the camera himself and taken pictures of me and the things that he found meaningful in the places we visited.

-Do you think so?, I ask. Do you feel that the photos represent what you wanted to communicate?

-Yes. There are so many feelings that also I see when I look at myself. Happiness, sorrow, stress, calmness, flirting, worry, anger. That was what I was after when we took the photos. Although I haven't realised that I look so sad, Asad replies. And my hair has started to turn grey. I bet that's because of all the stress; when the process is over, I think I'll have turned completely grey. I'm only 35, you know. Asad pauses for a while. Why is it that you never ask anything about my process?, he then suddenly inquires.

-Well, if you want to talk about that, I'm happy to do that. It's just that I'd like to talk about things that are important to you instead of determining what kind of things we discuss. I cannot know whether you want to talk about your process or whether meetings with me and us taking photos is a way for you to forget the process for a while. But if you want, we can talk about it.

The politico-corporeal struggle that takes place between sovereign practices and the human body is not limited to asylum seekers. It involves us all, because the struggle is a matter of organising our political existence in the world. The senses of the international that emerge through the struggle concern the asylum seeker and the citizen/resident alike. In the multiple ways and networks through which sovereignty is enacted, the human body is cut up by or caught up in competing narratives about security, identity and community, to mention a few. Yet, asylum

166 *Collage of a politico-corporeal struggle*

seekers make this struggle evident, as they are not in their claims and articulations able to rely on an understanding of politics that bases itself on a state. The struggle concerns representation: ways of articulating the self and its relations to others, political structures, historical developments and lived realities. Moreover, it concerns response: the need to be seen and addressed as a singular being, not simply as a representative of a particular group or status.

Each of the Chapters has reflected upon the constant loosening and tensioning that characterises the struggle between sovereign politics and practices that concern the body, and the politics that the body enacts, which disrupts and transcends the logic of sovereignty. An engagement with the struggle meant exploring the international in terms of sense(s). A focus on the senses involves both an exploration of the sensuous, embodied effects that sovereign practices evoke and the ways in which people make sense of those practices. Throughout the chapters, the main focus has been on the responses that evolve through the simultaneous processes of sensing and making sense, and how they shape human relations. I have been at pains to avoid representing asylum seekers in ways that withdraw them to abstract categories that would imply the status or position as delineating an unambiguous identity.

Asad takes a sip of coffee and stares over the river that calmly flows through the village and at the old warehouse where the café is located. The forest on the other side of the river is blazing with autumn colours, in various shades of yellow, orange and red. He comments: "I kind of like meeting with you because it offers me a break from the daily routines. It is something else that disrupts my waiting. And I don't want to go into details about the process. But you know, it has taken over a year now. Still no answer. Do you think that is a good sign?"

I look at him and decide to give as honest an answer as possible. –Impossible to say, really. I think that it only says that either the Immigration Service is overstretched or that your case is not simple and some extra work is needed in order to make a decision. The latter can mean either that they suspect something or that they find your story credible enough to investigate it further. But, just as for you, it is also impossible for me to know what is going on.

He nods and looks me in the eye. – I contacted the officials and they told me that my decision will come in three weeks. That was a month ago. It's hard to just wait. Sometimes I get so depressed that I don't want to get out of bed or eat. I feel exhausted. Because of that I have – run into arguments and fights with the men who share the apartment with me. I kicked the door in, because they never clean up after themselves in the kitchen. Just leave everything lying around. So I kicked the door in and threw their dirty plates on the floor. After that the staff told me that if I don't stop making trouble, I'll be transferred to another centre.

The reaction of the staff does not surprise me, and neither does the stress that Asad describes feeling nor the reactions to which it gives rise.

Asad puts the photos and his phone aside and takes a long look at me.–But how are you? You look really tired today. Is everything ok?

Over the years, the woes and worries related to the struggle of asylum seekers in relation to bureaucratic processes and governmental practices have become familiar to me. It would have been easier – and undoubtedly many would claim necessary – to filter my engagements with asylum seekers through theoretical concepts and a strict role made possible by my professional position. Yet, I have consciously chosen otherwise. The choice of transcending substantial identities in the lives of asylum seekers also meant renouncing secure points of self-identification. It has become a guiding principle in my work to allow myself to feel hurt, to be moved and care about people's lives. The choice still results in a great deal of personal agony, and overwhelms me to the point of exhaustion if I do not distance myself from it on a regular basis. The tirednessness that characterised my field experiences at the beginning (see Event 1) still catches up with me. However, my choice allows room for mutual exposure, which again allows room for an understanding that arises from lived and sensuous realities instead of theoretical concepts. It enables me to grasp more clearly what is at stake in the struggle of seeking asylum. Not only from the perspective of the asylum seeker, but also from the perspective of the state and the representatives of the state.

My exploration of the dynamic struggle began with a personal experience of being exposed to the demand to think about the ways in which our beings are related and the ultimately lacking foundations of making separations between people. It developed into a scrutiny of the potentiality embedded in preventing claims of authenticity and truth as the guidelines when thinking about political asylum within the international. Exposure puts into focus the relational moments during which the self-evidence of the body is questioned and its finiteness, limitations, transience and vulnerability are brought out. This, according to Steven Van Wolputte (2004), suggests a move from the abstract or ideal(ised) body towards a philosophical-praxical challenge to political belonging.

The events of evoking exposure lead into a mixing of roles and positions. Thus, very few asylum seekers with whom I have worked over the years have considered my relationship with them a purely professional one. Neither have they thought of my spending time with them as first and foremost my work. The setting has been incredibly demanding ethically. It has required constant reflection on my part to remember that our encounters were not coincidental, and at points people have shown that they understood this. Usually this understanding has been communicated through various kinds of requests concerning either the process or daily life. During fieldwork I have grown accustomed to being addressed as a channel or point of distraction, a way out of the daily routine of a life in a reception centre. I am addressed as a mirror in relation to which people formulate their thoughts and opinions, construct self-positions and lash out frustrations. People have not asked me if I were willing to take on this role. I have come to consider that the decision was not mine at all. Perhaps it represents a responsibility that I cannot escape.

> Today Asad is not in the mood for taking photos. He's too consumed with other things. He seems restless, full of anxious energy that is waiting to erupt. We are walking around the town where we had planned to take the next

168 *Collage of a politico-corporeal struggle*

portraits of him. Instead of posing, we end up walking for a long time. When we are walking by the river, we pass the rapids. There Asad stops.

-Can you take my photo here? With the water in the background? Asad asks. The torrent of water makes us elevate our voices a bit.

-Of course. What kind of photo do you have in mind? What do you want to see in it? I inquire as I get the camera from my backpack and adjust the settings: shutter speed, aperture, ISO sensitivity. I hope I don't forget to check anything.

-I don't know, but I want to see the rapids in the background not so much of the rest of the stuff, replies Asad as he is assuming a pose. He looks straight towards the camera, with a self-confident face.

-Ok. I'll try my best, I say and start looking for an angle that would highlight Asad and the falling water. I feel nervous; what if I do not manage to deliver the kind of picture that he wants and that seems important for him to have? I take a couple of shots and show them to him.

Asad examines the shots from the screen of my camera. – Great. I think they look really good, he contends. – Are you sure? Is this enough?, I ask, trying to find out whether he is really happy with the photos. But Asad is already getting restless: – Yes, let's continue walking.

I follow Asad as he chooses directions intutively as he does not know the town. He talks continuously. About his life in the reception centre, about the inutile things that he is expected to do and the kind of activities he is supposed to participate in. Asad tells me that a week ago he went to see a doctor, because he started having suicidal thoughts. – I'm sick of waiting. I'm so sick of waiting that I'm thinking about hurting somebody, either myself or someone else. Some time ago I ended up in a fight in the reception centre. There is just so much aggression in me right now, he confesses.

We end up walking for hours together. As the distance walked grows longer, Asad's talk shifts from experienced aggression to his hopes for the future and to growing older and about the relations that people have in their lives. – I think you cannot really know about a person, he ponders.

-What do you mean by saying that you can never know about a person? I ask, while we head for a café. We are both feeling cold so we decided to go for a cup of coffee and talk about how he wants to spend the rest of the day.

-I mean that people are like envelopes. You need to look inside, if you want to know what's there, Asad says and shrugs his shoulders.

(Research diary, September–November 2013)

Instead of trying to fit the struggle involved in seeking asylum into the framework of sovereign politics, exposure allows us to acquire evented understanding. Thus, the scope of understanding is not to analyse the asylum seeker's forms of agency from the perspective of the state or against a specific understanding of politics. Rather, the aim is to understand how asylum seekers and an engagement with them can put learned notions into flux and articulate in many different ways the vulnerability that characterises not only human life, but also ways of politically organising that life. Understanding does not, within the adopted framework, emerge from a conscious effort to know, make sense of or find out about something. Exposure, as the various parts of this book have illustrated, is largely an intuitive process that takes shape and direction through the sense and bodily responses that other people's presence and articulation evoke in us. It demands constant evaluation and questioning of our premises and preconceptions, which centralises the moment of disruption in which thought-systems are exposed to being as it happens, as the core of the political. The 'I' is not in total control over the process of understanding, which makes it ultimately a shared process.

The process through which evented understanding appears evokes different relations to the actual moment of engagement, which represents the present at the time of contact. The coming together of different bodies arises immediate affective and sensuous responses, of which neither of the parties is in total control (see also Damasio 2000, 2005). It takes a while, a transient moment, for the body to process and signify those reactions and begin to resonate with them consciously. A sensuous experience of the meeting arises, which can intuitively guide the research process onto unwarranted paths. It represents something that is not yet articulate and not yet imagined (see also Reyes Cruz 2008; Chapter 1). Understanding and knowledge lag behind. They take time and effort, and often they impose dominance and erasure. That is why Nancy claims that the body can never be known, that at the same time that it approaches us to make itself known, it also withdraws from our reach. A leap of creativity is needed if we are to understand how we live and are together.

Because understanding never happens at the moment of exposure, senses and the body can play such a great role in fathoming how we articulate ourselves and our connections to others. Being responsive forms an ethical position that articulates a political commitment (see also Devisch 2011). With regard to the politico-corporeal struggle that is involved in seeking asylum, the approach enables us to explore how the multiple ways of enacting sovereignty enter into people's lives, even in extremely intimate and mundane forms, how sovereign imaginaries construct particular types of visibilities for all of us and how people undermine the working of sovereign practices in their daily lives. Ultimately, exposure aims to challenge epistemologies that seem fixed and represent secure grounds for thinking and learning. By implying a different ontological order, which is in constant flux, it sensitises us to the vulnerability of our theories, ways of thinking and categories with which we construct meaning and order. In terms of asylum seeking and politics, exposure can result in an understanding about the mechanisms and ways of the struggle in the lives of asylum seekers. Perhaps even more importantly, it can help understand what matters in people's lives, why they struggle and how it would be possible for us to form a more accurate response to the demand with which they present our societies.

As asylum seekers are particularly constrained by sovereign imaginaries, my collage has struggled to illustrate how sovereign practices make bodily surfaces,

170   *Collage of a politico-corporeal struggle*

and how bodies sense and materialise politics as a corporeal practice. Sense, moves and acts that cross and cut through borders time and again in unforeseen places, in unexpected ways, undermine politics in which the body is contracted to a state. A politics of the body seeks to interpret and transform the political organisation of the world again and anew (see also Nancy 2004b: 53). The latter politics is necessarily one of openness, indetermination and the incomplete. It subjects identity and points of identification to change. It suggests change in the political organisation of the world, and not just in one of its manifestations, the sovereign state. Ultimately, an exploration of sovereignty, asylum seekers and the senses of the international concerns the ways in which the international and ourselves become accessible and meaningful through relations with the world and others in it. Through the notion of exposure, it has been possible to engage with political existence as evented and enacted relationally. The other becomes thinkable only when the self first appears as the self to itself. The politico-corporeal struggle that we all need to engage with concerns the foundations of our own identities and it *demands that we think of eventuality as actuality.*

References

Aaltola, Mika (2005) "The international airport: the hub-and-spoke pedagogy of the American empire", *Global Networks* 5 (3), pp. 261–278.

Abu-Lughod, Lila (1985) "Honor and the sentiments of loss in a Bedouin society", *American Ethnologist* 12 (2), pp. 245–261.

Abu-Lughod, Lila (1989) "The romance of resistance: tracing transformations of power through Bedouin women", *American Ethnologist* 17 (1), pp. 41–55.

Ackerly, Brooke A.; Maria Stern & Jacqui True (2006) "Conclusion", in Ackerly, Brooke A.; Maria Stern & Jacqui True (eds.) *Feminist Methodologies for International Relations*, pp. 261–263. Cambridge: Cambridge University Press.

Agamben, Giorgio (1993) *Stanzas: Word and Phantasm in Western Culture*. Minneapolis: University of Minnesota Press.

Agamben, Giorgio (1998) *Homo Sacer: Sovereign Power and Bare Life*. Stanford, CA: Stanford University Press.

Agamben, Giorgio (2005) *State of Exception*. Chicago: The University of Chicago Press.

Agathangelou, Anna M. & Lily H. M. Ling (2004) "Power, borders, security, wealth: lessons from September 11", *International Studies Quarterly* 48 (3), pp. 517–538.

Agathangelou, Anna M. & Lily H. M. Ling (2005) "Power and play through poisies: reconstructing self and other in the 9/11 commission report", *Millennium: Journal of International Studies* 33 (3), pp. 827–853.

Agier, Michel (2008) *On the Margins of the World: Refugee Experience Today*. Cambridge and Malden, MA: Polity Press.

Agnew, John (1999) "Mapping political power beyond state boundaries: territory, identity, and movement in world politics", *Millennium: Journal of International Studies* 28 (3), pp. 499–521.

Agnew, John (2007) "Know-where: geographies of knowledge of world politics", *International Political Sociology* 1 (2), pp. 138–148.

Ahmed, Sara (1999) "'She'll wake up one of these days and find out that she's turned into a nigger': passing through hybridity", *Theory, Culture & Society* 16 (2), pp. 87–106.

Ahmed, Sara (2004) *The Cultural Politics of Emotion*. Edinburgh: Edinburgh University Press.

Ahmed, Sara (2010) *The Promise of Happiness*. Durham: Duke University Press.

Ahmed, Sara; Claudia Castañeda, Anne-Mari Fortier & Mimi Sheller (eds.) (2003) *Uprootings/Regroundings: Questions of Home and Migration*. Oxford & New York: Berg.

Ahmed, Sara & Jackie Stacey (eds.) (2001) *Thinking through the Skin*. London & New York: Routledge.

172　*References*

Ahrens, Jörn (2005) "Freedom and sovereignty: a fatal relationship outlined with Jean-Luc Nancy and Marquis de Sade", *Law and Critique* 16 (3), pp. 301–313.

Anderson, Benedict (1991) *Imagined Communities: Reflections on the Origins and Spread of Nationalism.* London: Verso.

Andreas, Peter (2000) "Introduction: the wall after the wall", in Andreas, Peter & Timothy Snyder (eds.) *The Wall around the West: State Borders and Immigration Controls in North America and Europe*, pp. 1–11. Lanham, MD: Rowman and Littlefield.

Aradau, Claudia; Jef Huysmans & Vicki Squire (2010) "Acts of European citizenship: a political sociology of mobility", *Journal of Common Market Studies* 48 (4), pp. 945–965.

Ashley, Richard (1989) "Living on border lines: man, poststructuralism, and war", in Derian, James Der & Michael J. Shapiro (eds.) *International/Intertextual Relations. Postmodern Readings of World Politics*, pp. 259–322. New York: Lexington Books.

Atkinson, Paul & Amanda Coffey (2002) "Revisiting the relationship between participant observation and interviewing", in Gubrium, Jaber F. & James A. Holstein (eds.) *Handbook of Interview Research: Context and Method*, pp. 801–814. Thousand Oaks: Sage.

Bamberg, Michael (2004) "Positioning with Davie Hogan: stories, tellings, and identities", in Daiute, Colin & Cynthia Lightfoot (eds.) *Narrative Analysis: Studying the Development of Individuals in Society*, pp. 135–157. London: Sage.

Bartelson, Jens (1995) *A Genealogy of Sovereignty.* Cambridge: Cambridge University Press.

Bavelas, Janet B. (1994) "Gestures as part of speech: methodological implications", *Research on Language and Social Interaction* 27 (3), pp. 201–221.

Behar, Ruth (1996) *The Vulnerable Observer: Anthropology that Breaks Your Heart.* Boston, MA: Beacon Press.

Behar, Ruth (2003) "Ethnography and the book that was lost", *Ethnography* 4 (1), pp. 15–39.

Beier, J. Marshall (2005) "Beyond hegemonic state(ment)s of nature: indigenous knowledge and non-state possibilities in international relations", in Chowdhry, Geeta & Sheila Nair (eds.) *Power, Postcolonialism and International Relations: Reading Race, Gender and Class*, pp. 82–114. New York: Routledge.

Benhabib, Seyla (2004) *The Rights of Others: Aliens, Residents, and Citizens.* Cambridge: Cambridge University Press.

Benterrak, Krim; Benjamin Muecke & Paddy Roe (1984) *Reading the Country: Introduction to Nomadology.* With Ray Keogh, Butcher Joe (Nangan) & E. M. Lohe. Fremantle, Western Australia: Fremantle Arts Centre Press.

Berard, Tim J. (2006) "From concepts to methods: on the observability of inequality", *Journal of Contemporary Ethnography* 35 (3), pp. 236–256.

Biddle, Jennifer (2001) "Inscribing identity: skin as country in the Central Desert", in Ahmed, Sara & Jackie Stacey (eds.) *Thinking through the Skin*, pp. 177–193. London & New York: Routledge.

Bigo, Didier (2002) "Security and immigration: toward a critique of the governmentality of unease", *Alternatives: Global, Local, Political* 27 (supplement), pp. 63–92.

Bigo, Didier (2005) "Globalised-in-security: the field and the ban-opticon", in Solomon, John & Naoki Sakai (eds.) *Translation, Philosophy and Colonial Difference*, pp. 109–157. Hong Kong: Hong Kong University Press.

Bigo, Didier (2007) "Detention of foreigners, states of exception, and the social practices of control", in Rajaram, Prem Kumar & Carl Grundy-Warr (eds.) *Borderscapes: Hidden Geographies and Politics at Territory's Edge*, pp. 3–33. Minneapolis & London: University of Minnesota Press.

References 173

Bigo, Didier & Rob B. J. Walker (2007) "Political sociology and the problem of the international", *Millennium: Journal of International Studies* 35 (3), pp. 725–739.

Bleiker, Roland & Amy Kay (2007) "Representing HIV/AIDS in Africa: pluralist photography and local empowerment", *International Studies Quarterly* 51 (1), pp. 139–163.

Blom Hansen, Thomas & Finn Stepputat (eds.) (2005) *Sovereign Bodies: Citizens, Migrants and States in the Postcolonial World*. Princeton & Oxford: Princeton University Press.

Bögner Diana; Chris Brewin & Jane Herlihy (2010) "Refugees' experiences of Home Office interviews: a qualitative study on the disclosure of sensitive personal information", *Journal of Ethnic and Migration Studies* 36 (3), pp. 519–535.

Bohmer, Carol & Amy Shuman (2007) "Producing epistemologies of ignorance in the political asylum application process", *Identities: Global Studies in Culture and Power* 14 (5), pp. 603–629.

Brady, Ivan (2004) "In defense of the sensual: meaning construction in ethnography and poetics", *Qualitative Inquiry* 10 (4), pp. 622–644.

Brandt, Keri J. (2004) "The skin we live in: explorations of body modification, sexuality, and citizenship", *Symbolic Interaction* 27 (3), pp. 429–436.

Brigg, Morgan & Roland Bleiker (2008) "Expanding ethnographic insights into world politics", *International Political Sociology* 2 (1), pp. 89–90.

Brigg, Morgan & Roland Bleiker (2010) "Autoethnographic international relations: exploring the self as a source of knowledge", *Review of International Studies* 36 (3), pp. 779–798.

Briggs, Charles L. (2002) "Interviewing, power/knowledge, and social inequality", in Gubrium, Jaber F. & James A. Holstein (eds.) *Handbook of Interview Research: Context and Method*, pp. 911–922. Thousand Oaks: Sage.

Brinkmann, Svend (2009) "Literature as qualitative inquiry: the novelist as researcher", *Qualitative Inquiry* 15 (8), pp. 1376–1394.

Brown, Wendy (2002) "At the edge", *Political Theory* 30 (4), pp. 556–576.

Budgeon, Shelley (2003) "Identity as an embodied event", *Body & Society* 9 (1), pp. 35–55.

Burke, Anthony (2002) "Prisoners of paradox: thinking for the refugee", *Social Alternatives* 21 (4), pp. 21–27.

Bürkner, Hans-Joachim (2011) "Intersectionality: how gender studies might inspire the analysis of social inequality among migrants", *Population, Space and Place* 18 (2), pp. 181–195.

Butalia, Urvashi (1998) *The Other Side of Silence: Voices from the Partition of India*. New Delhi: Penguin Books.

Butler, Judith (1997) *The Psychic Life of Power: Theories in Subjection*. Stanford, CA: Stanford University Press.

Butler, Judith (2001) "Giving an account of oneself", *Diacritics* 31 (4), pp. 22–40.

Butler, Judith (2003a) "Violence, mourning, politics", *Studies in Gender and Sexuality* 4 (1), pp. 9–37.

Butler, Judith (2003b) "Afterword: after loss, what then?", in Eng, David L. & David Kazanjian (eds.) *Loss: The Politics of Mourning*, pp. 467–473. Berkeley & Los Angeles: University of California Press.

Butler, Judith (2004) *Precarious Life: The Powers of Mourning and Violence*. London & New York: Verso.

Calhoun, Craig (2003) "'Belonging in the cosmopolitan imaginary'", *Ethnicities* 3 (4), pp. 531–568.

Campbell, David (2005) "Beyond choice: the onto-politics of critique", *International Relations* 19 (1), pp. 127–134.

174 *References*

Campbell, Howard & Josiah Heyman (2007) "Slantwise: beyond domination and resistance on the border", *Journal of Contemporary Ethnography* 36 (1), pp. 3–30.

Caruth, Cathy (1996) *Unexclaimed Experience: Trauma, Narrative and History*. Baltimore: The Johns Hopkins University Press.

Caruth, Cathy (2001) "Parting worlds: trauma, silence and survival", *Cultural Values* 5 (1), pp. 7–27.

Cavarero, Adriana (2002) "Politicizing theory", *Political Theory* 30 (4), pp. 506–532.

Caygill, Howard (1997) "The shared world: philosophy, violence, freedom", in Sheppard, Darren; Simon Sparks & Colin Thomas (eds.) *The Sense of Philosophy: On Jean-Luc Nancy*, pp. 19–31. London: Routledge.

Cerwonka, Allaine & Liisa H. Malkki (2007) *Improvising Theory: Process and Temporality in Ethnographic Fieldwork*. Chicago & London: The University of Chicago Press.

Ceyhan, Anna & Anastasia Tsoukala (2002) "The securitisation of migration in Western societies: ambivalent discourses and policies", *Alternatives: Global, Local, Political* 27 (supplement), pp. 21–39.

Chambers, Iain (1994) "Leaky habitats and broken grammar", in Robertson, George (ed.) *Travellers' Tales: Narratives of Home and Displacement*, pp. 243–247. London: Routledge.

Chan, Stephen (2003a) "A new triptych for international relations in the 21st century: beyond Waltz and beyond Lacan's Antigone, with a note on the Falun Gong of China", *Global Society* 17 (2), pp. 187–208.

Chan, Stephen (2003b) "A problem for IR: how shall we narrate the saga of the bestial man?", *Global Society* 17 (4), pp. 385–413.

Chen, Boyu; Ching-Chane Hwang & Lily H. M. Ling (2009) "Lust/caution in IR: democratising world politics with culture as method", *Millennium: Journal of International Studies* 37 (3), pp. 743–766.

Choo, Hae Yeon & Myra Marx Ferree (2010) "Practicing intersectionality in sociological research: a critical analysis of inclusions, interactions, and institutions in the study of inequalities", *Sociological Theory* 28 (2), pp. 129–149.

Clifford, James (2007) "On ethnographic authority", in Robben, Antonius C. G. M. & Jeffrey A. Sluka (eds.) *Ethnographic Fieldwork: An Anthropological Reader*, pp. 476–492. Malden, MA & Oxford: Blackwell Publishing.

Cohn, Carol (1987) "Sex and death in the rational world of defense intellectuals", *Signs* 12 (4), pp. 687–718.

Coker, Elizabeth (2004) "'Traveling pains': embodied metaphors of suffering among Southern Sudanese refugees in Cairo", *Culture, Medicine and Psychiatry* 28 (1), pp. 15–39.

Connolly, William (2010) "Materialities of experience", in Coole, Diana and Samantha Frost (eds.) *New Materialisms: Ontology, Agency, and Politics*, pp. 178–200. Durham, NC: Duke University Press.

Coole, Diana (2005) "Rethinking agency: a phenomenological approach to embodiment and agentic capacities", *Political Studies* 53 (1), pp. 124–142.

Coole, Diana & Samantha Frost (eds.) (2010) *New Materialisms: Ontology, Agency, and Politics*. Durham: Duke University Press.

Coutin, Susan Bibler (2001) "The oppressed, the suspect, and the citizen: subjectivity in competing accounts of political violence", *Law & Social Inquiry* 26 (1), pp. 63–94.

Coward, Martin (2009) "Jean-Luc Nancy", in Edkins, Jenny & Nick Vaughan-Williams (eds.) *Critical Theorists and International Relations*, pp. 251–262. Oxon & New York: Routledge.

References   175

Critchley, Simon (1993) "Retracing the political: politics and community in the works of Lacoue-Labarthe and Jean-Luc Nancy", in Campbell, David & Michael Dillon (eds.) *The Political Subject of Violence*, pp. 73–93. Manchester: Mancherster University Press.

Csordas, Thomas (1994) *The Sacred Self: A Cultural Phenomenology of Charismatic Healing*. Berkeley: University of California Press.

Curtis, Barry & Claire Pajaczkowska (1994) " 'Getting there': travel, time and narrative", in Robertson, George (ed.) *Travellers' Tales: Narratives of Home and Displacement*, pp. 197–214. London: Routledge.

Dallmayr, Fred (1997) "An 'inoperative' global community? Reflections on Nancy", in Sheppard, Darren; Simon Sparks & Colin Thomas (eds.) *The Sense of Philosophy: On Jean-Luc Nancy*, pp. 174–196. London: Routledge.

Damasio, Antonio (2000) *The Feeling of What Happens: Body and Emotion in the Making of Consciousness*. New York: Mariner Books.

Damasio, Antonio (2005 [1994]) *Descartes' Error: Emotion, Reason, and the Human Brain*. New York: Penguin Books.

Darby, Phillip (2003) "Reconfiguring 'the international': knowledge machines, boundaries, and exclusions", *Alternatives: Global, Local, Political* 28 (1), pp. 141–166.

Darby, Phillip (2004) "Pursuing the political: a postcolonial rethinking of relations international", *Millennium: Journal of International Studies* 33 (1), pp. 1–32.

Das, Veena (1998) "Language and body: transactions in the construction of pain", in Kleinman, Arthur; Veena Das & Margaret Lock (eds.) *Social Suffering*, pp. 67–91. Delhi: Oxford University Press.

Dauphinee, Elizabeth (2010) "The ethics of autoethnography", *Review of International Studies* 36 (3), pp. 799–818.

Dauphinee, Elizabeth (2013) *The Politics of Exile*. London & New York: Routledge.

Dauphinee, Elizabeth & Cristina Masters (eds.) (2006) *The Logics of Biopower and the War on Terror: Living, Dying, Surviving*. London: Palgrave MacMillan.

de Genova, Nicholas P. (2002) "Migrant illegality and deportability in everyday life", *Annual Reviews in Anthropology* 31, pp. 419–447.

de Genova, Nicholas P. (2004) "The legal production of Mexican/migrant 'illegality'", *Latino Studies* 2 (2), pp. 160–185.

de Genova, Nicholas P. (2007) "The production of culprits: from deportability to detainability in the aftermath of 'homeland security'", *Citizenship Studies* 11 (5), pp. 421–448.

Denton, Diana (2005) "Toward a sacred discourse: reconceptualizing the heart through metaphor", *Qualitative Inquiry* 11 (5), pp. 752–770.

Denzin, Norman K. (1994) "The art and politics of interpretation", in Denzin, Norman K. & Yvonna S. Lincoln (eds.) *Handbook of Qualitative Research*, pp. 500–515. Thousand Oaks, CA: Sage.

Denzin, Norman K. (2009) *Qualitative Inquiry under Fire: Toward a New Paradigm Dialogue*. Walnut Creek: Left Coast Press.

Derrida, Jacques (2005) *On Touching – Jean-Luc Nancy*. Stanford, CA: Stanford University Press.

Despret, Vinciane (2013) "Responding bodies and partial affinities in human-animal worlds", *Theory, Culture & Society* 30 (7–8), pp. 51–76.

Devisch, Ignaas (2011) "Doing justice to existence: Jean-Luc Nancy and 'the size of humanity'", *Law and Critique* 22 (1), pp. 1–13.

Didur, Jill & Teresa Heffernan (2003) "Revisiting the subaltern in the new empire", *Cultural Studies* 17 (1), pp. 1–15.

176   *References*

Dikeç, Mustafa (2005) "Space, politics, and the political", *Environment and Planning D: Society and Space* 23 (2), pp. 171–188.

Dillon, Michael (2004) "Correlating sovereign and biopower", in Edkins, Jenny; Véronique Pin-Fat & Michael J. Shapiro (eds.) *Sovereign Lives: Power in Global Politics*, pp. 41–60. London & New York: Routledge.

Dossa, Parin (2003) "The body remembers: a migratory tale of social suffering and witnessing", *International Journal of Mental Health* 32 (3), pp. 50–73.

Doty, Roxanne L. (1997) "Aporia: a critical exploration of the agent-structure problematique in international relations theory", *European Journal of International Relations* 3 (3), pp. 137–139.

Doty, Roxanne L. (1999) "Racism, desire, and the politics of immigration", *Millennium: Journal of International Studies* 28 (3), pp. 585–606.

Doty, Roxanne L. (2001) "Desert tracts: statecraft in remote places", *Alternatives: Global, Local, Political* 26 (4), pp. 523–543.

Doty, Roxanne L. (2004) "Maladies of our souls: identity and voice in the writing of academic international relations", *Cambridge Review of International Affairs* 17 (2), pp. 377–392.

Doty, Roxanne L. (2006) "Fronteras compasivas and the ethics of unconditional hospitality", *Millennium: Journal of International Studies* 35 (1), pp. 53–74.

Doty, Roxanne L. (2010) "Autoethnography – making human connections", *Review of International Studies* 36 (4), pp. 1047–1050.

Dugan, Kimberly & Jo Reger (2006) "Voice and agency in social movement outcomes", *Qualitative Sociology* 29 (4), pp. 467–484.

Eades, Diana (2009) "Testing the claims of asylum seekers: the role of language analysis", *Language Assessment Quarterly* 6 (1), pp. 30–40.

Eckl, Julian (2008) "Responsible scholarship after leaving the veranda: normative issues faced by field researchers – and armchair scientists", *International Political Sociology* 2 (2), pp. 185–203.

Edkins, Jenny (1999) *Poststructuralism and International Relations: Bringing the Political Back In*. Boulder, CO: Lynne Rienner.

Edkins, Jenny (2000) "Sovereign power, zones of indistinction, and the camp", *Alternatives: Global, Local, Political* 25 (1), pp. 3–25.

Edkins, Jenny (2003) *Trauma and the Memory of Politics*. Cambridge: Cambridge University Press.

Edkins, Jenny (2005a) "Ethics and practices of engagement: intellectuals as experts", *International Relations* 19 (1), pp. 64–69.

Edkins, Jenny (2005b) "Exposed singularity", *Journal for Cultural Research* 9 (4), pp. 359–386.

Edkins, Jenny (2013) "Dismantling the face: landscape for another politics?", *Environment and Planning D: Society and Space* 31 (3), pp. 538–553.

Edkins, Jenny & Maja Zehfuss (2005) "Generalising the international", *Review of International Studies* 31 (3), pp. 451–472.

Edkins, Jenny & Véronique Pin-Fat (2005) "Through the wire: relations of power and relations of violence", *Millennium: Journal of International Studies* 34 (1), pp. 1–24.

Edwards, Derek & Elizabeth Stokoe (2011) "'You don't have to answer': lawyers' contributions in police interrogations of suspects", *Research on Language and Social Interaction* 44 (1), pp. 21–43.

Elliott, Brian (2011) "Community and resistance in Heidegger, Nancy and Agamben", *Philosophy and Social Criticism* 37 (3), pp. 259–271.

References 177

Ellis, Carolyn & Leigh Berger (2002) "Their story/my story/our story: including the researcher's experience in interview research", in Gubrium, Jaber F. & James A. Holstein (eds.) *Handbook of Interview Research: Context and Method*, pp. 849–875. Thousand Oaks: Sage.

Enloe, Cynthia (1999) "Margins, silences and bottom rungs: how to overcome the underestimation of power in the study of international relations", in Smith, Steve; Ken Booth & Marysia Zalewski (eds.) *International Theory: Positivism and Beyond*, pp. 186–202. Cambridge: Cambridge University Press.

Epstein, Charlotte (2007) "Guilty bodies, productive bodies, destructive bodies: crossing the biometric borders", *International Political Sociology* 1 (1), pp. 149–164.

Epstein, Charlotte (2010) "Who speaks? Discourse, the subject and the study of identity in international politics", *European Journal of International Relations* 17 (2), pp. 327–350.

Evans, Christine (2003) "Asylum seekers and 'border panic' in Australia", *Peace Review* 15 (2), pp. 163–170.

Farber, Leona (2006) "Skin aesthetics", *Theory, Culture & Society* 23 (2–3), pp. 247–250.

Fischer, Francis (1997) "Jean-Luc Nancy: the place of a thinking", in Sheppard, Darren; Simon Sparks & Colin Thomas (eds.) *The Sense of Philosophy: On Jean-Luc Nancy*, pp. 32–37. London: Routledge.

Foster, Susan (1995) "Choreographing history", in Foster, Susan (ed.) *Choreographing History*, pp. 3–21. Bloomington: Indiana University Press.

Foster, Susan (ed.) (1996) *Corporealities: Dancing Knowledge, Culture and Power*. New York: Routledge.

Foucault, Michel (1978) *The History of Sexuality, Volume I: An Introduction*. New York: Pantheon.

Foucault, Michel (1979) *Discipline and Punish: The Birth of the Prison*. New York: Pantheon.

Foucault, Michel (1980) *Power/Knowledge: Selected Interviews & Other Writings 1972–1977*. New York: Pantheon Books.

Foucault, Michel (1982) "The subject and power", *Critical Inquiry* 8 (4), pp. 777–795.

Fox O'Mahony, Lorna & James A. Sweeney (2010) "The exclusion of (failed) asylum seekers from housing and home and oppositional discourse", *Journal of Law and Society* 37 (2), pp. 285–314.

Fraser, Nancy (1984) "The French Derrideans: politicizing deconstruction or deconstructing the political?", *New German Critique* 33 (Autumn), pp. 127–154.

French, Lindsay (1994) "The political economy of injury and compassion: amputees on the Thai-Cambodian border", in Csordas, Thomas (ed.) *Embodiment and Experience: The Existential Ground of Culture and Self*, pp. 69–99. Cambridge: Cambridge University Press.

Frost, Samantha (2010) "Fear and the illusion of autonomy", in Coole, Diana & Samantha Frost (eds.) *New Materialisms: Ontology, Agency, and Politics*, pp. 158–177. Durham, NC: Duke University Press.

Fynsk, Christopher (2004/1991) "Foreword: experiences of finitude", in Nancy, Jean-Luc (ed.) *The Inoperative Community*, pp. vii–xxxv. Minneapolis: University of Minnesota Press.

Gagnon, John H. (1992) "The self, its voices, and their discord", in Ellis, Carolyn & Michael G. Flaherty (eds.) *Investigating Subjectivity: Research on Lived Experience*, pp. 221–243. Newbury Park: Sage.

Gatens, Moira (1996) *Imaginary Bodies: Ethics, Power, Corporeality*. London & New York: Routledge.

178 References

Gergen, Mary (2004) "Once upon a time: a narratologist's tale", in Daiute, Colin & Cynthia Lightfoot (eds.) *Narrative Analysis: Studying the Development of Individuals in Society*, pp. 267–285. London: Sage.

Gergen, Mary & Kenneth Gergen (2002) "Ethnographic representation as relationship", in Bochner, Arthur P. & Carolyn Ellis (eds.) *Ethnographically Speaking: Autoethnography, Literature, and Aesthetics*, pp. 11–33. Walnut Creek, CA: Altamira Press.

Gerritsen, Annette A.; Inge Bramsen, Walter Devillé, Loes H. M. van Willigen, Johannes E. Hovens & Henk M. van der Ploeg (2006) "Physical and mental health of Afghan, Iranian and Somali asylum seekers and refugees living in the Netherlands", *Social Psychiatry and Psychiatric Epidemiology* 41 (1), pp. 18–26.

Good, Anthony (2004) "Expert evidence in asylum and human rights appeals: an expert's view", *International Journal of Refugee Law* 16 (3), pp. 358–380.

Goodwin, Charles (1981) *Conversational Organization: Interaction between Speakers and Hearers*. Academic Press: New York.

Granhag Pär Anders; Leif A. Strömvall & Maria Hartwig (2005) "Granting asylum or not? Migration board personnel's beliefs about deception", *Journal of Ethnic and Migration Studies* 31 (1), pp. 29–50.

Grayson, Kyle (2010) "Dissidence, Richard K. Ashley, and the politics of silence", *Review of International Studies* 36 (4), pp. 1005–1019.

Grimwood, Tom (2004) "The body as a lived metaphor: interpreting Catherine of Siena as an ethical agent", *Feminist Theology* 13 (1), pp. 62–76.

Grosz, Elizabeth (2010) "Feminism, materialism, and freedom", in Coole, Diana & Samantha Frost (eds.) *New Materialisms: Ontology, Agency, and Politics*, pp. 139–157. Durham, NC: Duke University Press.

Grovogui, Siba N. (2005) "Postcolonial criticism: international reality and modes of inquiry", in Chowdhry, Geeta & Sheila Nair (eds.) *Power, Postcolonialism and International Relations: Reading Race, Gender and Class*, pp. 33–55. New York: Routledge.

Guillaume, Xavier (2007) "Unveiling the 'international': process, identity and alterity", *Millennium: Journal of International Studies* 35 (3), pp. 741–759.

Haddad, Emma (2007) "Danger happens at the border", in Rajaram, Prem Kumar & Carl Grundy-Warr (eds.) *Borderscapes: Hidden Geographies and Politics at Territory's Edge*, pp. 119–136. Minneapolis & London: University of Minnesota Press.

Haddad, Emma (2008) *The Refugee in International Society: Between Sovereigns*. Cambridge: Cambridge University Press.

Hall, Alexandra (2010) "'These people could be anyone': fear, contempt (and empathy) in a British immigration removal centre", *Journal of Ethnic and Migration Studies* 36 (6), pp. 881–898.

Halla, Tapio (2007) "Psyykkisesti sairas maahanmuuttaja", *Duodecim* 123 (4), pp. 469–475.

Hamacher, Werner (1997) "Ou, séance, touche de Nancy, ici", in Sheppard, Darren; Simon Sparks & Colin Thomas (eds.) *The Sense of Philosophy: On Jean-Luc Nancy*, pp. 38–62. London: Routledge.

Harker, Christopher (2007) "'A close and unbreachable distance': witnessing everything and nothing", *ACME: An International E-Journal for Critical Geographies* 6 (1), pp. 51–72.

Heikkilä, Martta (2007) *At the Limits of Presentation: Coming-into-Presence and Its Aesthetic Relevance in Jean-Luc Nancy's Philosophy*. Helsinki: Helsinki University Printing House, available at <http://urn.fi/URN:ISBN:978-952-10-3570-8>, accessed 11th September 2016.

References 179

Heritage, John (1996) *Harold Garfinkel ja Etnometodologia*. Gaudeamus: Helsinki. (Original English version: *Garfinkel and Ethnomethodology*, 1984. Cambridge: Polity Press.)

Herlihy, Jane & Stuart Turner (2006) "Should discrepant accounts given by asylum seekers be taken as proof of deceit?", *Torture* 16 (2), pp. 81–92.

Herlihy, Jane & Stuart Turner (2007) "Memory and seeking asylum", *European Journal of Psychotherapy and Counselling* 9 (3), pp. 267–276.

Herzfeld, Michael (2007) "Senses", in Robben, Antonius C. G. M. & Jeffrey A. Sluka (eds.) *Ethnographic Fieldwork: An Anthropological Reader*, pp. 431–441. Malden, MA & Oxford: Blackwell Publishing.

Hewett, Heather (2004) "'In search of an 'I': embodied voice and the personal essay", *Women's Studies* 33 (6), pp. 719–741.

Hewitt, Kim (1997) *Mutilating the Body: Identity in Blood and Ink*. Bowling Green: Bowling Green State University Popular Press.

Hill, Djanna A. (2005) "The poetry in portraiture: seeing subjects, hearing voices, and feeling contexts", *Qualitative Inquiry* 11 (1), pp. 95–105.

Honkasalo, Marja-Liisa (1998) "Space and embodied experience: rethinking the body in pain", *Body & Society* 4 (2), pp. 35–57.

Howarth, David (2006) "Space, subjectivity, and politics", *Alternatives: Global, Local, Political* 31 (2), pp. 105–134.

Howell, Alison (2011) *Madness in International Relations: Psychology, Security, and the Global Governance of Mental Health*. London & New York: Routledge.

Humphreys, Adam R. C. (2010) "The heuristic application of explanatory theories in international relations", *European Journal of International Relations* 17 (2), pp. 257–277.

Huynh, Kim (2007) *Where the Sea Takes Us: A Vietnamese-Australian Story*. London, New York, Sydney & Auckland: Harper Collins.

Huynh, Kim (2010) "Refugeeness: what's so good and not so good about being persecuted and displaced", *Local-Global: Identity, Security, Community* 8, pp. 52–74.

Huysmans, Jef (2006) *The Politics of Insecurity: Fear, Migration and Asylum in the EU*. London: Routledge.

Huysmans, Jef (2008) "The jargon of exception: on Schmitt, Agamben and the absence of political society", *International Political Sociology* 2 (1), pp. 165–183.

Inayatullah, Naeem & David L. Blaney (2004) *International Relations and the Problem of Difference*. London & New York: Routledge.

Isin, Engin F. & Greg M. Nielsen (eds.) (2008) *Acts of Citizenship*. London & New York: Zed Books.

Isin, Engin F. & Kim Rygiel (2006) "Abject spaces, frontiers, zones, camps", in Dauphinee, Elizabeth & Cristina Masters (eds.) *The Logics of Biopower and the War on Terror: Living, Dying, Surviving*, pp. 181–203. Basingstoke: Palgrave Macmillan.

Jackson, Patrick T. (2008) "Can ethnographic techniques tell us distinctive things about world politics", *International Political Sociology* 2 (1), pp. 91–93.

Jackson, Patrick T. & Daniel H. Nexon (2009) "Paradigmatic faults in international relations theory", *International Studies Quarterly* 53 (4), pp. 907–930.

James, Ian (2002) "The persistence of the subject: Jean-Luc Nancy", *Paragraph* 25 (1), pp. 125–141.

James, Ian (2006) *The Fragmentary Demand: An Introduction to the Philosophy of Jean-Luc Nancy*. Stanford, CA: Stanford University Press.

James, Ian (2010) "Naming the nothing: Nancy and Blanchot on community", *Culture, Theory and Critique* 51 (2), pp. 171–187.

180 References

Jenkins, Mercilee M. (2010) "Ethnographic writing is as good as ten mothers", *Qualitative Inquiry* 16 (2), pp. 83–89.

Joseph, Jonathan (2010) "The limits of governmentality: social theory and the international", *European Journal of International Relations* 16 (2), pp. 223–246.

Junka, Laura (2006) "Camping in the third space: agency, representation, and the politics of Gaza beach", *Public Culture* 18 (2), pp. 348–359.

Jutila, Matti; Samu Pehkonen & Tarja Väyrynen (2008) "Resuscitating a discipline: an agenda for critical peace research", *Millennium: Journal of International Studies* 36 (3), pp. 623–640.

Kearney, Richard (2007) "Narrating pain: the power of catharsis", *Paragraph: A Journal of Modern Critical Theory* 30 (1), pp. 51–66.

Kearney, Richard (2015) "What is carnal hermeneutics?", *New Literary History* 46 (1), pp. 99–124.

Keller, Allen S.; Douglas Ford, Emily Sachs, Barry Rosenfeld, Chau Trinh-Shevrin, Chris Meserve, Jonathan A. Leviss, Elizabeth Singer, Hawthorne Smith, John Wilkinson, Glen Kim, Kathreen Allden & Paul Rockline (2003) "The impact of detention on the health of asylum seekers", *The Journal of Ambulatory Care Management* 23 (4), pp. 383–385.

Kellogg, Catherine (2005) "Love and communism: Jean-Luc Nancy's shattered community", *Law and Critique* 16 (3), pp. 339–355.

Kendon, Adam (1990) *Conducting Interaction: Patterns of Behavior in Focused Encounters.* Cambridge: Cambridge University Press.

Khosravi, Shahram (2010) *"Illegal" Traveller: An Auto-Ethnography of Borders.* Basingstoke: Palgrave Macmillan.

Kleinman, Arthur (1989) *The Illness Narratives: Suffering, Healing, and the Human Condition.* New York: Basic Books.

Kristeva, Julia (1991) *Strangers to Ourselves.* New York: Harvester Wheatsheaf.

Kvale, Steinar (2006) "Dominance through interviews and dialogues", *Qualitative Inquiry* 12 (3), pp. 480–500.

Kynsilehto, Anitta (2011) "Negotiating intersectionality in highly educated migrant Maghrebi women's life stories", *Environment and Planning-Part A* 7: pp. 1547–1561.

Kynsilehto, Anitta & Eeva Puumala (2013) "Persecution as experience and knowledge: the ontological dynamics of asylum interviews", *International Studies Perspectives*, doi:10.1111/insp.12064.

Kynsilehto, Anitta & Eeva Puumala (2016) "Intimate economies of state practice: materialities of migrant detention in Finland", in Conlon, Deirdre & Nancy Hiemstra (eds.) *Intimate Economies: Critical Perspectives on Migrant Detention*, pp. 203–218. London & New York: Routledge.

Lacoue-Labarthe, Philippe & Jean-Luc Nancy (1997) *Retreating the Political.* London: Routledge.

Lash, Scott (1998) "Being after time: towards a politics of melancholy", in Lash, Scott; Andrew Quick & Richard Roberts (eds.) *Time and Value*, pp. 147–161. Oxford & Malden, MA: Blackwell.

LeDoux, Joseph (1996) *The Emotional Brain: The Mysterious Underpinnings of Emotional Life.* New York: Simon & Schuster.

Librett, Jeffrey S. (1997) "Interruptions of necessity: being between meaning and power in Jean-Luc Nancy", in Sheppard, Darren; Simon Sparks & Colin Thomas (eds.) *The Sense of Philosophy: On Jean-Luc Nancy*, pp. 103–139. London: Routledge.

Löwenheim, Oded (2010) "The 'I' in IR: an autoethnographic account", *Review of International Studies* 36 (4), pp. 1023–1045.

References 181

Lukkaroinen, Riitta (2005) *"Muutos on pysyvä olotila"*: *Turvapaikanhakijoiden vastaanottona järjestettävät palvelut ja niiden järjestämisestä aiheutuvat kustannukset*. Työpoliittinen tutkimus 292. Työministeriö: Helsinki.

MacLure, Maggie; Rachel Holmes, Liz Jones & Christina MacRae (2010) "Silence as resistance to analysis: or, not opening one's mouth properly", *Qualitative Inquiry* 16 (6), pp. 492–500.

Maggio, Joe (2007) " 'Can the subaltern be heard?': political theory, translation, representation, and Gayatri Chakravorty Spivak", *Alternatives: Global, Local, Political* 32 (4), pp. 419–443.

Malkki, Liisa H. (1995) "Refugees and exile: from "refugee studies" to the national order of things", *Annual Review of Anthropology* 24, pp. 495–523.

Malkki, Liisa H. (1996) "Speechless emissaries: refugees, humanitarianism, and dehistoricization", *Cultural Anthropology* 11 (3), pp. 377–404.

Mallot, Edward (2006) "Body politics and the body politic", *Interventions: The International Journal of Postcolonial Studies* 8 (2), pp. 165–177.

Manning, Erin (2000) "Beyond accommodation: national space and recalcitrant bodies", *Alternatives: Global, Local, Political* 25 (1), pp. 51–74.

Manning, Erin (2007) *Politics of Touch: Sense, Movement, Sovereignty*. Minneapolis & London: University of Minnesota Press.

Manning, Erin (2009) *Relationscapes: Movement, Art, Philosophy*. Cambridge, MA & London: The MIT Press.

Marcus, George E. (2004) "What comes (just) after 'post'?: the case of ethnography", in Daiute, Colin & Cynthia Lightfoot (eds.) *Narrative Analysis: Studying the Development of Individuals in Society*, pp. 563–574. London: Sage.

Marcus, George E.; W. Russell Neuman & Michael Mackuen (2000) *Affective Intelligence and Political Judgment*. Chicago: Chicago University Press.

Massey, Doreen (2004) "Geographies of responsibility", *Geografiska Annaler* Series B, 86 (1), pp. 5–18.

Masters, Cristina (2006) "Body counts: the biopolitics of death", in Dauphinee, Elizabeth & Cristina Masters (eds.) *The Logics of Biopower and the War on Terror*, pp. 43–59. Basingstoke: Palgrave Macmillan.

Matteo, Perin (2005) "The sense of freedom: the surprise of being-in-common", *Law and Critique* 16 (3), pp. 315–338.

Mazzei, Lisa A. (2003) "Inhabited silences: in pursuit of a muffled subtext", *Qualitative Inquiry* 9 (3), pp. 355–368.

Mbembe, Achille (2003) "Necropolitics", *Public Culture* 15 (1), pp. 11–40.

McAllister, Margaret (2003) "Multiple meanings of self-harm: a critical review", *International Journal of Mental Health Nursing* 12 (3), pp. 177–185.

McCarthy, John; Paul Sullivan & Peter Wright (2006) "Culture, personal experience and agency", *British Journal of Social Psychology* 45 (2), pp. 421–439.

McLane, Janice (1996) "The voice on the skin: self-mutilation and Merleau-Ponty's theory of language", *Hypatia* 11 (4), pp. 107–118.

McNay, Lois (2008) "The trouble with recognition: subjectivity, suffering, and agency", *Sociological Theory* 26 (3), pp. 271–296.

McNevin, Anne (2010) "Becoming political: asylum seeker activism through community theatre", *Local-Global: Identity, Security, Community* 8, pp. 142–159.

McNevin, Anne (2012) *Contesting Citizenship: Irregular Migrants and New Frontiers of the Political*. New York: Columbia University Press.

182 References

Meyer, John W. & Ronald L. Jepperson (2000) "The 'actors' of modern society: the cultural construction of social agency", *Sociological Theory* 18 (1), pp. 100–120.

Mezzadra, Sandro (2010) "The gaze of autonomy: Capitalism, migration and social struggles", *UniNomade* 19.9.2010, available at: <http://www.uninomade.org/the-gaze-of-autonomy-capitalism-migration-and-social-struggles/>, accessed 15th December 2015.

Mezzadra, Sandro & Brett Neilson (2003) "Né qui, né altrove – migration, detention, desertation: a dialogue", *Borderlands e-journal* 2 (1), available at <http://www.borderlands.net.au/vol2no1_2003/mezzadra_neilson.html>, accessed 20th December 2015.

Mezzadra, Sandro & Brett Neilson (2012) "Between inclusion and exclusion: on the topology of global space and borders", *Theory, Culture & Society* 29 (4–5), pp. 58–75.

Moon, J. Donald (1991) "Constrained discourse and public life", *Political Theory* 19 (2), pp. 202–229.

Moorehead, Caroline (2006) *Human Cargo: A Journey among Refugees*. London: Vintage.

Moreira, Claudio (2005) "Made for sex", *Qualitative Inquiry* 13 (1), pp. 48–57.

Morin, Marie-Eve (2009) "Thinking things: Heidegger, Sartre, Nancy", *Sartre Studies International* 15 (2), pp. 35–53.

Morris, Lydia (2009) "Asylum, welfare and civil society: a case study in civil repair", *Citizenship Studies* 13 (4), pp. 365–379.

Motha, Stewart (2002) "The sovereign event in a nation's law", *Law and Critique* 13 (3), pp. 311–338.

Moulin, Carolina & Peter Nyers (2007) " 'We live in a country of UNHCR' – refugee protests and global political society", *International Political Sociology* 2 (1), pp. 356–372.

Mountz, Alison (2010) *Seeking Asylum: Human Smuggling and the Bureaucracy at the Border*. Minneapolis & London: University of Minnesota Press.

Muldoon, Paul (2001) "Between speech and silence: the postcolonial critic and the idea of emancipation", *Critical Horizons* 2 (1), pp. 33–59.

Munro, Daniel (2007) "Norms, motives and radical democracy: Habermas and the problem of motivation", *Journal of Political Philosophy* 15 (4), pp. 447–472.

Nail, Thomas (2012) "Violence at the borders: Nomadic solidarity and non-status migrant resistance", *Radical Philosophy Review* 15 (1), pp. 241–257.

Nail, Thomas (2015) *The Figure of the Migrant*. Stanford: Stanford University Press.

Nancy, Jean-Luc (1990) "Exscription", in Stoekl, Allan (ed.) *On Bataille*, Yale French Studies 78, pp. 47–65. New Haven: Yale University Press.

Nancy, Jean-Luc (1992) "La comparution/the compearance: from the existence of 'communism' to the community of 'existence'", *Political Theory* 20 (3), pp. 371–398.

Nancy, Jean-Luc (1993a) *The Birth to Presence*. Stanford, CA: Stanford University Press.

Nancy, Jean-Luc (1993b) "You ask me what it means today . . . : an epigraph for *Paragraph*", *Paragraph* 16 (2), pp. 108–110.

Nancy, Jean-Luc (1998) *The Sense of the World*. Minneapolis: University of Minnesota Press.

Nancy, Jean-Luc (1999) "Responding for existence", *Studies in Practical Philosophy* 1 (1), pp. 1–11.

Nancy, Jean-Luc (2000) *Being Singular Plural*. Stanford, CA: Stanford University Press.

Nancy, Jean-Luc (2003a) "The confronted community", *Postcolonial Studies* 6 (1), pp. 23–36.

Nancy, Jean-Luc (2003b) *A Finite Thinking*. Stanford, CA: Stanford University Press.

Nancy, Jean-Luc (2004a/1991) *The Inoperative Community*. Minneapolis & London: University of Minnesota Press.

Nancy, Jean-Luc (2004b) "Banks, edges, limits (of singularity)", *Journal of the Theoretical Humanities* 8 (2), pp. 41–53.

References   183

Nancy, Jean-Luc (2007) "Church, state, resistance", *Journal of Law and Society* 34 (1), pp. 3–13.

Nancy, Jean-Luc (2008) *Corpus*. New York: Fordham University Press.

Nancy, Jean-Luc (2010) "Body as theatre", lecture, April 2010. Helsinki, Finland.

Nancy, Jean-Luc & Peter Connor (1993) "On one side/D'un côté", *Assemblage* 20, pp. 58–59.

Nast, Heidi J. & Steve Pile (1998) "Introduction: MakingPlacesBodies", in Nast, Heidi J. & Steve Pile (eds.) *Places through the Body*, pp. 1–19. London & New York: Routledge.

Nayak, Meghana & Eric Selbin (2010) *Decentering International Relations*. London & New York: Zed Books.

Neocosmos, Michael (2012) "Are those-who-do-not-count capable of reason? Thinking political subjectivity in the (neo-)colonial world and the limits of history", *Journal of Asian and African Studies* 47 (5), pp. 530–547.

Neumann, Iver B. (2010) "Autobiography, ontology, autoethnology", *Review of International Studies* 36 (4), pp. 1051–1055.

Nevins, Joseph (2008) *Dying to Live: A Story of U.S. Immigration in an Age of Global Apartheid*. San Francisco: City Lights Books.

Newland, Kathleen (2010) "The governance of international migration: mechanisms, processes, and institutions", *Global Governance* 16 (3), pp. 331–343.

Noland, Carrie (2009) *Agency and Embodiment: Performing Gestures/Producing Culture*. London & Cambridge, MA: Harvard University Press.

Norris, Andrew (2000a) "Jean-Luc Nancy and the myth of the common", *Constellations* 7 (2), pp. 272–295.

Norris, Andrew (2000b) "Giorgio Agamben and the politics of living dead", *Diacritics* 30 (4), pp. 38–58.

Nyers, Peter (2003) "Abject cosmopolitanism: the politics of protection in the anti-deportation movement", *Third World Quarterly* 24 (6), pp. 1069–1093.

Nyers, Peter (2008) "In solitary, in solidarity: detainees, hostages and contesting the anti-policy of detention", *European Journal of Cultural Studies* 11 (3), pp. 333–349.

Odysseos, Louiza (2007) *The Subject of Coexistence: Otherness in International Relations*. Minneapolis: University of Minnesota Press.

Oliver, Sophie Anne (2010) "Trauma, bodies, and performance art: towards an embodied ethics of seeing", *Continuum: Journal of Media & Cultural Studies* 24 (1), pp. 119–129.

Olsson, Gunnar (1991) *Lines of Power: Limits of Language*. Minneapolis & Oxford: University of Minnesota Press.

Olsson, Gunnar (2007) *Abysmal: A Critique of Cartographic Reason*. Chicago: The University of Chicago Press.

Osella, Caroline & Filippo Osella (1998) "Friendship and flirting: micro-politics in Kerala, South India", *The Journal of the Royal Anthropological Institute* 4 (2), pp. 189–206.

Palladino, Paolo & Tiago Moreira (2006) "On silence and the constitution of the political community", *Theory & Event* 9 (2), online publication.

Panagia, Davide (2009) *The Political Life of Sensation*. Durham & London: Duke University Press.

Panelli, Ruth & Richard Welch (2005) "Why community? Reading difference and singularity with community", *Environment and Planning A* 37 (9), pp. 1589–1611.

Panelli, Ruth & Richard Welch (2007) "Questioning community as a collective antidote to fear: Jean-Luc Nancy's 'singularity' and 'being singular plural'", *Area* 39 (3), pp. 349–356.

Papastergiadis, Nikos (2000) *The Turbulence of Migration: Globalisation, Deterritorialisation and Hybridity*. Cambridge: Polity Press.

184 *References*

Parr, Hester (2001) "Feeling, reading, and making bodies in space", *The Geographical Review* 91 (1–2), pp. 158–167.

Parviainen, Jaana (2010) "Choreographing resistances: spatial-kinaesthetic intelligence and bodily knowledge as political tools in activist work", *Mobilities* 5 (3), pp. 311–329.

Perera, Suvendrini (2002) "What is a camp . . .?", *Borderlands e-journal* 1 (1), available at <http://www.borderlands.net.au/vol1no1_2002/perera_camp.html>, accessed 20th December 2015.

Perera, Suvendrini (2006) " 'They give evidence': bodies, borders and the disappeared", *Social Identities* 12 (6), pp. 637–656.

Perpich, Diane (2005) "*Corpus Meum*: disintegrating bodies and the ideal of integrity", *Hypatia* 20 (3), pp. 75–91.

Philipose, Liz (2007) "The politics of pain and the end of empire", *International Feminist Journal of Politics* 9 (1), pp. 60–81.

Pirinen, Ilkka (2008) *Turvapaikanhakijoiden terveydentila: tutkimus Tampereen kaupungin ulkomaalaistoimiston terveydenhuoltoyksikössä*. Acta Universitatis Tamperensis; 1289. Tampere: Tampere University Press.

Pitts, Victoria (2003) *In the Flesh: The Cultural Politics of Body Modification*. Basingstoke: Palgrave Macmillan.

Poindexter, Cynthia Cannon (2002) "Research as poetry: a couple experiences HIV", *Qualitative Inquiry* 8 (6), pp. 707–714.

Pugliese, Joseph (2002) "Penal asylum: refugees, ethics, hospitality", *Borderslands e-journal* 1 (1), available at <http://www.borderlands.net.au/vol1no1_2002/pugliese.html>, accessed 20th December 2015.

Pugliese, Joseph (2004) "Subcutaneous law: embodying the migration amendment act 1992", *The Australian Feminist Law Journal* 21, December 2004, pp. 23–34.

Pupavac, Vanessa (2001) "Therapeutic governance: psycho-social intervention and trauma risk management", *Disasters* 25 (4), pp. 358–372.

Pupavac, Vanessa (2008) "Refugee advocacy, traumatic representations and political disenchantment", *Government & Opposition* 43 (2), pp. 270–292.

Puumala, Eeva (2012) *Corporeal conjunctures no-w-here: Failed asylum seekers and the senses of the international*. Acta Universitatis Tamperensis 1744. Tampere: Tampere University Press.

Puumala, Eeva (2013) "Political life beyond accommodation and return: re-thinking relations between the political, the international and the body", *Review of International Studies* 39 (4), doi:10.1017/S026021051200037X.

Puumala, Eeva & Anitta Kynsilehto (2015) "Does the body matter? Determining the right to asylum and the corporeality of political communication", *European Journal of Cultural Studies*, doi:10.1177/1367549415592898.

Puumala, Eeva & Samu Pehkonen (2010) "Corporeal choreographies: failed asylum seekers moving from body politics to body spaces", *International Political Sociology* 4 (1), pp. 50–65.

Puumala, Eeva; Tarja Väyrynen, Anitta Kynsilehto & Samu Pehkonen (2011) "Events of the body politic: a Nancian reading of asylum-seekers' bodily choreographies and resistance", *Body & Society* 17 (4), pp. 83–104.

Rabinow, Paul (1986) "Representations are social facts: modernity and post-modernity in anthropology", in Clifford, James & George E. Marcus (eds.) *Writing Culture: The Poetics and Politics of Ethnography*, pp. 234–261. Berkeley: University of California Press.

Radhakrishnan, Rajagopalan (1993) "Postcoloniality and the boundaries of identity", *Callaloo* 16 (4), pp. 750–771.

References   185

Rajaram, Prem Kumar (2013) "Historicising 'asylum' and responsibility", *Citizenship Studies* 17 (6–7), pp. 681–696.

Rajaram, Prem Kumar & Carl Grundy-Warr (2004) "The irregular migrant as homo sacer: migration and detention in Australia, Malaysia, and Thailand", *International Migration* 42 (1), pp. 33–64.

Rajaram, Prem Kumar & Carl Grundy-Warr (eds.) (2007) *Borderscapes: Hidden Geographies and Politics at Territory's Edge*. Minneapolis & London: University of Minnesota Press.

Rajchman, John (1988) "Foucault's art of seeing", *October* 44 (Spring), pp. 88–117.

Rancatore, Jason P. (2010) "It is strange: a reply to Vrasti", *Millennium: Journal of International Studies* 39 (1), pp. 65–77.

Redclift, Victoria (2013) "Abjects or agents? Camps, contests and the creation of 'political space'", *Citizenship Studies* 14 (3–4), pp. 308–321.

Reischer, Erica & Kathryn S. Koo (2004) "The body beautiful: symbolism and agency in the social world", *Annual Review of Anthropology* 33, pp. 297–317.

Reyes Cruz, Mariolga (2008) "What if I just cite Graciela? Working toward decolonizing knowledge through a critical ethnography", *Qualitative Inquiry* 14 (4), pp. 651–658.

Richardson, Laurel (1992) "The consequences of poetic representation: writing the other, rewriting the self", in Ellis, Carolyn & Michael G. Flaherty (eds.) *Investigating Subjectivity: Research on Lived Experience*, pp. 125–137. Newbury Park: Sage.

Richardson, Laurel (1994) "Nine poems: marriage and the family", *Journal of Contemporary Ethnography* 23 (1), pp. 3–13.

Richardson, Laurel (1998) "The politics of location: where am I now?", *Qualitative Inquiry* 4 (1), pp. 41–48.

Richardson, Laurel (2002) "Poetic representation of interviews", in Gubrium, Jaber F. & James A. Holstein (eds.) *Handbook of Interviewing*, pp. 877–891. Thousand Oaks, CA: Sage.

Richardson, Laurel (2004) "Writing: a method of inquiry", in Daiute, Colin & Cynthia Lightfoot (eds.) *Narrative Analysis: Studying the Development of Individuals in Society*, pp. 516–529. London: Sage.

Riessman, Catherine Kohler (2002a) "Analysis of personal narratives", in Gubrium, Jaber F. & James A. Holstein (eds.) *Handbook of Interview Research: Context and Method*, pp. 695–710. Thousand Oaks: Sage.

Riessman, Catherine Kohler (2002b) "Narrative analysis", in Huberman, A. Michael & Matthew B. Miles (eds.) *The Qualitative Researcher's Companion*, pp. 217–270. Thousand Oaks, CA: Sage.

Robben, Anthonius C. G. M. (1996) "Ethnographic seduction, transference, and resistance in dialogues about terror and violence in Argentina", *Ethos* 24 (1), pp. 71–106.

Robinson, Fiona (2011) "Stop talking and listen: discourse ethics and feminist care ethics in international political theory", *Millennium: Journal of International Studies* 39 (3), pp. 845–860.

Rosaldo, Renato (1986) "From the door of his tent: the fieldworker and the inquisitor", in Clifford, James (ed.) *Writing Culture: The Poetics and Politics of Ethnography*, pp. 77–97. Berkeley: University of California Press.

Rosenblatt, Paul C. (2002) "Interviewing at the border of fact and fiction", in Gubrium, Jaber F. & James A. Holstein (eds.) *Handbook of Interview Research: Context and Method*, pp. 893–909. Thousand Oaks: Sage.

Ross, Andrew A. G. (2010) "Why they don't hate us: emotion, agency and the politics of 'anti-americanism'", *Millennium: Journal of International Studies* 39 (1), pp. 109–125.

186   References

Rygiel, Kim (2011) "Bordering solidarities: migrant activism and the politics of movement and camps at Calais", *Citizenship Studies* 15 (1), pp. 1–19.

Said, Edward W. (1978) *Orientalism*. London & New York: Penguin Books.

Said, Edward W. (2000) *Out of Place: A Memoir*. New York: Vintage Books.

Said, Edward W. (2001) *Ajattelevan ihmisen vastuu*. [Representations of the Intellectual] Trans. Matti Savolainen. Helsinki: Loki-Kirjat.

Salis Gross, Corina (2004) "Struggling with imaginaries of trauma and trust: the refugee experience in Switzerland", *Culture, Medicine and Psychiatry* 28 (2), pp. 151–167.

Salter, Mark B. (2006) "The global visa regime and the political technologies of the international self: borders, bodies, biopolitics", *Alternatives: Global, Local, Political* 31 (2), pp. 167–189.

Sarbin, Theodore R. (2004) "The role of imagination in narrative construction", in Daiute, Colin & Cynthia Lightfoot (eds.) *Narrative Analysis: Studying the Development of Individuals in Society*, pp. 5–20. London: Sage.

Scarry, Elaine (1985) *The Body in Pain: The Making and Unmaking of the World*. New York & Oxford: Oxford University Press.

Schick, Kate (2011) "Acting out and working through: trauma and (in)security", *Review of International Studies* 37 (4), pp. 1837–1855.

Schildkrout, Enid (2004) "Inscribing the body", *Annual Review of Anthropology* 33, pp. 319–344.

Schwarzmantel, John (2007) "Community as communication: Jean-Luc Nancy and 'Being-in-Common'", *Political Studies* 55 (6), pp. 459–476.

Scott, Gwen Gustafson (2004) "Undocumented immigrants in the 21st century: perceptions of spatial legitimacy", in Janelle, Donald G.; Barney Warf & Kathy Hansen (eds.) *WorldMinds: Geographical Perspectives on 100 Problems*, pp. 589–593. Dordrecht, Boston & London: Kluwer Academic Publishers.

Sermijn, Jasmina; Patrick Devlieger & Gerrit Loots (2008) "The narrative construction of the self: selfhood as a rhizomatic story", *Qualitative Inquiry* 14 (4), pp. 632–650.

Shapiro, Ian (2002) "Problems, methods, and theories in the study of politics, or what's wrong with political science and what to do about it", *Political Theory: An International Journal of Political Philosophy* 30 (4), pp. 596–619.

Shapiro, Kam (2003) *Sovereign Nations, Carnal States*. Cornell University: Cornell University Press.

Shapiro, Michael J. (1997) *Violent Cartographies: Mapping Cultures of War*. Minneapolis: University of Minnesota Press.

Shuman, Amy & Carol Bohmer (2004) "Representing trauma: Political asylum narrative", *Journal of American Folklore* 466, pp. 394–414.

Smith, Michael P. (1992) "Postmodernism, urban ethnography, and the new social space of ethnic identity", *Theory and Society* 21 (4), pp. 493–531.

Smith, Phil (1999) "Food truck's party hat", *Qualitative Inquiry* 5 (2), pp. 244–261.

Smith, Walt Nopalito (2002) "Ethno-poetry notes", *International Journal of Qualitative Studies in Education* 15 (4), pp. 461–467.

Soguk, Nevzat (1999) *States and Strangers: Refugees and Displacements of Statecraft*. Minneapolis & London: University of Minnesota Press.

Soguk, Nevzat (2000) "Poetics of a world of migrancy: migratory horizons, passages, and encounters of alterity", *Global Society* 14 (3), pp. 415–442.

Soguk, Nevzat (2005) "On the task of politics as a 'project': politics, hegemony, embedded lives and fugitive agency", *Theory & Event* 8 (4), online publication.

Soguk, Nevzat (2007) "Border's capture: insurrectional politics, border-crossing humans, and the new political", in Rajaram, Prem Kumar & Carl Grundy-Warr (eds.) *Borderscapes:*

References 187

Hidden Geographies and Politics at Territory's Edge, pp. 283–308. Minneapolis & London: University of Minnesota Press.

Solis, Jocelyn (2004) "Narrating and counternarrating illegality as an identity", in Daiute, Colin & Cynthia Lightfoot (eds.) *Narrative Analysis: Studying the Development of Individuals in Society*, pp. 181–199. London: Sage.

Solomin, Nina (2005) *Gränsen: En Resa bland Människor som Kallas Illegala*. Stockholm: Wahlström & Widstrand.

Spivak, Gayatri Chakravorty (1988) "Can the subaltern speak?", in Nelson, Cary & Lawrence Grossberg (eds.) *Marxism and the Interpretation of Culture*, pp. 271–313. Basingstoke: MacMillan Education.

Spivak, Gayatri Chakravorty (1998) "Gender and international studies", *Millennium: Journal of International Studies* 27 (4), pp. 819–824.

Squire, Vicki (2009) *The Exclusionary Politics of Asylum*. Basingstoke: Palgrave Macmillan.

Squire, Vicki (2014) "Desert 'trash': posthumanism, border struggles, and humanitarian politics", *Political Geography* 39, pp. 11–21.

Squire, Vicki (2015) "Reshaping critical geopolitics? The materialist challenge", *Review of International Studies* 41 (1), pp. 139-159.

Squire, Vicki (ed.) (2010) *The Contested Politics of Mobility: Borderzones and Irregularity*. London: Routledge.

Squire, Vicki & Jonathan Darling (2013) "The 'minor' politics of rightful presence: justice and relationality in city of sanctuary", *International Political Sociology* 7 (1), pp. 59–74.

Steel, Z.; S. Momartin, C. Bateman, A. Hafshejani, D. M. Silove, N. Everson, K. Roy, M. Dudley, L. Newman, B. Blick & S. Mares (2004) "Psychiatric status of asylum seeker families held for a protracted period in a remote detention centre in Australia", *Australia and New Zealand Journal of Public Health* 6, pp. 527–536.

Stokoe, Elizabeth (2014) "The conversation analytic role-play method (CARM): a method for training communication skills as an alternative to simulated role-play", *Research in Language and Social Interaction* 47 (3), pp. 255–265.

Stoller, Paul (1997) *Sensuous Scholarship*. Philadelphia: University of Pennsylvania Press.

Sullivan, Nikki (2001) *Tattooed Bodies: Subjectivity, Textuality, Ethics, and Pleasure*. Westport, CT & London: Praeger.

Sullivan, Paul & John McCarthy (2004) "Toward a dialogical perspective on agency", *Journal for the Theory of Social Behaviour* 34 (3), pp. 291–309.

Svašek, Maruška (2010) "On the move: emotions and human mobility", *Journal of Ethnic and Migration Studies* 36 (6), pp. 865–880.

Sylvester, Christine (2007) "Whither the international at the end of IR", *Millennium: Journal of International Studies* 35 (3), pp. 551–573.

Sylvester, Christine (2013) *War as Experience: Contributions from International Relations and Feminist Analysis*. London: Routledge.

Tabar, Linda (2007) "Memory, agency, counter-narrative: testimonies from Jenin refugee camp", *Criticalarts* 21 (1), pp. 6–31.

Takhar, Shaminder (2007) "Expanding the boundaries of political activism", *Contemporary Politics* 13 (2), pp. 123–137.

Tanggaard, Lene (2009) "The research interview as a dialogical context for the production of social life and personal narratives", *Qualitative Inquiry* 15 (9), pp. 1498–1515.

Tate, Shirley Anne (2001) "That's my star of David': skin, abjection and hybridity", in Ahmed, Sara & Jackie Stacey (eds.) *Thinking through the Skin*, pp. 209–222. London & New York: Routledge.

Tate, Shirley Anne (2007) "Translating melancholia: a poetics of black interstitial community", *Community, Work and Family* 10 (1), pp. 1–15.

188   *References*

Tatman, Lucy (1998) "The yearning to be whole-enough or to feel something, not nothing: a feminist theological consideration of self-mutilation as an act of atonement", *Feminist Theology* 6 (January), pp. 25–38.

Taylor, Janelle S. (2005) "Surfacing the body interior", *Annual Review of Anthropology* 34, pp. 741–756.

Teleky, Richard (2001) " 'Entering the silence': voice, ethnicity and the pedagogy of creative writing", *Melus* 26 (1), pp. 205–219.

Threadgold, Terry (1997) *Feminist Poetics: Poiesis, Performance, Histories.* New York & London: Routledge.

Tickner, Arlene (2003) "Seeing IR differently: notes from the Third World", *Millennium: Journal of International Studies* 32 (3), pp. 295–324.

Turp, Maggie (2007) "Self-harm by omission: a question of skin containment", *Psychodynamic Practice* 13 (3), pp. 229–244.

Tyler, Imogen (2006) " 'Welcome to Britain': the cultural politics of asylum", *European Journal of Cultural Studies* 9 (2), pp. 185–202.

Uçarer, Emek M. (2006) "Burden-shirking, burden-shifting, and burden-sharing in the emergent European asylum regime", *International Politics* 43, pp. 219–240.

Vaittinen, Tiina (2015) "The power of the vulnerable body: a new political economy of care", *International Feminist Journal of Politics* 17 (1), pp. 100–118.

Van Den Abbeele, Georges (1997) "Lost horizons and uncommon grounds: for a poetics of finitude in the work of Jean-Luc Nancy", in Sheppard, Darren; Simon Sparks & Colin Thomas (eds.) *The Sense of Philosophy: On Jean-Luc Nancy*, pp. 12–18. London: Routledge.

van der Walt, Johan (2005) "Interrupting the myth of partage: reflections on sovereignty and sacrifice in the work of Nancy, Agamben and Derrida", *Law and Critique* 16 (3), pp. 277–299.

Van Wolputte, Steven (2004) "Hang on to your self: of bodies, embodiment, and selves", *Annual Review of Anthropology* 33, pp. 251–269.

Vaughan-Williams, Nick (2007) "Beyond a cosmopolitan ideal: the politics of singularity", *International Politics* 44 (1), pp. 107–124.

Väyrynen, Tarja (2013) "Keeping the trauma of war open in the male body – resisting the hegemonic forms of masculinity and Finnish national identity", *Journal for Gender Studies* 22 (2), pp. 137–151.

Väyrynen, Tarja & Eeva Puumala (2015) "Bodies of war, the past continuous and (ar)rhythmic experiences", *Alternatives: Global, Local, Political* 40 (3–4), pp. 237–250.

Vidler, Anthony (1993) "Spatial violence", *Assemblage* 20, pp. 84–85.

Vrasti, Wanda (2008) "The strange case of ethnography and international relations", *Millennium: Journal of International Studies* 37 (2), pp. 279–301.

Vrasti, Wanda (2010) "Dr. Strangelove, or how I learned to stop worrying about methodology and love writing", *Millennium: Journal of International Studies* 39 (1), pp. 79–88.

Vuori, Jaana & Anu Hirsiaho (2012) "Stories of alphabetisation, stories of everyday citizenship", *Nordic Journal of Migration Research* 2 (3), pp. 1–11.

Wagner, Andreas (2006) "Jean-Luc Nancy: a negative politics?", *Philosophy & Social Criticism* 32 (1), pp. 89–109.

Walker, Rob B. J. (1993) *Inside/Outside: International Relations as Political Theory.* Cambridge: Cambridge University Press.

Walker, Rob B. J. (2006a) "Lines of insecurity: international, imperial, exceptional", *Security Dialogue* 37 (1), pp. 65–82.

References 189

Walker, Rob B. J. (2006b) "The double outside of the modern international", *Ephemera* 6 (1), pp. 56–69.

Walker, Rob B. J. (2009) *After the Globe, Before the World*. London: Routledge.

Wall, Illan rua (2008) "On pain and the sense of human rights", *Australian Feminist Law Journal* 29 (2), pp. 53–76.

Walters, William (2002) "Deportation, expulsion, and the international police of aliens", *Citizenship Studies* 6 (3), pp. 265–292.

Walters, William (2006) "Rethinking borders beyond the state", *Comparative European Politics* 4 (2–3), pp. 141–159.

Walters, William (2015) "Reflections on migration and governmentality", *Movements: Journal für Kritische Migrations- und Grenzregimeforschung* 1 (1), available at <http://movements-journal.org/issues/01.grenzregime/04.walters – migration.governmentality. html>, accessed 19th December 2015.

Watkin, Christopher (2009) *Phenomenology or Deconstruction: The Question of Ontology in Maurice Merleay-Ponty, Paul Ricoeur and Jean-Luc Nancy*. Edinburgh: Edinburgh University Press.

Weber, Cynthia (2008) "Designing safe citizens", *Citizenship Studies* 12 (2), pp. 125–142.

Wedeen, Lisa (2010) "Reflections on ethnographic work in political science", *Annual Review of Political Science* 13, pp. 255–272.

Wettergren, Åsa & Hanna Wikström (2014) "Who is a refugee? Political subjectivity and the categorization of Somali asylum seekers in Sweden", *Journal of Ethnic and Migration Studies* 40 (4), pp. 566–583.

White, Lucie (2007) "Mourning becomes resistance", *Unbound* 3, available at <http://www.legalleft.org/wp-content/uploads/2008/04/3unb001-white.pdf>, accessed 5th October 2011.

Wikström, Hanna (2014) "Gender, culture and epistemic injustice: The institutional logic in assessment of asylum applications in Sweden", *Nordic Journal of Migration Research* 4 (4), doi:10.2478/njmr-2014-0024.

Wright, Jeannie K. (2009) "Autoethnography and therapy writing on the move", *Qualitative Inquiry* 15 (4), pp. 623–640.

Zarowsky, Christina (2004) "Writing trauma: emotion, ethnography, and the politics of suffering among Somali returnees in Ethiopia", *Culture, Medicine and Psychiatry* 28 (2), pp. 189–209.

Zetter, Roger (1991) "Labelling refugees: forming and transforming a bureaucratic identity", *Journal of Refugee Studies* 4 (1), pp. 39–62.

Zetter, Roger (2007) "More labels, fewer refugees: remaking the refugee label in an era of globalisation", *Journal of Refugee Studies* 20 (2), pp. 172–192.

Zevnik, Andreja (2009) "Sovereign-less subject and the possibility of resistance", *Millennium: Journal of International Studies* 38 (1), pp. 83–106.

Žižek, Slavoj (2000) "Melancholy and the act", *Critical Inquiry* 26 (4), pp. 657–681.

Appendix

Transcription symbols used:

[	the beginning of overlapping speech
]	overlapping speech ends
(.)	microbreak: 0.2 seconds or less
=	two turns, speaking acts without a break
ye::s	long vowel
ye-	(dash) unfinished word
(yeah)	single parenthesis marks an unclear period or speaker
(-)	an unclear word
((cries))	the transcriber's comments and explanations of the situation are presented in double parentheses

Index

academic writing 24
Ackerly, Brooke 10
affinity of goals 15
Agamben, Giorgio 35, 103, 121
agency in corporeal refusals and aversion 157–60
Agier, Michel 38
Ahmed, Sara 16, 151
Anderson, Benedict x
anger: in asylum seekers 149, 151; directed at asylum seekers 102–3
articulation: movement as corporeal 105–8; passivity in 159–60; of the political, sensuous 160–4; representation and 70–3; of space, movement as 98–9, 129
asylum seekers: anger directed toward 102–3; anger in 149, 151; claim for authority and right to control one's life among 29–31; compearance 46–8, 130, 141; contestation and connection in the determination process 59–60; countries of origin 8; demands of 10–12, 51–2; deportspora 36–7; discontent towards the determination process 65–70; Dublin protocol and 1, 4n1, 118; emotional discomfort from fieldwork on 22–3; exposure and 38–41; facing life and death situations 34; field of study of 6–9; gaping discord between perceptions of the state and 60–5; hopelessness, helplessness and haplessness in 18, 28n4, 29, 153–7, 165; interviews of 55–7, 68–80, 148; justice and fairness for 11–12; lack of control in determination process 60; media image of x–xi; narrative of hopelessness, helplessness and haplessness among 18, 28n4, 29; ontologically potent bodies of 25–8;

otherness of 35; outrage felt by 97; political engagement by 125–8; political subjectivity of 41–2, 43; reception centers for 1, 3, 7–8, 101–2; relational ethics towards xiii–xiv; representation of 11; responsible scholarship on xv–xvi; retention of identity, traditions and culture 37–8; rumours surrounding 17; scrutinizing the international in terms of xii–xiii, 14–15; self-harm among 138–9, 143–4, 146–7, 155, 161; stereotypes of 103; struggle of 2; surveillance and governance over 103–4, 122–3, 128, 150; taken into police custody 1; truthfulness of 69–70, 72; using fake documents 36; ways of engagement and presence 40; on witnessing war 10, 52; *see also* body/bodies; health of asylum seekers, mental and physical
asylum syndrome 138
authority, right to 29–31
autoethnography 25
axes of demarcation 87

Behar, Ruth 11
being: local 128; as movement of sense 45–6
belonging: ontological 73; political mode of 106
Bleiker, Roland 25
body/bodies: central role in politics of asylum seeking 89–93; compearance of 46–8, 130; corporeal refusals and aversion 157–60; exceeding totality 31; existence and 48–9; as a limit 111–13; local being and 128; movement as articulation of space 98–9; movement as corporeal articulation 105–8; ontological 25–8, 44–6; passivity of 159–60;

192   *Index*

performing different positionalities 49–50; as point of reflection 73–5; political engagement and 125–8; politics of the 41–4; as question of politics 43–4; representing tension between being as it happens and as it is politically designed to happen 163; sovereign control and 35–8, 56; surveillance and governance over 103–4, 122–3, 150; turned into active agents of meaning-giving 146; voice of the marginalised 151–3; withdrawal from grasp of sovereign power 163–4; *see also* movement
border(s): as an active site 116–17; as central to sovereignty 101; *see also* sovereignty
Brigg, Morgan 25
Butler, Judith 87, 119

"Can the subaltern speak?" (Spivak) 6, 42
Carvalho, Márcio x
co-existence of the self and the other 38–9
Common European Asylum system 150
compearance 46–8, 130, 141
conjunctures, deep 17
corporeal articulation, movement as 105–8, 119–20

Dallmayr, Fred 40
Das, Veena 161
deep conjunctures 17
demands of asylum seekers 10–12, 51–2
Denzin, Norman 15
deportspora 36–7
Despret, Vinciane 27
determination process, the: asylum seekers cut off from past and future during 159; body as point of reflection in 73–5; compearance and 46–8, 130; contestation and connection in 59–60; equal discontent towards 65–70; gaping discord between perceptions of the state and asylum seekers in 60–5; interviews in 55–7, 68–73, 148; national order of things and 64; representation and articulation in 70–3
Dossa, Parin 144
Dublin Convention 1, 4n1, 118, 150
dynamics of asylum interviews 76–80

embodied involvement 15, 70
endistic narratives 73
Epstein, Charlotte 35–6
essentialist politics 46–8
ethics: professional 30–1; relational xiii–xiv

ethnographic research 1–4; affinity of goals in 15; field of study in 6–9; hermeneutics of the ontologically potent body in 25–8; *Lines of life* 18–22, 24; local colour in 141–5; motivation for 9–10; participants 8; points of departure 5–6; sensuous scholarship and the seduction of 13–18; the writing 'I' in 22–5
ethnographic seduction 13–18
Eurodac system 150, 152
European Asylum Support Office (EASO) 67
European Union: asylum regime in 26–7; countries of origin of refugees in 8; failures in responding to people's movement 108–9; restrictive asylum measures implemented in x–xi, 36–7, 118, 150
evented positionalities 80–9
exposure 26–8; approaching asylum through 38–41, 166–70; categories of analysis of 50–1; as a demand to think of 'being' 40; exploring the event of 48–51; movement as modality of 129–30; as political event of existence 163; sense of place and 31; sharing and 42–3, 47, 50; sovereignty and 40–1, 107
exscription 47

fake documents 36
fingerprints 150
Finland xi, 8, 19, 28n2, 56; data collection 28n3; Immigration Service policies 61–5
Foucault, Michel 87–8

Gatens, Moira 42
gesturing 127–9, 154

Haddad, Emma x
health of asylum seekers, mental and physical 133–6; anger and 149, 151; asylum syndrome and 138; emotional outbursts and 146, 149; melancholy and 155–7; self-harm and 138–9, 143–4, 146–7, 155, 161; sense of vulnerability and 153–7; trauma and 145–8, 158
hermeneutics of the ontologically potent body 25–8
hopelessness, helplessness and haplessness 18, 28n4, 29, 153–7, 165

identification, politics of 6
identities: asylum seekers retaining their 37–8; interdependency of political 41–2;

Index 193

shared 50; unfolding in relation to one
another in encounters 39, 166–7
in-different positionalities 93–5
interiority/exteriority 50
international, the: challenged from
below 33–4; ethnography exposing
25–6; organizing people through 56;
scrutinized in terms of asylum seekers
xii–xiii, 14–15; senses of 51–4
intersubjectivity 40
interviews, asylum 55–7, 68–73, 148;
dynamics of 76–80

Khosravi, Shahram 25

limit, body as 111–13
Lines of life 18–22, 24, 26, 52
"local being" 128
local colour 141–5, 148
logic of selective opposition x
Lukkaroinen, Riitta 138

Mallot, Edward 63
Manning, Erin 103
McCarthy, John 141, 152
meaning and sense 137, 156–7
melancholy 155–7
mentality of erasure 161
mezzanine spaces of sovereignty 36,
38, 101
migration, turbulence of 92
migration officers 56–7, 61–3; discontent
towards the determination process
65–70
Moorehead, Caroline 17, 22, 114
motivation, research 9–10
Moulin, Carolina 64
Mountz, Alison 5, 60, 114
movement: as articulation of space 98–9,
129; as both resistance and only viable
option 120; as corporeal articulation
105–8, 119–20; as modality of exposure
129–30; seeing states through 114–22;
seen like a state 101–4; sensing space
through 121–8; *see also* body/bodies

Nancy, Jean-Luc 15, 39, 40, 41, 121–2,
169; on human existence 48–9, 54;
on "local being" 128; on notion of the
state 46; ontological body and 45; on
presence 47, 70; refusal to be labeled
a political thinker 48–9; on sense and
meaning 121–2, 144; on shared identities
26–7, 28nn6–7, 50; on sovereignty and

exposure 40–1, 107; sovereignty as
"nothing but the *com-*" 109; on space
and spatiality 43; on voice 72, 152;
we-world and 42
national order of things 54, 64
Noland, Carrie 146
Nyers, Peter 36, 37, 64, 101

objectivity 68, 94
officers, migration 56–7, 61–3; discontent
towards the determination process
65–70
ontological belonging xi, 73
ontological bodies 25–8, 44–6
otherness 35; existence of the self and
38–9, 50

Panagia, Davide 42, 93
passivity 159–60
Perera, Suvendrini 73
Perpich, Diane 42, 144
poetry 18–22, 24, 26, 52, 106–7
politico-corporeal struggle of asylum
seeking 37, 40, 47, 92, 161; the body and
104, 106, 113, 114; collage of 165–70;
movement as ability to speak out of
place and 130–1; trauma and 145–6
politics 34; and bodily event of the
political 128–31; the body and
sovereign 35–6; compearance and
46–8; connections between the senses
and 139–41; essentialist 46–8; ethical
commitment in 130; of identification 6;
local colour and 141–5; of mobility 41,
110; multiple forms of engagement by
asylum seekers in 125–8; of voice and
the body 41–4, 63–4, 68
positionalities: body performing different
49–51; evented 80–9; in-different 93–5
prepersonal motor system 146
professional ethics 30–1
protests, sensuous 148–53
Pugliese, Joseph 138, 146–7
Pupavac, Vanessa 139

Rabinow, Paul 23
Rajaram, Prem Kumar 42
reception centers 1, 3, 7–8; as constructed
space of visibility 101–2; physical and
mental health in 133–6
reflection, body as point of 73–5
relating, ethnographic seduction as 15–16
relational ethics xiii–xiv
representation and articulation 70–3

194 *Index*

responsible scholarship xv–xvi
Richardson, Laurel 23
Robben, Antonius 13

Schick, Kate 138
scrutiny of the international xii–xiii, 14–15
seduction, ethnographic 13–18
self: co-existence of the other and the
    38–9, 50; harm 138–9, 143–4, 146–7,
    155, 161; as source of knowledge 25
self-harm among asylum seekers 138–9
sense(s): being as movement of 45–6;
    connection between politics and 139–41;
    in corporeal refusals and aversion
    157–60; of the international 51–4;
    making sense of sentiment and the 145–8;
    meaning and 137, 156–7; melancholy
    155–6; of vulnerability, shared 153–7
sensing of space 121–8
sensuous articulations of the political
    160–4
sensuous protests 148–53
sensuous scholarship 13–18
sentiment, making sense of 145–8
sharing: exposure and 42–3, 47, 50; sense
    of vulnerability 153–7
Soguk, Nevzat 39
sovereignty: borders as central to 101;
    control and the body 35–8, 56;
    deportspora and 36–7; dichotomy
    between interiority/exteriority and self/
    other 50; distinction between inside and
    outside 33–4; exposure and 40–1, 107;
    how societies are formed and bordered
    and 37; the international and 51–4;
    local colour and 141–5; mezzanine
    spaces of 36, 38, 101; practice 30–1,
    33; spatiotemporal practices of 53; in
    transition 107–10
space(s): irregular migratory movement
    subverting fixed notions of 113;
    movement as articulation of 98–9, 129;

sensing 121–8; of sovereignty, mezzanine
    36, 38, 101; and spatiotemporal practices
    of sovereignty 53
Spivak, Gayatri Chakravorty 6, 28n1, 42
Squire, Vicki x, 124
state, the 55–7; asylum interviews by
    55–7; determination process 59–60;
    discontent towards the determination
    process 65–70; gaping discord between
    perceptions of asylum seekers and 60–5;
    notion of 46–8; seen through movement
    114–22; *see also* sovereignty
stereotypes, gendered and racialised 103
Stern, Maria 10
Stoller, Paul 13
Sullivan, Paul 141, 152
surveillance 103–4, 122–3, 128, 150
Sylvester, Christine xiv

transition, sovereignty in 107–10
trauma 145–8, 158
True, Jacqui 10
truth 69–70, 72
turbulence of migration 92

Van Den Abbeele, Georges 110, 121
Van Wolputte, Steven 167
voice: of the marginalised body 151–3;
    politics of 41–4, 63–4, 68; as world-
    making 72
vulnerability, shared sense of 153–7

Walker, Rob 48, 80
Walters, William 105
war, witnesses to 10, 53; *see also Lines
    of life*
Weber, Cynthia 51
we-world 42
writing 22–5; academic 24; autoethnography
    25; poetry 18–22, 24, 26, 52, 106–7; that
    illustrates the state seen as movement
    115–17, 120–1